State Administrative Law in Indonesia

This book examines Indonesian laws regulating state administration, in other words, the relationship between the Indonesian government and its citizens.

This book uses public administration science to explain state administrative law. It covers the historical evolution of state administrative law in Indonesia, the political and legal acceptance of the Universal Declaration of Human Rights in Indonesia as well as the ratification of the 2020 Omnibus Law reforms. It evaluates both the benefits and drawbacks of establishing laws through the Omnibus Law model, and the challenges of its adoption by the Indonesian statutory system. The book also examines state administrative law in other Southeast Asian countries, to provide a more nuanced understanding of how human rights implementation occurs in the respective legal regimes.

Covering the legal reforms and changes to state administrative law in Indonesia, this book will be of keen interest to scholars of state administrative law, public administration, and constitutional law.

M. Zaenul Muttaqin is a senior lecturer of public administration at Cenderawasih University, Indonesia.

Routledge Studies in Asian Law

Civil Unrest and Governance in Hong Kong
Law and Order from Historical and Cultural Perspectives
Edited by Michael H.K. Ng and John D. Wong

Writing Chinese Laws
The Form and Function of Legal Statutes Found in the Qin Shuihudi Corpus
Ernest Caldwell

National Identity and Japanese Revisionism
Abe Shinzō's Vision of a Beautiful Japan and its Limits
Michal Kolmaš

Constitutional Remedies in Asia
Edited by Po Jen Yap

Chinese Legal Culture and Constitutional Order
Shiping Hua

Land Law and Disputes in Asia
In Search of an Alternative for Development
Edited by Brian Z. Tamanaha, Narufumi Kadomatsu, and Yuka Kaneko

China's Foreign Investment Legal Regime
Progress and Limitations
Yuwen Li and Cheng Bian

Philosophy of Law in Korea
Acceptance, Engagement and Social Change
Jeong-Oh Kim, Hak-Tai Kim, Joon-Seok Park, and Dong-Ryong Shin

The Law and Regulation of Public Health
Global Perspectives on Hong Kong
Eric C. Ip

State Administrative Law in Indonesia
M. Zaenul Muttaqin

For more information about this series, please visit: https://www.routledge.com/Routledge-Studies-in-Asian-Law/book-series/RSIAL

State Administrative Law in Indonesia

M. Zaenul Muttaqin

Routledge
Taylor & Francis Group
LONDON AND NEW YORK

First published 2025
by Routledge
4 Park Square, Milton Park, Abingdon, Oxon, OX14 4RN

and by Routledge
605 Third Avenue, New York, NY 10158

Routledge is an imprint of the Taylor & Francis Group, an informa business

British Library Cataloguing-in-Publication Data
A catalogue record for this book is available from the British Library

Library of Congress Cataloging-in-Publication Data
Names: Muttaqin, M. Zaenul, author.
Title: State administrative law in Indonesia/M. Zaenul Muttaqin.
Description: Abingdon, Oxon [UK]; New York, NY: Routledge, 2025. | Series: Routledge studies in Asian law | Includes bibliographical references and index. | Contents: Concept of state administrative law – Scope of state administrative law – Administrative law in Southeast Asia – State administrative law in Indonesia – State administrative law in corruption eradication – Omnibus law and its influence on state administrative law.
Identifiers: LCCN 2024037965 (print) | LCCN 2024037966 (ebook) | ISBN 9781032855301 (hardback) | ISBN 9781032855318 (paperback) | ISBN 9781003518563 (ebook)
Subjects: LCSH: Administrative law–Indonesia.
Classification: LCC KNW2720.M88 2025 (print) | LCC KNW2720 (ebook) | DDC 342.598/06–dc23/eng/20240815
LC record available at https://lccn.loc.gov/2024037965
LC ebook record available at https://lccn.loc.gov/2024037966

ISBN: 978-1-032-85530-1 (hbk)
ISBN: 978-1-032-85531-8 (pbk)
ISBN: 978-1-003-51856-3 (ebk)

DOI: 10.4324/9781003518563

Typeset in Galliard
by Deanta Global Publishing Services, Chennai, India

Contents

Abbreviations

ACE:	Alignment, Creativity, and Empowerment
AJI:	Aliansi Jurnalis Independen
AUPB:	*Asas Umum Pemerintahan yang Baik*/the Principles of Good Governance
BLBI:	Bantuan Likuiditas Bank Indonesia
BPPLHK:	Balai Pengamanan dan Penegakan Hukum Lingkungan Hidup dan Kehutanan
BPUPKI:	Investigating Body for Preparatory Work for Independence
COP:	Control, Order, and Prediction
CPF:	The Central Provident Fund
DPD:	The Regional Representative Council
DPMPTSP:	Dinas Penanaman Modal dan Pelayanan Terpadu Satu Pintu
DPR:	People's Representative Council
DPR-GR:	The Provisional People's Representative Council
GBHN:	*Garis Besar Haluan Negara*/The General Guidelines of State Policy
HAM:	*Hak Asasi Manusia*/Human Rights
HTP:	*Hukum Tata Pemerintahan*/Governance Law
ICW:	Indonesian Corruption Watch
IS:	The *Indische Stratsregeling*
ITE:	*Internet dan Transaksi Elektronik*/Internet and Electronic Transactions
Jatam:	*Jaringan Advokasi Tambang*/The Mining Advocacy Network
JCAC:	The Judicial Commission of the Administrative Court
Kemenkominfo:	*Kementerian Komunikasi dan Informasi*/Ministry of Communication and Information
KIP:	*Komisi Informasi Publik*/Public Information Commission
KPA:	*Konsorsium Pembaruan Agraria*/The Agrarian Reform Consortium

KPBI: *Konfederasi Persatuan Buruh Indonesia*/Confederation of Indonesian Labor Associations
Komnas HAM: The National Commission on Human Rights
KPK: Corruption Eradication Commission
KTUN: *Keputusan Tata Usaha Negara*/Administrative Decrees
KUH Perdata: Civil Code
LBH: *Lembaga Bantuan Hukum*/Legal Aid Institute
LN: League of Nations
LPHN: The National Law Development Institute
MAS: Malaysian Airline System (now Malaysia Airlines Berhad)
MPR: The People's Consultative Assembly
MPRS: The Provisional People's Consultative Assembly
MSMEs: Micro, Small, and Medium Enterprises
NPM: New Public Management
PAFHRIER: Policy analysis, Financial, Human Resources, Information, and External Relations
Perma: Supreme Court Regulation
Perpres: *Peraturan Presiden*/Presidential Decree
Perpu: Government Regulations in Lieu of Law
PNS: *Pegawai Negeri Sipil*/Government employees
POSDCORB: Planning, Organizing, Staffing, Directing, Coordinating, Reporting, and Budgeting
P4D: Regional Labor Dispute Settlement Committee
P4P: Central Labor Dispute Settlement Committee
PTUN: The State Administrative Court
PTUN Militer: Military Administrative Court
RO: The *Reglemen op de rechterlijke Organisatie en het beleid der justitie*
RUU: A Draft of Law
SafeNet: Southeast Asia Freedom of Expression Network
SAL: State Administrative Law
Surpres: *Surat Presiden*/President's Letter
TAP MPR: Resolutions of the People's Consultative Assembly
TPA: Traditional Public Administration
TUN: *Tata Usaha Negara*/State Administration
UN: The United Nations
UU: *Undang-Undang*/Law
WTO: World Trade Organization

Acknowledgments

This book is the result of the collective efforts of many individuals. While the author played a pivotal role in its creation, numerous others also played a part in the book's development. Some of them contributed directly, while others participated in intellectual discussions. Social and emotional support were also crucial elements in the process. Those who made significant contributions were not only the author's closest associates but also senior lecturers, including several public administration students at Cenderawasih University.

A senior lecturer who provided invaluable input was Professor Dr. Vince Tebay. As a Papuan woman, Professor Tebay provides many references to writings on human rights in state administrative law, almost all of which are cited in this book. The stories and reflections in her writings provide an overview of the scope of study and practice of state administration, which is continuously developing.

Then there is my senior colleague, Dr. Yosephina Ohoiwutun, who I have to say contributed greatly as Chair of the Master of Public Administration Program. Dr. Ohoiwutun provided invaluable moral support from the very first time I expressed the idea of writing this book. As part of my teaching team with Dr. Ohoiwutun, we have often engaged in in-depth discussions on comprehensive material that is suitable for students.

My colleague, Johni R. V. Korwa, who is currently pursuing his doctoral studies at Southampton, has been a great source of inspiration and guidance regarding the contents of this book. I would also like to extend my gratitude to the public administration students of Cenderawasih University. By hearing these students'stories, including discussions on current issues regarding state administrative law, it has helped us to understand the concepts that are difficult for us to grasp. Long-term discussions with these students have also encouraged me to examine the final two chapters of this book, about corruption and the Omnibus Law. I would be remiss if I did not mention my fellow students of the Public Administration Doctoral Program at Makassar State University, who have provided invaluable support for my studies and exploration of the field of public administration research.

I would also like to extend my gratitude to Mr. Kendrick Loo, the editor of this book at Routledge. His support was invaluable in helping me to complete this project. Initially, this book was proposed as a textbook for campuses with subjects in the field of state administrative law. Additionally, I must admit that I lack confidence in my ability to write a book on this topic, given that I am not an academic with a legal background. My legal knowledge is limited to policy products that align with public policy science. Kendrick Loo was extremely supportive of this book proposal, suggesting an option to make it widely accepted in monograph form.

I would also like to thank the anonymous reviewers who evaluated the book proposal and the finished draft of the book that I submitted to Routledge. Their insights and corrections were invaluable in helping me improve the content and material in this book.

Finally, I would like to express my sincerest gratitude to my family, especially to Pungky Eka Febrina, my wife, and to my late brother, M. Hasanaen Hidayatullah. Without their unwavering support and guidance, this book would not have been possible. Even though it is simple, I hope that this book will provide a valuable introduction to the development of state administrative law studies in Indonesia and facilitate a concise understanding for international audiences regarding the nature of Indonesian state administrative law.

Preface

State administrative law examines governmental actions from a juridical perspective, focusing on the legal ramifications of such actions. These legal consequences manifest as rights and obligations conferred upon both the actors involved and the subjects of their actions, which affects both the administrative bodies and the governed entities that are subject to administrative regulations. From a governmental perspective, there is a rationale underlying the implementation of such regulatory frameworks, and their resultant effects constitute another primary area of focus for state administrative law. Paramount among these concerns is the imperative for the state to embed a thorough comprehension of governmental duties within the framework of applicable laws, which necessitates an preexisting understanding of governmental concepts and their interrelationship with state administrative law as a field of study.

The domain of state administrative law encompasses various aspects of governmental operations, particularly in the realm of governance management. Its scope extends to all governmental acts and decisions executed through legal enforcement mechanisms. State administrative law provides a normative foundation for accountable governance and is characterized by a unique authority relationship, manifest in the government's power to make unilateral decisions that are binding on citizens.

To facilitate a greater understanding of this subject across an international readership, this book presents an examination of state administrative law in Southeast Asian nations, elucidating the legal contexts across various regimes. This includes countries with authoritarian, economic development-oriented approaches, as well as those adhering to more democratic ideologies. An analysis of these distinctions will help guide readers toward an appreciation of Indonesia's administrative legal framework, which operates within a democratic system.

Concern about the dearth of state administrative law research was the motivational basis for the author's desire to write about this field. The findings in research by Ardiansyah, Wandi, Suparto, M. Rafi, and Pahmi Amri show that the weakness of studies in this field has occurred due to the minimal level of collaboration between researchers.[1] Research clearly shows that the United States dominates the field of state administrative law studies, with up to 40 studies, followed by the United Kingdom, which has yielded a total of 31 studies. Even though the database used originates from literature indexed in Scopus, these findings indicate that this field of study attracts little research interest. Furthermore, these findings suggest that research in this field is equally difficult to find in the Asian region. One research paper called for integrated research partnership systems between countries in Asia to expand the scope of research. However, research into state administration (outside of legal scholarship) may be limited due to a number of different factors. As Raadschelders points out in, his review of Newbold and Rosenbloom's *The Constitutional School of American Public Administration*, public administration scholars tend to focus more on the immediate past and future, taking political-administrative superstructures for granted rather than critically evaluating them, and thus they focus only on operational issues. Decision-makers often feel the pressure to remediate immediate problems and focus on short-term results.[2] Raadschelder calls for more attention to the constitutional contexts in which the contemporary administrative state operates. Indeed, the very phrase "state administrative law" belies a key barrier that discourages research, which isthat researchers with academic backgrounds outside of law are often less interested in pursuing studies in this sub-discipline.

On a national scale, investigations into the number and substance of state administrative law books in Indonesia are predominantly based on legal science. The science of state administrative law indeed owes a lot to the study of law, and an in-depth analysis of relevant articles will form a solid basis for identifyingpatterns and developments in state administrative law in each regime. From the legal historical landscape, state administrative law appeared around the 18th and 19th centuries.[3] Cicero provides a clear explanation of the evolution of legal thought through his works, titled *De Re Publica*, and, *De Legibus*.[4] Unlike the ancient Greek tradition developed by Aristotle, which envisioned the law as something outside the concept of the state, ancient Roman law used the term *lex* with a broader scope. Constitutions began to be understood as determinants of the construction and development of the state in accordance with the principle of this higher law. Ancient Roman philosophers also

1 Ardiansyah et al., "Bibliometric Analysis and Visualization of State Administrative Law in Scopus Database from 2017–2021," *Cogent Social Sciences* 10, no. 1 (2024), https://doi.org/https://doi.org/10.1080/23311886.2024.2310935.

2 Jos C N Raadschelders, "The United States of America as Rechtsstaat: State and Administrative Law as Key to Understanding the Administrative State" (HeinOnline, 2017).

3 Luca Mannori and Bernardo Sordi, "Science of Administration and Administrative Law," in *A Treatise of Legal Philosophy and General Jurisprudence: Vol. 9: A History of the Philosophy of Law in the Civil Law World, 1600-1900; Vol. 10: The Philosophers' Philosophy of Law from the Seventeenth Century to Our Days* (Springer, 2009), 225–61.

4 Asshiddiqie, *Pengantar Ilmu Hukum Tata Negara* (Jakarta: Konstitusi Press, 2006).

emphasized the principle of the hierarchy of laws and thepractical application of this legal hierarchy in exercising power. Additionally, Roman philosophers laid a foundation that distinctly separates and differentiates between public law and private law. Public law defends the general interest, reflected in the state's interest, while private law concerns both public and private interests.

Jimly Asshiddiqe explains that the historical experience of Roman constitutionalism provides an understanding of the actual conception of, "the spirit of our constitutional antecedents" throughout history.[5] Legal science should be regarded as necessary and at least as important as dialogues about the substance of the law. Furthermore, a fundamental principle developed in Roman legal science is the doctrine of popular sovereignty, which posits that the people are the source of all legitimacy underpinning the state's political authority. Thus, in Roman jurisprudence, the populace was regarded as the ultimate wellspring of both legal and power structures. In the early historical period, state administrative law functioned as a basis for state action and provided freedom for bureaucrats from the hegemony of the *ancien* French regime. In the 19th century, the development of legal studies born in France quickly spread to other parts of the world. Since then, legal research has developed further and moved away from political and state science into various new approaches such as in the social sciences, economics, history, and statistics. Legal science as a discipline extends from the civil law to various parts of state administrative law.[6] The development of legal studies at the end of the 19th century marked the particular characteristics of legal studies, including developments in Germany and Italy.[7] Legal studies in 19th-century Germany were characterized by a growing interest in the development of the civil law as well as a shift in focus, from the ultimate purpose of the state, to what the state actually in fact does.[8] The public law curriculum has also established state administrative law as a university discipline for further development in specific sub-disciplines, such as in technology and in industry. Bureaucrats are required to master legal knowledge to reason with information about society and the state's policy framework in national development.

Italian administrative law in the 19th century was influenced by the unification of the various states and by political events such as uprisings. The Albertine Statute of 1848, first granted to the Kingdom of Sardinia, soon disseminated throughout the various kingdoms,[9] eventually becoming the

5 Asshiddiqie.

6 David F Lindenfeld, *The Practical Imagination: The German Sciences of State in the Nineteenth Century* (University of Chicago Press, 2008).

7 Arthur Barrêtto de Almeida Costa, "Citation Networks in Administrative Law Books from the Civil Law World (Nineteenth Century)," *Comparative Legal History* 11, no. 2 (2023): 154–85.

8 David F Lindenfeld, *The Practical Imagination: The German Sciences of State in the Nineteenth Century* (University of Chicago Press, 2008).

9 Bernardo Giorgio Mattarella, "Administrative Law in Italy: An Historical Sketch," *Rivista Trimestrale Di Diritto Pubblico* 4 (2010).

Constitution of the United Kingdom of Italy. Although this constitution did not explicitly provide efficient protections, subsequent law-making laid a groundwork for a roadmap for personal rights related to power. In 1853, Law No. 1483 established the principle of ministerial responsibility. During the tenure of Prime Minister Francesco Crispi, the administrative organization became increasingly complex, with the establishment of a central administration, local government, administrative courts, and laws that articulated the state's role in controlling private activities. Scholars of this period have developed a classification of legal theories into public and private law. Crispi's most significant contribution was forming administrative judicial law, which played a role in reviewing administrative actions and had a hand in the general jurisdiction of the Fourth Section of the Council of State. Efforts to protect citizens through administrative law further developed in the last two decades of the 19th century. Laws intervened when private companies provoked concerns about insurance and worker safety, further prompting the creation of new public bodies to curb insurance monopolies.

Recently, the field of state administrative law has attracted scholarly attention in Indonesia.[10] I Gusti Ayu Ketut Rachmi Handayani, a Professor of Administrative Law at Universitas Negeri Surakarta, explains that current administrative law requires the development of comparative law education.[11] This aims to support national legal reform efforts to enhance citizens' welfare, especially in response to changes following the Omnibus Law.[12] Richo Andi Wibowo, an expert in administrative law at Universitas Gadjah Mada, emphasizes the urgency of Indonesian administrative law education due to the expanding executive powers and the consequent potential for abuse.[13] With the decline in democratic quality and with various instances of government aid misappropriation during the pandemic, Wibowo highlights the importance of

10 I Nyoman Gede Remaja, *Hukum Administrasi Negara, Singaraja: Fakultas Hukum Universitas Panji Sakti* (Singaraja: Universitas Panji Sakti, 2017); F C Susila Adiyanta, "Hukum Dan Studi Penelitian Empiris: Penggunaan Metode Survey Sebagai Instrumen Penelitian Hukum Empiris," *Administrative Law and Governance Journal* 2, no. 4 (2019): 697–709; Sri Nurhari Susanto, "Komponen, Konsep Dan Pendekatan Hukum Administrasi Negara," *Administrative Law & Governance Journal* 4, no. 1 (2021): 144–57; Muhammad Iqbal Ashari, "Theory and Practice of State Administrative Law," *Riwayat: Educational Journal of History and Humanities* 6, no. 3 (2023): 823–30.

11 Richo Andi Wibowo and Anak Agung Savita Padma, "Bagaimana Sebaiknya Arah Pengembangan Pembelajaran Hukum Administrasi Di Indonesia," law.ugm.ac.id, 2024.

12 Abdul Wahid, I Gusti Ayu Ketut Rachmi Handayani, and Lego Karjoko, "Legal Politics of Changes in Land Ownership Rights Regulations Post Omnibus Law Based on Pancasila Justice," in *International Conference On Law, Economic & Good Governance (IC-LAW 2023)* (Atlantis Press, 2024), 339–45.

13 Richo Andi Wibowo, *Tata Kelola Pemerintahan Yang Baik Dan Pengadaan Barang Jasa Pemerintah: Pendekatan Perbandingan Hukum* (UGM PRESS, 2022); Richo Wibowo, "Good Governance as a Conceptual Framework to Address the Discussion of Public Private Distinction in Public Procurement," in *The 6th Public Procurement Student Research Conference*, 2014.

addressing the very immediate challenges facing administrative law as a field of study.[14] Adriaan Bedner, a Professor at Leiden School of Law and a researcher of Indonesian law, provides a broader perspective. He asserts that the study of administrative law must adhere to fundamental aspects of the rule of law and to the general principles of good governance.[15] Consequently, educators are required to have a critical understanding of current situations and also to engage in discussions of specific case studies to ground administrative law concepts in the classroom.[16] There is an impression that state administrative law is parallel to public law.[17]

There is also another assumption that state administrative law is a branch of criminal law. From a public law perspective, state administrative law guides public officials in implementing policies and public services.[18] From a criminal law perspective, state administrative law is a representation of administrative justice that bridges the establishment of truth.[19] In the legal literature, state administrative law acts as an interface between criminal and private law.[20] Criminal law also encompasses norms that are essential for societal functioning, such that their enforcement cannot be delegated to private parties and must instead be executed by state authorities. Conversely, the civil law contains norms whose enforcement can be entrusted to private entities. Administrative law occupies a position between these two domains: civil law and criminal law. Therefore, state administrative law can be characterized as "intermediate law."

Indonesia's recently reelected government, led by Joko Widodo, recently used the omnibus law technique in 2020 to revise laws inhibiting job creation. The use of the Omnibus Law offers new grounds to reexamine state administrative law theories. Economic development in Indonesia, from the time of establishing independence to the present,has focused on state power rather than on market power. However, adopting the Omnibus Law shows a significant shift in weakening the state's control, particularly as it relates toadministrative justice. There are three reasons why the Omnibus Law is important whendiscussing the context of state administrative law:

14 Wibowo and Padma, "Bagaimana Sebaiknya Arah Pengembangan Pembelajaran Hukum Administrasi Di Indonesia."

15 Adriaan Bedner, "An Elementary Approach to the Rule of Law," *Hague Journal on the Rule of Law* 2, no. 1 (2010): 48–74.

16 Wibowo and Padma, "Bagaimana Sebaiknya Arah Pengembangan Pembelajaran Hukum Administrasi Di Indonesia."

17 Remaja, *Huk. Adm. Negara.*

18 I Wayan Suandi, "Eksistensi Kebijakan Publik Dan Hukum Dalam Penyelenggaraan Pemerintahan Daerah," *Jurnal Ilmiah Fakultas Ilmu Sosial Dan Ilmu Politik* 1, no. 1 (2010).

19 Abdul Latief, *Hukum Administrasi Dalam Praktik Tindak Pidana Korupsi* (Jakarta: Kencana, 2016).

20 Philipus M Hadjon, "Pengantar Hukum Administrasi Indonesia (Introduction to the Indonesian Administrative Law)" (Gadjah Mada University Press, Yogyakarta, 2002).

1) Although discretion is believed to provide normative strength for government action in providing fair public services, through the Omnibus Law, excessive government discretion fosters the growth of criminal acts of corruption.
2) The Job Creation Law, which houses the Omnibus Law, tends to weaken the role of administrative justice, which in the Indonesian context is carried out by the State Administrative Court (PTUN).
3) The Job Creation Law, in centralizing power in the executive branch, runs counter to the decentralization drive pursued by Indonesia after the end of Suharto's New Order regime in 1998. This book posits that this change is a reflection of the impact of international economic development on the state administration system. This dynamic also impactsthe study the reasons for the formation and resilience of administrative justice.

Why are economic factors relevant to the Indonesian context? To answer this question, we need to reflect on Ginsburg's writings regarding the expanding role of administrative justice in the Asian region.[21] Economic globalization in Asian countries has an impact on the development of national policies and regulations. The logic of globalization discourse maps the route for capital to be absorbed at the national policy level and paves the way for capital flows from the inside out. When the government has minimal involvement in providing public services, the government's influence over the private sector will also weaken, making disputes challenging to contain. In this situation, the courts must be more advanced and adaptive in response to the complex changes of economic globalization. Further to this, global economic changes must also encourage fundamental policy reforms at the national level.

The Indonesian government has made fundamental leaps in economic development regulation through the omnibus law technique. Overlapping national regulations require government intervention to increase the speed and responsiveness of the national economy. The Indonesian government has used the Omnibus Law unilaterally to revise around 80 articles in laws that are seen as unfriendly to investment. This situation challenges the role of administrative justice and requires one to test the theory and practice of this concept. After all, state administrative law fortifies the state's interaction with its citizens and serves as a guide facilitating citizen participation, which ishow the state protects the human rights of its citizens.[22] As inGinsburg's view,

21 Tom Ginsburg, "The Judicialization of Administrative Governance: Causes, Consequences and Limits," in *Administrative Law and Governance in Asia* (Routledge, 2008), 11–30.

22 Tom Ginsburg, "Written Constitutions and the Administrative State: On the Constitutional Character of Administrative Law," in *Comparative Administrative Law* (Edward Elgar Publishing, 2010); Tom Ginsburg and Albert H Y Chen, "Administrative Law and Governance in Asia," *Comparative Perspectives*, 2009.

state administrative law determines the limits of government actions within society.[23] Ginsburg highlights a growingshift toward a more liberal regulatory model, which builds on the context of Asia during the 1990s and poses a sharper challenge for the Indonesian context. The administrative courts in Indonesia do not fall merely between interventionist and liberal market models. Instead, Indonesia's administrative courts reflect an open engagement with both the interventionist and liberal market contexts.

This book argues that the weakening of administrative courts through the Omnibus Law provides evidence that Indonesian regulation tends toward the liberal market model: it grants discretion that exceeds authority under the pretext of good governance, and it fosters conditions for corruption as well as human rights violations within the judiciary.

This book remains open to continuous refinement, and the author acknowledges that there is potential for enhancement through dissemination of concepts and interpretations developed thus far. The author also anticipates and welcomes reader feedback and corrections. While numerous texts on state administrative law are available, particularly in Indonesia, this book offers the following novel contributions to the field:

1) This book examines the significant changes brought about by Law No. 30/2014 on Government Administration, which expands the jurisdiction of administrative courts in Indonesia beyond the scope outlined in Law No. 51/2009 on State Administrative Courts (PTUN). The new legislation broadens the purview of PTUN to include written determinations and factual actions by administrative institutions or officials, even within the judiciary itself. Two controversial aspects of this expanded authority are covered here: the role of administrative courts in examining corruption cases that intersect with criminal corruption courts, and the application of decisions to citizens.
2) The book provides a critical analysis of specific administrative court cases related to human rights, offering a nuanced assessment of judicial decisions that either uphold or neglect the protection of citizens' rights.
3) The book delves into the intersection of administrative courts and corruption cases, revealing potential vulnerabilities created by the Law No. 30/2014 system whichmay be exploited for particular purposes.
4) Lastly, the book presents novel insights into the evolving authority of administrative courts following the enactment of Indonesia's Job Creation Law.

Structurally, the work is divided into six chapters. Brief abstracts of these chapters are provided in the following secions.

23 Ginsburg, "The Judicialization of Administrative Governance: Causes, Consequences and Limits."

Chapter 1. Concept Of State Administrative Law. This chapter presents a comprehensive examination of the conceptual framework and general understanding of state administrative law. It incorporates an analysis of the terminological intersection between the law and state administration. To exemplify the function of administrative courts, this chapter provides a detailed exposition of a landmark decision rendered by the Pekanbaru Administrative Court, which ruled in favor of the plaintiffs from an agrarian collective in a land dispute case. Furthermore, this chapter delineates several trends in the conceptualization of governmental paradigms concerning state administration. In this context, "paradigm" encompasses the developmental trajectory of state administrative concepts. The chapter also introduces the foundational principles of state administrative law, categorized into three distinct conceptual frameworks based on geographical and national characteristics. This tripartite classification serves as a prelude to understanding the specific model of state administrative law employed in Indonesia.

Chapter 2. Scope of State Administrative Law. This chapter examines the scope and breadth of administrative law within the broader legal framework. It begins by presenting the dichotomy between public and private law within national legal systems, positioning administrative law firmly within the public law domain. This classification stems from state administrative law's focus on regulating public interests, encompassing the legal relationships between the state and its constituent entities, as well as between the state and individual citizens, with particular emphasis on civic rights and obligations. The chapter then shifts to an analysis of the Universal Declaration of Human Rights and its reception in developing nations, including Indonesia. This section explores how the Declaration's principles, reflecting common moral imperatives such as freedom of expression, religious and ethnic equality, and gender parity, have been integrated into both political and legal frameworks. In delineating the boundaries of administrative law as a distinct discipline, the chapter aims to highlight its unique characteristics vis-à-vis other legal sciences. To illustrate these concepts, the chapter presents a case study of an administrative court ruling concerning governmental misconduct in the context of an internet shutdown in Papua. This example serves as a practical demonstration of state administrative law's scope and application.

Chapter 3. Administrative Law in Southeast Asia. This chapter extends the analysis to the evolution of administrative law across Southeast Asia, with a particular focus on the historical context and legal frameworks of state administration in the Philippines, Thailand, Malaysia, Singapore, and Vietnam. This comparative examination serves as a prelude to the book's central focus: an in-depth study of administrative law within Indonesia's democratic system. The chapter posits a key argument: that there exists a correlation between the inefficacy of administrative courts and the pervasiveness of corruption. This hypothesis is explored through a comparative lens, examining the varying degrees of judicial independence and corruption across the aforementioned Southeast Asian nations. To illustrate the practical implications of these concepts, the chapter concludes with an analysis of a land dispute case in which the government prevailed. This case study is utilized to highlight the discernible trend of executive populism within administrative court rulings, which raises questions about the balance of power between the judiciary and the executive branch. By juxtaposing the Indonesian system against its regional counterparts, this chapter provides a nuanced understanding of the challenges and complexities inherent in administrative law across Southeast Asia.

Chapter 4. State Administrative Law in Indonesia. This chapter provides a comprehensive examination of the foundational elements, enforcement mechanisms, and protective functions of state administrative law in Indonesia. It begins by elucidating the sources of state administrative law, followed by an analysis of its enforcement protocols and legal safeguards. The chapter then expands its discussion to the scope of protection and accountability within state administrative law, contextualizing these concepts within their historical frameworks. This historical perspective is particularly emphasized in the exploration of the administrative court's evolution. Central to this chapter is an in-depth investigation of the concept of administrative justice and its role in safeguarding citizens' rights. This focus stems from the intrinsic relationship between state administrative law and the dynamic interplay between governmental entities and the citizenry. The chapter proceeds to examine critically the challenges inherent in Indonesia's state administrative judicial system. To illustrate these issues, the chapter presents a case study of a land dispute ruling that favored municipal authorities, providing a practical example of the complexities within the system. The final section of the chapter is dedicated to a detailed discussion of the Peradilan Tata Usaha Negara (PTUN), or administrative court, with particular emphasis on the limitations of Keputusan Tata Usaha Negara (KTUN), or administrative decrees. This analysis serves to highlight the practical constraints and potential areas for reform within the current administrative law framework.

Chapter 5. State Administrative Law in Corruption Eradication. This chapter examines corruption as a fundamental challenge to democratic governance, with a particular focus on Indonesia. It provides a systematic analysis of the functions and roles of state administrative law in both preventing and combating corruption, interweaving this discussion with the principles of good governance, notably transparency and accountability. The chapter posits that good governance emerges from clean governance, which can only be achieved through the actions of a competent government adhering to principles of transparency and accountability. This theoretical framework sets the stage for the chapter's exploration of the various forms of legal oversight, including internal oversight (conducted by entities within the governmental structure) and external oversight (carried out by independent organizations or institutions). These forms of oversight comprise avital system of checks and balances within the administrative system. A portion of the chapter is dedicated to a critical analysis of state administrative law in relation to corruption offenses following the implementation of Law No. 30/2014. This section examines the phenomenon of convicted corrupt officials appealing to restore their status as public officials, highlighting the complexities and potential shortcomings in the current legal framework. The chapter concludes by exploring the potential of state administrative law to act as a preventive measure against corruption, and outlines potential strategies for anti-corruption law implementation.

Chapter 6. Omnibus Law and Its Influence on State Administrative Law. This chapter serves as both a reflective analysis and a conclusion to the book's examination of administrative law reform in Indonesia, specifically focusing on the implementation of the Omnibus Law. The introduction of this legislative approach has elicited diverse societal reactions, primarily due to the inherent tension between Indonesia's civil law tradition and the common law origins of the omnibus law concept. This divergence in philosophical, juridical, and sociological foundations presents significant challenges in maintaining consistency within the omnibus law framework. The chapter explores the opportunities and challenges associated with adopting this legislative approach within the Indonesian legal system. It highlights four primary benefits of the omnibus law model: streamlining the legislative process; mitigating parliamentary deadlock in draft law discussions; enhancing cost efficiency in legislation; and facilitating regulatory harmonization. It also highlights several issues that have arisen both prior to and following the implementation of the Omnibus Law. To illustrate the practical implications of these challenges, the chapter presents two significant case studies involving violations of indigenous land rights for palm oil plantations in Papua. Despite its purported benefits, the chapter argues that the omnibus law approach is not without substantial weaknesses. These include: a potentially less democratic nature; a tendency to limit public participation (thus conflicting with principles of deliberative democracy); reduced precision; caution in its formulation; and the risk of overstepping constitutional boundaries due to limited participation and insufficient scrutiny during the development of the Omnibus Law.

References

Almeida Costa, Arthur Barrêtto de. "Citation Networks in Administrative Law Books from the Civil Law World (Nineteenth Century)." *Comparative Legal History* 11, no. 2 (2023): 154–85. https://doi.org/10.1080/2049677X.2023.2270388

Ardiansyah, Wandi, Suparto, M. Rafi, and Pahmi Amri. "Bibliometric Analysis and Visualization of State Administrative Law in Scopus Database from 2017–2021." *Cogent Social Sciences* 10, no. 1 (2024). https://doi.org/10.1080/23311886.2024.2310935.

Asshiddiqie, Jimly. *Omnibus Law Dan Penerapannya Di Indonesia*. Jakarta: Konstitusi Press, 2020.

Bedner, Adriaan. "An Elementary Approach to the Rule of Law." *Hague Journal on the Rule of Law* 2, no. 1 (2010): 48–74. https://doi.org/10.1017/S1876404510100037

Ginsburg, Tom. "The Judicialization of Administrative Governance: Causes, Consequences and Limits." In *Administrative Law and Governance in Asia*, 11–30. Routledge, 2008. https://doi.org/10.4324/9780203888681

———. "Written Constitutions and the Administrative State: On the Constitutional Character of Administrative Law." In *Comparative Administrative Law*. Edward Elgar Publishing, 2010.

Ginsburg, Tom, and Albert H Y Chen. "Administrative Law and Governance in Asia." *Comparative Perspectives*, 2009. https://doi.org/10.4324/9780203888681

Latief, Abdul. *Hukum Administrasi Dalam Praktik Tindak Pidana Korupsi*. Jakarta: Kencana, 2016.

Lindenfeld, David F. *The Practical Imagination: The German Sciences of State in the Nineteenth Century*. University of Chicago Press, 2008.

Mannori, Luca, and Bernardo Sordi. "Science of Administration and Administrative Law." In *A Treatise of Legal Philosophy and General Jurisprudence: Vol. 9: A History of the Philosophy of Law in the Civil Law World, 1600-1900; Vol. 10: The Philosophers' Philosophy of Law from the Seventeenth Century to Our Days*, 225–61. Springer, 2009. https://doi.org/10.1007/978-90-481-2964-5_6

Mattarella, Bernardo Giorgio. "Administrative Law in Italy: An Historical Sketch." *Rivista Trimestrale Di Diritto Pubblico* 4 (2010). https://papers.ssrn.com/sol3/papers.cfm?abstract_id=2199888

Raadschelders, Jos C N. "The United States of America as Rechtsstaat: State and Administrative Law as Key to Understanding the Administrative State." HeinOnline, 2017. https://doi.org/10.1111/puar.12763

Suandi, I Wayan. "Eksistensi Kebijakan Publik Dan Hukum Dalam Penyelenggaraan Pemerintahan Daerah." *Jurnal Ilmiah Fakultas Ilmu Sosial Dan Ilmu Politik* 1, no. 1 (2010). http://portalgaruda.fti.unissula.ac.id/index.php?ref=browse&mod=viewarticle&article=12780

Wahid, Abdul, I Gusti Ayu Ketut Rachmi Handayani, and Lego Karjoko. "Legal Politics of Changes in Land Ownership Rights Regulations Post Omnibus Law Based on Pancasila Justice." In *International Conference On Law, Economic & Good Governance (IC-LAW 2023)*, 339–45. Atlantis Press, 2024. https://doi.org/10.2991/978-2-38476-218-7_57

Wibowo, Richo. "Good Governance as a Conceptual Framework to Address the Discussion of Public Private Distinction in Public Procurement." In *The 6th Public Procurement Student Research Conference*, 2014. https://www.nottingham.ac.uk/pprg/documentsarchive/phdconference2014/wibowo.pdf

Wibowo, Richo Andi. *Tata Kelola Pemerintahan Yang Baik Dan Pengadaan Barang Jasa Pemerintah: Pendekatan Perbandingan Hukum*. UGM PRESS, 2022.

Wibowo, Richo Andi, and Anak Agung Savita Padma. "Bagaimana Sebaiknya Arah Pengembangan Pembelajaran Hukum Administrasi Di Indonesia." law.ugm. January 20, 2024. https://law.ugm.ac.id/bagaimana-sebaiknya-arah-pengembangan-pembelajaran-hukum-administrasi-di-indonesia/

1 Concept of State Administrative Law

Introduction

Since the shift in the paradigm of the state as a, "night watchman," or what in the literature is often termed a, "watchdog state," there has been a fundamental change in the function of the state, from serving initially only in the field of internal security, to becoming manager of the citizens' welfare. This change in state function must, of course, enter the realm of the private lives of citizens and so far this has been in the context of the night watchman state isolated from the reach of the state. The state implements an administrative system to manage all government activities and aims to create prosperity for its citizens. Ginsburg provides a simple analogy to understand state administrative law through a hierarchy of retail and wholesale characteristics.[1] State administrative law at the retail level refers to government interaction with the private sector. At the wholesale level, state administrative law is related to the judicial control unit and to rule-making at a level below the legislature. This analogy provides a straightforward understanding of how state administrative law works in state life. In another article, Ginsberg and Chen explained that the fundamental convergence of the state administrative law system provides space for the right to submit cases to institutions, accept adverse decisions, and appeal third-party administrative decisions.[2] The essence of the state administrative law system is to empower government interaction with citizens and provide solutions to protect citizens' rights and participation.

The entry of state administration into citizens' private lives aims to enable the management of citizens' welfare. This certainly requires an instrument that will provide a legal basis for and a formal justification of the state's activities in attempting to regulate private matters, one which takes the form of a system of state administrative law.

1 Tom Ginsburg, "The Judicialization of Administrative Governance: Causes, Consequences and Limits," in *Administrative Law and Governance in Asia* (London: Routledge, 2008), 11–30, https://doi.org/10.4324/9780203888681.
2 Tom Ginsburg and Albert H. Y. Chen, "Administrative Law and Governance in Asia," in *Comparative Perspectives* (London: Routledge, 2009), https://doi.org/10.4324/9780203888681.

DOI: 10.4324/9781003518563-1

Administrative courts ensure justice for citizens in lawsuits against the government in specific cases, such as in land use disputes. As stipulated in Article 53 of Law No. 51/2009 on the State Administrative Court, lawsuits brought to administrative courts essentially aim to annul a state administrative decision. The administrative court ruling in Pekanbaru in 2020 exemplifies how a group of Tuasai farmers contested the development and expansion of self-funded community plantations in partnership with the private sector. Through the Pekanbaru State Administrative Court Ruling No. 23/G/TF/2020/PTUN/PBR, the court decided to halt activities and prohibit the use of partnership land between the Sumatra Environmental Law Enforcement Agency (BPPHLHK) and the private sector, which was proven to harm the Tuasai farmers. In this case, BPPHLHK Sumatra argued that the plaintiffs occupied an area that was part of the Riau Province Forest. Meanwhile, the plaintiffs argued that the defendants acted without a Boundary Determination Report. In this case, the panel of judges granted all of the plaintiffs' demands and ordered the defendants to pay damages.[3] In this context, the administrative court provided a solution for protecting the rights and participation of citizens, represented by the group of Tuasai farmers as the plaintiffs.

Before discussing how to develop a greater understanding of state administrative law, it is important to realize that the phrase, "state administrative law," refers to two units: namely the law and state administration. To gain a comprehensive understanding of this area of the law, it is necessary to understand each unit separately. The law and state administration are then synergized to comprehend state administrative law as a whole. The interpretation of the concept of the law in the academic literature is extensive, but fundamentally some interpretations are more narrow than others because they relate to the perspectives of experts assigning meaning to concepts of the law.

Conceptual Framework of Law and State Administration

In his analysis, Susanto delineates the fundamental concept of state administrative law into three distinct categories.[4] The first of these, rooted in the American perspective, defines administrative law according to its regulatory function. This approach emphasizes that state administrative law serves to delineate and govern the extent of governmental authority and actions. Crucially, the American perspective encompasses a legal framework for scrutinizing and reviewing administrative practices. The American conceptualization underscores the role of administrative law as a mechanism for both empowering and

3 Muhammad Arauf and H. B. Gusliana, "Penerapan Ganti Rugi Terhadap Warga Masyarakat Akibat Perbuatan Melanggar Hukum Pemerintah (Onrechtmatige Overheidsdaad) Melalui Peradilan Tata Usaha Negara," *Riau Law Journal* 7, no. 2 (2019): 231–47.

4 Sri Nurhari Susanto, "Komponen, Konsep Dan Pendekatan Hukum Administrasi Negara," *Administrative Law & Governance Journal* 4, no. 1 (2021): 144–57.

constraining governmental entities. The American tradition also highlights the dual nature of administrative law: on the one hand, it provides the legal basis for government operations, while on the other hand it establishes parameters within which these operations must occur. The inclusion of provisions for reviewing administrative practices further emphasizes the accountability aspect of this legal framework.[5] American administrative law is fundamentally rooted in the Administrative Procedure Act of 1946. The United States administrative law framework prioritizes formal legal processes over broader public regulatory and administrative functions. It further reflects a legalistic orientation that emphasizes procedural aspects and statutory compliance in administrative actions. By contrast, the English tradition pioneered by A.V. Dicey presents a distinct perspective on administrative law.[6] Dicey's approach, emerging from the British legal system, offers a different lens through which to view the relationship between administrative bodies and the law.

The juxtaposition of American and English concepts highlights the diverse theoretical underpinnings of administrative law across different legal traditions. The American model, with its focus on formal procedures and statutory frameworks, stands in potential contrast to Dicey's English approach, which emphasize different aspects of administrative legal theory. According to the English framework, administrative law is a form of legal discrimination between the government and the people. However, this concept lacks a clear focus on either substantive or formal law, leading modern English administrative law to move gradually away from Dicey's interpretation toward the concept pioneered by Ivor Jennings, who explains that this law relates to issues of state administration. The fundamental difference between the English and American concepts is that the American concept starts from the administrative process, while the English concept emphasizes the role of power. This means that the focus of administrative law in the English system relies on *ultra vires*, affecting the use of regulatory functions and public administration. The development of the English legal concept has progressed instages. Currently, English administrative law focuses on the public service with an emphasis on rights in public service, which considers both physical and psychological elements. The physical element refers to the availability of resources, while the psychological element refers to the behaviors or actions of administrative officials. A third conceptualization, rooted in the French tradition, was pioneered by André de Laubadère.[7] Laubadère posited that administrative law constitutes a branch of internal public law governing organizational structures

5 Kenneth Culp Davis, "Behavioral Science and Administrative Law," *Journal of Legal Education* 17, no. 2 (1964): 137–54.

6 Albert Venn Dicey, *Introduction to the Study of the Law of the Constitution* (London: Macmillan, 1956).

7 André de Laubadère, "B. Droit Administratif," *Revue Internationale de Droit Comparé* 16, no. 4 (1964): 771–73.

and administrative functions. The French conceptualization encompasses the organization of state administration, the examination of administrative activities, the mechanisms of administrative action, and patterns of administrative litigation and judicial oversight.[8]

The Netherlands, drawing from the French tradition, adopted a comprehensive approach to state administrative law. The Dutch model has subsequently exerted significant influence on Indonesia's administrative legal framework. The historical colonial relationship between the Netherlands and Indonesia serves as a conduit for this legal influence, resulting in Indonesia's legal system being closely affiliated with Dutch legal concepts.

The French concept of state administrative law, as adopted by the Netherlands and consequently influencing Indonesia, is characterized by its expansive scope. It encompasses both formal and material aspects of administrative law, including:

1. Administrative processes
2. Adaptive administrative changes in response to societal evolution
3. Regulatory mechanisms
4. Supervisory functions
5. Administrative judiciary

A distinguishing feature of the Dutch model is the establishment of specialized administrative courts, a practice also implemented in France to address the unique complexities of administrative law cases. This comprehensive approach represents a more holistic view of administrative law compared with some other legal traditions. It not only governs procedural aspects but also addresses the substantive elements of administrative actions, regulatory frameworks, and the means of resolving administrative disputes. The adoption of this model in Indonesia, through Dutch colonial influence, underscores the lasting impact of colonial legal systems on postcolonial nations' administrative structures. It also highlights the transnational nature of these legal concepts, particularly in the realm of administrative law.

Definitional Analysis of State Administrative Law

1. Definition of the Law
The concept of the law in Indonesia, as discussed by various scholars, extends beyond simple rules and regulations. Initially, thinkers like Simorangkir, Sastropranoto, and Tirtaatmidjaja defined the law as a set of enforceable rules governing social behaviors, with consequences for violations.

8 Horace B. Jacobini, *An Introduction to Comparative Administrative Law* (New York: Oceana Publications, 1991).

Sjahran Basah expanded this view, outlining the following five key functions of the law:[9]

1. Guiding society toward national goals
2. Building national unity
3. Preserving social harmony
4. Refining state and citizen behavior
5. Providing justice

The narrative then contrasts between narrow and broad interpretations of the law. The narrow view defines the law as state-created written regulations for maintaining order. The broader understanding and definition, however, includes both written and unwritten rules, created by both state and non-state entities, and encompasses as well thebehaviors, symbols, and cultural norms that contribute to social order. This comprehensive view suggests that the law is more than just a set of rules orformal regulations, and further comprises law enforcement behaviors and cultural perceptions of the law as a value system.

This analytical approach recognizes that the law's effectiveness depends not just on formal codes, but also on how it interacts with social norms and cultural values. For Indonesia, with its diverse cultural landscape, this broad understanding is particularly relevant. It implies that developing effective laws requires considering not only their content but also their cultural reception and social impact. This perspective can lead to a more nuanced, culturally appropriate, and effective legal system that truly serves the needs of Indonesia's diverse and dynamic society.

2. Definition and Paradigm of State Administration

State administration is portrayed as a vital tool used by governments to manage their countries and ensure the well-being of their citizens. This concept goes beyond simple governance to focus on how governments can effectively meet society's needs, especially in terms of welfare services. The narrative describes state administration as encompassing various aspects of running a country, including organization of the bureaucracy, planning of government activities, implementation of policies, and oversight of government actions.

A key emphasis is placed on creating a stable and measurable system. This ensures that government activities achieve their intended outcomes with predictable quality and quantity. The ultimate goal of state administration is to support the government in implementing policies designed to improve citizens' welfare. This view is reinforced by Leonard D. White's broader definition, which includes all state activities aimed at carrying out government

9 Basah, Sjachran. *Eksistensi Dan Tolak Ukur Badan Peradilan Administrasi Di Indonesia* (Bandung: Alumni, 1989).

policies.[10] This understanding of state administration reflects the following important ideas:

1. The government should actively work to meet citizens' needs.
2. Efficiency and measurability in government operations are crucial.
3. There should be a clear link between policy-making and implementation.
4. The focus should always be on benefiting citizens.

For a country like Indonesia, with its diverse population and complex challenges, this view of state administration is particularly relevant. It suggests that the government should:

- Develop systems that respond well to citizens' needs.
- Ensure efficient implementation of policies.
- Address a wide range of societal issues.
- Regularly measure and evaluate its performance.

State administration is essentially a comprehensive tool for achieving societal goals and ensuring citizen welfare, emphasizing efficiency, measurability, and citizen-focused outcomes.[11] Prajudi Atmosudirdjo views state administration in its broader function, which is to implementate and execute the government's wills, strategies, policies, and decisions in a tangible manner.[12] According to Atmosudirdjo, the state administrative function also includes implementing and administrating laws according to their articles as per established implementing regulations. To clarify the meaning of state administration, Atmosudirdjo details the context of implementing government policies, which includes the state apparatus as government apparatus, andthe role of state political institutions. State administration serves as a function of the government and its operational activities, and thereby governs the technical process of implementing the laws. This definition interprets state administration from two perspectives: as an organization and as an administration dedicated to achieving state and public objectives. This means that the goals established by the law are pursued through mandatory legal enforcement, or *dwingend recht*.[13]

10 Leonard D. White, "Public Administration Under the Federalists," *Boston University Law Review* 24 (1944): 144.

11 Leonard D. White, "Public Administration Under the Federalists," *Boston University Law Review* 24 (1944): 144.

12 S. Prajudi Atmosudirdjo, *Hukum Administrasi Negara* (Jakarta: Ghalia Indonesia, 1981).

13 Philipus M. Hadjon, *Pemerintahan Menurut Hukum, Surabaya, Universitas Airlangga* (Surabaya: Yuridika, 1992); Philipus M. Hadjon and R Sri Soemantri Marto Soewgnjo, *Pengantar Hukum Administrasi Negara Indonesia, Surabaya: Yuridika* (Surabaya: Yuridika, 2002); Fajlurrahman Jurdi, *Pengantar Hukum Administrasi Negara* (Jakarta Timur: Prenada Media, 2023).

This clarifies that while state administration is not merely about the actors who perform administrative functions, it is also about the methods, procedures, and prerequisites that collectively transform all available resources to achieve the state's goals. Ultimately, state administration is better understood as a system that involves all available elements and characteristics of the system to achieve a specific objective.

As a system, state administration naturally also fulfills the characteristics of that system, which includes having a purpose, having boundaries, generally being open (although in some cases it may be closed), consisting of various parts or subsystems, being holistic, having interconnectedness, performing transformation activities, having control mechanisms, and having the ability to regulate and adapt.[14]

The state administration system must be able to harmonize all of these primary objectives to achieve its goals. These system objectives are oriented toward quality, quantity, time, and the costs incurred. Of course, the state administration system has limitations in achieving its objectives. Every country has limitations in certain areas. Therefore, the state administration system must be able to determine the main objectives it intends to achieve within its limitations.

State administration is a dynamic system that evolves alongside changes in government and society. It emphasizes how shifts in governmental concepts and functions directly influence administrative systems. This text introduces the idea of paradigm shifts in state administration. A paradigm is defined as a set of views, values, methods, and principles adopted by a community at a given time. In society, paradigms encounter challenges that can lead to distrust and eventual change.

This concept of paradigms as applied to state administration suggests that administrative systems also undergo transitions from one paradigm to another. These paradigmatic shifts are seen as responses to external challenges and changing societal needs. Key implications of this perspective may include:

1. Adaptability: State administration must be flexible to respond to changing governmental concepts and societal needs.
2. Continuous Evolution: Administrative systems are not static and undergo ongoing development.
3. Reflection of Society: Changes in administration mirror broader societal and governmental shifts.
4. Awareness: Understanding paradigm shifts is crucial for the effective management of administrative systems.
5. Interconnectedness: There is a close link between governmental functions, societal needs, and administrative practices.

14 Tatang M. Amirin, *Pokok-Pokok Teori Sistem* (Denpasar: Rajawali, 1989).

For diverse and complex nations like Indonesia, this view also suggests that:

- Administrative systems should be responsive to changing societal needs.
- Ongoing evaluation and adaptation of practices is necessary.
- Administrators should be prepared for and open to paradigm shifts.

This presents state administration as a field that must evolve to remain effective and relevant in meeting the changing needs of both citizens and government. It encourages a proactive and flexible approach to public administration, which is particularly valuable in rapidly developing nations.[15]

In the development of the state administration paradigm, the stages of development and shifts in the state administration paradigm are divided into five levels: the paradigm of the dichotomy between politics and state administration; the paradigm of administrative principles; the paradigm of state administration as political science; the paradigm of public administration as administrative science; and the paradigm of state administration as state administration.

The initial paradigm of state administration was marked by the emergence of state administration as a dichotomy between politics and state administration. This paradigm occurred between 1900 and 1926 and was pioneered by Frank J. Goodnow and Leonard D. White.[16] In his book, *Politics and Administration*, Goodnow argues that politics should focus on policy or the expression of the people's will, while administration concerns the implementation of that policy or will. The separation between politics and administration is manifested by the division between the legislative body, which is responsible for expressing the people's will, and the executive body, which is responsible for implementing that will.[17] In this context, the judiciary assists the legislative body in determining goals and formulating policy.

A significant paradigm in state administration thought is known as the politics-administration dichotomy.This paradigm and its subsequent evolution reflect changing perspectives on the role and nature of public administration. Key aspects of this paradigm include:

1. Separation of Politics and Administration: The paradigm posits that administration should be kept separate from politics, free from value judgments or political influences.

15 Gopesh Anand, Eric C. Larson, and Joseph T. Mahoney, "Thomas Kuhn on Paradigms," *Production and Operations Management* 29, no. 7 (2020): 1650–57.

16 Herbert J. Storing, "Leonard D. White and the Study of Public Administration," *Public Administration Review* (1965): 38–51, https://doi.org/10.2307/974006

17 Frank J. Goodnow, *Politics and Administration: A Study in Government* (London: Routledge, 2017).

2. Value-Free Administration: It advocates for a "pure" administration, untainted by subjective values or political considerations.
3. Efficiency and Economy: The primary goals are achieving efficiency and economy in government bureaucracy.
4. Focus on Locus: This paradigm emphasizes the "where" of public administration, focusing on government bureaucracy as its primary domain.
5. Less Attention to Methods: It pays less attention to the "how" or the methods of public administration.

This narrative introduces the concept of paradigm shift in state administration. It suggests that such a paradigm, like all paradigms, undergoes a process of classification or change due to societal changes. Specifically, the source mentions a shift toward a new paradigm of administrative principles. This shift implies the following important points:

1. Dynamic Nature of Administrative Thought: Public administration theory is not static but evolves in response to changing societal needs and understandings.
2. Limitations of the Dichotomy: The shift suggests recognition of limitations in the politics-administration dichotomy.
3. Evolving Goals: While efficiency remains important, other goals may gain prominence in newer paradigms.
4. Broadening Focus: The shift might indicate a move toward considering both the "where" (locus) and the "how" (focus) of public administration.
5. Reintegration of Values: New paradigms may reintroduce consideration of values in administrative practice.

For countries like Indonesia, understanding this paradigm shift is crucial because:

- It suggests a need for flexible administrative systems that can adapt to changing theoretical understandings.
- It highlights the importance of balancing efficiency with other considerations in public administration.
- It implies that administrative practices should evolve to meet changing societal expectations and needs.

This captures a key moment in the evolution of public administration thought. It describes a shift from a paradigm that emphasized a strict separation of politics and administration, focusing on efficiency and bureaucracy, to a potentially more nuanced set of approaches that might reintegrate political considerations and broaden the focus of administrative practice. This evolution reflects the ongoing challenges of public administration in balancing efficiency with responsiveness to political and societal needs.

Some key experts have significantly influenced this discussion of paradigm changes in administrative principles, particularly those who supported its development:Willoughby, Gulick, and Urwick.[18] One such major paradigm shift in state administration occurred between 1927 and 1937. The core ideas of this paradigm were influenced by classical management concepts such as those of Henry Fayol and Frederick Taylor.[19] The two classical management experts introduced principles with the simple acronym POSDCORB (Planning, Organizing, Staffing, Directing, Coordinating, Reporting, and Budgeting). This view clearly shows that state administration issues are considered to be part of a process within the governmental system, which naturally starts with planning, followed by organizing, staffing, directing, coordinating, reporting, and budgeting. However, this thinking pattern is considered simplistic, as it treats state administration matters merely as administrativemanagement issues. Moreover, in this paradigm's view, the existence of POSDCORB is essentially universal and can be applied anywhere. This paradigm thereby no longer prioritizes locus, as it is considered applicable universally. This is a flawed assumption, because it suggests that administrative issues can be handled uniformly. This is problematic, because underlying state administration issues there are human factors in a society whose changeability or diversity may be difficult to predict.

In subsequent developments, a new paradigm emerged: state administration as political science. The emergence of this new paradigm was marked by a significant question posed by Fritz Morstein Marx, the editor of the book, *Elements of Public Administration*.[20] Marx questioned the separation of politics and administration and found the separation between state administration and politics to be impossible or unrealistic. How could state administration be separated in such a way from politics, given that state administration executes orders that are delivered by the politics of the state? Another supporter of this state administration paradigm as political science is Herbert Simon, who emphasized the inconsistency of administrative principles prioritizing classical management andconsidered those principles *not* to be universally applicable.[21]

Yeremias T. Keban asserts that state administration is not universally applicable or value-neutral and is instead shaped by specific values.[22] This view

18 William Franklin Willoughby, *Principles of Public Administration: With Special Reference to the National and State Governments of the United States* (Baltimore, MD: Johns Hopkins Press, 1927); Luther Gulick and Lyndall Urwick, *Papers on the Science of Administration* (London: Routledge, 2004).

19 Raymond Edwards, "An Elaboration of the Administrative Theory of the 14 Principles of Management by Henri Fayol," *International Journal for Empirical Education and Research* 1, no. 1 (2018): 41–51.

20 Fritz Morstein Marx, *Elements of Public Administration* (New York: Prentice-Hall, 1946).

21 Herbert A. Simon, *Administrative Behavior: A Study of Decision-Making Processes in Administrative Organizations*, 4th ed. (New York: The Free Press, 1997).

22 Yeremias T. Keban, *Dimensi Strategis Administrasi Publik Konsep, Teori, Dan Isu Edisi Kedua* (Yogyakarta: Gaya Media, 2008).

contradicts the earlier paradigm that advocated for a strict separation between politics and administration. The source text highlights a tension between the ideas of value-free administration and value-laden politics. It suggests that contemporary governance practices demonstrate the impossibility of truly value-neutral administration. Friedman's systems theory is further cited to emphasize that culture, which is inherently value-laden, is an inseparable element of administrative systems.[23] John Gaus's perspective that public administration theory is also political theory also reinforces this interconnectedness between politics and administration.[24]

This viewpoint has a number of implications:

1. It challenges the notion of administration as a purely technical, apolitical process.
2. It emphasizes the importance of cultural context in administration.
3. It suggests a more integrated approach to studying and practicing public administration.
4. It highlights the complex nature of public administration, involving technical, political, and cultural elements.
5. It implies a need for adaptive approaches that can accommodate different value systems and cultural contexts.

For diverse countries like Indonesia, administrative practices should be sensitive to local cultural values and political realities. The conceptualization above cautions against implementing universal administrative practices without considering local contexts, presenting instead a more nuanced view of public administration that acknowledges the intrinsic connection to values, culture, and politics. This challenges earlier paradigms that sought to separate these interconnected factors.

Public administration's evolution as an administrative science occurred between 1956 and 1970, introducing implementation of contemporary methodologies including quantitative analysis, systems theory, operations research, and econometrics. Public administration emphasized the study of organizational behavior and management analysis and posited that management principles were universally applicable across both private and public sectors. The most recent paradigm, emerging in the 1970s and continuing to evolve, is known as, "state administration as state administration." In contrast to its predecessor, which viewed state administration through the lens of political science, Keban argues that this new paradigm exhibits a more defined focus and

23 Lawrence M. Friedman, "Legal Culture and Social Development," *Law and Society Review* (1969): 29–44, https://doi.org/10.2307/3052760.

24 John M. Gaus, "Trends in the Theory of Public Administration," *Public Administration Review* 10, no. 3 (1950): 161–68.

locus. It centers on public policy theory, management, organizational theory, and related issues, and is firmly rooted in the public interest.

Gerald E. Caiden states that alongside the periodization of state administration paradigms, several streams within state administration should be considered alongside efforts to understand the science of state administration.[25] These streams include: the administrative process; the empirical; human behavior; bureaucratic analysis; social systems, decision-making; the mathematical; and the integrative.

Each stream has characteristics that differentiate it from the other streams. Keban notes that the administrative process stream relies on POSDCORB to ensure public administration succession.[26] The empirical stream relies on various cases or studies of public administration practices that can guide public administration succession and which do not rely solely on theories or generalizations. The human behavior stream also focuses on communication, conflict, motivation, leadership, status, and social interaction. These elements contribute to achieving certain goals. Meanwhile, the bureaucratic analysis stream focuses on applying Weberian bureaucratic principles, which are considered superior due to their reliance on a rationality that governs structures and processes based on technical knowledge and efficiency. Furthermore, the social systems stream sees organizations as open and closed social systems. Its development expands upon an understanding of the relationship between public administration and society. The decision-making stream then aims to prevent organizations from making wrong decisions. The mathematical stream utilizes mathematical and statistical models so that administrators no longer rely solely on traditional methods. Lastly, the integrative stream attempts to consolidate various iterations of the above-mentioned streams in public administration practice.

Caiden further develops these streams by dividing them into two major groups: the administrative process stream, which includes the empirical, decision-making, and mathematical streams, and the other streams, which are classified as holistic administrative system streams. Subsequent developments were driven by advancements in administrative practices at the time, prompting G. D. Garson and E. S. Overman to refine their previous opinions and unveil the existence of a new paradigm in 1983.[27] There was a refinement in using the term POSDCORB, which was revised to PAFHRIER (Policy analysis, Financial, Human Resources, Information, and External Relations). In subsequent years, state administration evolved concurrently with global and societal

25 Gerald E. Caiden, *Administrative Reform Comes of Age*, vol. 28 (Berlin: Walter de Gruyter GmbH & Co KG, 2014).

26 Yeremias T. Keban, *Enam Dimensi Strategis Administrasi Publik: Konsep, Teori Dan Isu* (Yogyakarta: Gava Media, 2004).

27 G. David Garson and E. Samuel Overman, *Public Management Research in the United States* (New York: Praeger, 1983).

progress. This evolution culminated in a paradigmatic shift within state administration, which Barzelay and Armajani characterized as a transition from a bureaucratic to a post-bureaucratic paradigm.[28] These two paradigms exhibit significant distinctions. The bureaucratic paradigm emphasizes:

1. Public interest, efficiency, administration, and control
2. Functions, authority, and structure
3. Cost assessment and responsibility
4. Adherence to rules and procedures
5. Operation of administrative systems

In contrast, the post-bureaucratic paradigm prioritizes:

1. Valuable societal outcomes, quality, and values
2. Products and adherence to norms
3. Missions, services, and outcomes
4. Providing societal value, building accountability, and strengthening work relationships
5. Understanding and applying norms, problem identification and resolution, and continuous improvement processes
6. Separation of service from control norm support; customer choice expansion; collective activity promotion; incentive provision; outcome measurement and analysis; and feedback enrichment

This demonstrates that there was a fundamental change in the approach to state administration, reflecting broader societal and organizational trends toward more flexible, outcome-oriented, and citizen-centric governance models.

Simultaneous with the development and shift in paradigms of state administration, D. Osborne and T. Gaebler introduced a highly renowned paradigm known for its reformative nature which reinvented government.[29] Imagine a government transforming from a rigid, power-wielding entity into a nimble, responsive organization that operates more like a well-oiled business. This is the paradigmatic shift in public administration that Osborne and Gaebler envisioned. They portrayed a government that sparks change, belongs to its community, thrives on healthy competition, and stays laser-focused on its mission and results.

In this reimagined landscape, the government doesn't just serve its citizens—it empowers them. The government is not afraid of competition and instead embraces competition to drive innovation. Rather than getting bogged

28 Michael Barzelay, *Breaking through Bureaucracy: A New Vision for Managing in Government* (Berkeley: University of California Press, 1992).

29 David Osborne and Ted Gaebler, *Reinventing Government: The Five Strategies for Reinventing Government* (Penguin, 1993).

down in bureaucratic processes, a reimagined government keeps its eyes on the prize, delivering results that matter. This new government also thinks like an entrepreneur, always looking ahead to anticipate challenges, and not afraid to decentralize power to be more effective.

This revolutionary idea of, "reinventing government," shares a lot of DNA with a concept called New Public Management (NPM). Both of these approaches laid the groundwork for what we now call, "good governance." Hood, a respected voice in public administration, breaks down NPM into several key ingredients. He talks about bringing professional management techniques from the business world into government offices, using hard data to measure performance and focusing on what the government produces rather than on how it operates.

Hood's vision extends to breaking large, unwieldy government departments down into smaller, more manageable units. He advocates for injecting a dose of healthy competition into public services and borrowing best practices from the private sector. All of this, Hood argues, should be done while keeping an eye on using resources wisely and maintaining discipline in operations.

This new approach to governance represents a seismic shift in how we think about the role of government in society. It involves creating a government that is efficient, responsive, innovative, and truly at the service of its citizens.[30] According to Ferlie, Ashburner, Fitzgerald, and Pettigrew, NPM has undergone a shift in orientation toward an efficiency drive, which prioritizes efficiency in performance measurement, downsizing, and decentralization, emphasizing simplifying structures, enriching functions, and delegating authority to smaller units to function more quickly and accurately.[31] "In Search of Excellence" is a movement that prioritizes optimal performance by leveraging science and technology and a public service orientation which emphasizes quality, mission, and values. It further prioritizes the aspirations and needs of individual users and citizens.By granting higher authority to officials elected by the community, including their representatives, this reimagined governance system emphasizes social learning in public service delivery and underscores continuous performance evaluation, community participation, and accountability.

Warsito Utomo explains that a paradigm shift in public administration has occurred from traditional public administration (TPA) toward NPM.[32] Suppose TPA emphasizes the orientation of public administration on control, order, and prediction (COP) and is bound to political authority, tightening

30 Christopher Hood, "A Public Management for All Seasons?," *Public Administration* 69, no. 1 (1991): 3–19.

31 Ferlie Ewan et al., "The New Public Management in Action," *Long Range Planning* 30, no. 1 (1997): 145.

32 Warsito Utomo, *Administrasi Publik Baru Indonesia: Perubahan Paradigma Dari Administrasi Negara Ke Administrasi Publik* (Yogyakarta: Pustaka Pelajar, 2009).

control, and following instructions. In that case, NPM instead emphasizes alignment, creativity, and empowerment (ACE).

According to Utomo, the state administration used by the government in governing the country has undergone a shift in emphasis from, "administration of public," which designates the state as the sole agent implementing state functions, to, "administration for public," which emphasizes state functions or government serving in the public service.An, "administration by public" is oriented toward the differentiation of public demands. This means that the state's role is to act merely as a facilitator and catalyst, putting customers in the driver's seat. In other words, the state is no longer the primary driving force.

Utomo's opinion emphasizes a significant paradigm shift in which the state, which initially acted as the sole actor in government administration, now becomes a facilitator. The field of economics reflects this shift in roles. Some private sector roles have helped create balance in the economy, especially in influencing macro and microeconomic life and regulation. Jim Schiller asserts that the entry of the private sector into governance has yielded rapid adaptation and innovation in public participation, especially in the context of world after the New Order regime in Indonesia.[33] The post-New Order period brought about a challenging economic situation that led Indonesia to seek assistance from the International Monetary Fund (IMF). Furthermore, the government continues to face significant challenges in overcoming the inherent politics of racism that emerged in the early days of reform. The government must find a way to convince the public that economic growth is still needed to restore legitimacy, while also ensuring that its policies will not lose public support.

The shift in the paradigm of state administration has also led to a shift in the meaning of the word, "public." The understanding of the term, "public," previously perceived as the state or government, has shifted to a more complex meaning: namely, society. Society is no longer just the target object of state administration but also the actor in state administration activities. This approach to state administration is no longer focused solely on the state but more on society or a customer-oriented approach.[34]

Utomo states that in the new paradigm of state administration, all processes, systems, procedures, hierarchies, or the lawful state are no longer the primary reference points. However, they still need to be known and remain essential.[35] Results, teamwork, and flexibility must be prioritized and driven by the pressure, influence, and differentiation of public demand. The new paradigm of state administration is indeed based on tangible evidence of the

33 Jim Schiller, "Indonesia: Living with Uncertainty," *Policy, Organisation and Society* 18, no. 1 (1999): 123–39.

34 Hetifah Sj Sumanto, *Inovasi, Partisipasi Dan Good Governance* (Jakarta: Yayasan Obor Indonesia, 2006).

35 Warsito Utomo, *Administrasi Publik Baru Indonesia: Perubahan Paradigma Dari Administrasi Negara Ke Administrasi Publik* (Yogyakarta: Pustaka Pelajar, 2009).

functioning of a defined process, system, and procedure. Consequently, flexibility in various aspects is required to achieve the goals of state administration.

J. V. Denhardt and R. B. Denhardt state that to transition from the classical administration paradigm and reinvent the government toward the New Public Service paradigm, public administration must adhere to several principles: serve citizens, not customers; seek the public interest; value citizenship over entrepreneurship; think strategically; act democratically; recognize that accountability is not simple; serve rather than steer; and value people, not just productivity.[36] The rapid paradigm shift over the past few decades thus indicates that an increasing focus on the influence of public administration is due to a growing number of state failures producing administrative dysfunction.

3. Definition of State Administrative Law

In the Netherlands, the term, ***administratifrecht***, or ***bestuursrecht***, refers to the administrative environment or administrative law separate from the legislative and judicial environments. The term, ***droit administratif***, as it is used in France means administrative law. In English, the phrase administrative law is used and is similar to the term used in German: ***verwaltung recht.***

Indonesian experts use various terms in the literature of this field. Wirjono Prodjodikoro once used the term, "hukum tata usaha pemerintahan," or government administrative law, while Djulal Husein prefers to use the term, "hukum tata usaha negara," or state administrative law.[37] The term, "hukum administrasi negara," or state administrative law, was emphasized in Utrecht, although initially, "hukum tata usaha Indonesia" and later "hukum tata usaha negara Indonesia" were used, which mean Indonesian administrative law and Indonesian state administrative law respectively.[38] The term, "hukum administrasi negara," or state administrative law, stemmed from a collective agreement made during a faculty staff meeting of law faculties from all over Indonesia in March 1973 in Cirebon.[39] This agreement was based on the idea that state administrative law is broader and more in line with the legal development climate in Indonesia.[40]

The term "state administrative law," as the name of a course in the law faculty curriculum, did not go smoothly. The Minister of Education and

36 Janet Vinzant Denhardt, *The New Public Service, Expanded Edition: Serving, Not Steering* (New York: ME Sharpe, 2007); Robert B Denhardt and Janet Vinzant Denhardt, "The New Public Service: Serving Rather than Steering," *Public Administration Review* 60, no. 6 (2000): 549–59.

37 Wirjono Prodjodikoro, *Asas-Asas Ilmu Negara Dan Politik* (Bandung: PT. Eresco, 1971).

38 Ernst Utrecht, *Pengantar Hukum Tatausaha Negara Indonesia* (Jakarta: NV Bali Buku Indonesia, 1957).

39 Yos Johan Utama, Hukum Administrasi Negara, Universitas Terbuka (Tangerang Selatan: Tangerang Selatan, 2018).

40 W. Riawan Tjandra, *Hukum Administrasi Negara* (Jakarta: Sinar Grafika, 2021); Yusri Munaf, *Hukum Administrasi Negara* (Pekanbaru: Marpoyan Tujuh, 2016); Nur Asyiah, *Hukum Administrasi Negara* (Yogyakarta: Deepublish, 2018).

Culture's Decree No. 0198/U/1972 Regarding the Guidelines for the Minimum Curriculum of State and Private Higher Education Institutions used the course name, ***Hukum Tata Pemerintahan*** (HTP), or administrative law, as a compulsory subject in law faculties.[41] Until 1983, the use of the name "HAN" was reinstated with the Minister of Education and Culture's Decree No. 31/1983 Regarding the Core Curriculum of the Bachelor of Law Education Program. Along the way, these terms did not become universally accepted. Some legal products at that time, such as the, "Garis Besar Haluan Negara (GBHN)," or the Outline of State Policy, Law No. 14/1970, Concerning the Basic Principles of the Judiciary, and Law No. 5/1986, used the phrase "peradilan tata usaha negara," rather than, "peradilan administrasi negara," both of which mean, "administrative court." This proves that using the phrase "state administrative law" is not absolute and final. The striking differences among experts have contributed to the evolution in the use of different terminology.

Interrelationship between State Administrative Law and Public Law

It would be beneficial to gain an understanding of the correlation between state administrative law and public law by analyzing the actions and authority of the government in order to identify this linkage. Material administrative law is situated somewhere between private law and criminal law. Criminal law contains norms that are of such importance to society that it would not be appropriate to entrust their enforcement to private individuals, and therefore enforcement must be carried out by the authorities. Private law contains norms whose enforcement *can* be entrusted to private individuals. Between these two fields of law lies administrative law (intermediary law). In the opinion of Wahid, the substance of administrative law is located somewhere between private law and criminal law.[42] One illustrative example of administrative law as an intermediary is in the issuance of building permits. When granting building permits, the government ensures the safety aspects of the building from the planning to the construction stages. The government ensures that safety requirements are designed before granting the permit. Conversely, if the conditions or requirements are not met, the government can impose criminal sanctions. W.F. Prins stated that every regulation based on administrative law is primarily accompanied by several criminal provisions, as in the Latin term, ***in cauda venenum***, which means, "there is poison in the tail end."[43]

41 Fakhruddin Razy, *Buku Ajar Hukum Administrasi Negara* (Purwokerto Selatan: Pena Persada, 2020).

42 Ali Abdul Wahid, "Kedudukan Hukum Administrasi Negara Dalam Tata Hukum Indonesia," *Jurnal Sosial Dan Humanis Sains (JSHS)* 2, no. 1 (2017).

43 W. F. Prins and R. Kosim Adisapoetra, *Pengantar Ilmu Hukum Administrasi Negara, Cet* (V. Jakarta: PT. Pradnya Paramita, 1993).

The necessity for state administrators to understand the boundaries and essence of the power inherent in their roles, including the purposes, nature, and sanctions associated with their obligations, is of paramount importance. Additionally, state administrative law furnishes insight into the regulations or standards that safeguard rights and interests. The categorization of state administrative law as either private or public law is contingent upon the content and nature of the relationships being governed. This classification is based on the protection of various interests. These interests are both individual and general to some extent.

The classification of state administrative law into private and public law is inextricably linked to the content and nature of the relationships governed and is based on the interests being protected. In some instances, these interests are individual, while in others they are general. It is therefore necessary to provide a clear delineation of these legal relationships, encompassing the rights and obligations of the individuals involved. Initially, state administrative law was a branch of constitutional law that evolved in response to societal demands and the emergence of new legal principles within this field of legal studies. Consequently, state administrative law has evolved into a distinct field that has surpassed constitutional law andis now a subset of public law, encompassing regulations pertaining to general issues. In the context of the public interest, the collective good of the nation, society, and the state must take precedence over any individual, group, or regional set of interests. This implies that individual interests must be protected in a balanced manner to achieve the goals of the state and government.

The correlation between state administrative law and international law is related to the regulation of the relationship between the authorities and society.[44] The implementation of conventions and international agreements, such as those on human rights that have been ratified, is inextricably linked to state administrative law. However, a distinctive feature of state administrative law in Indonesia is its instrumental nature within a dualistic legal system. Consequently, the reflection of state administrative law in international agreements only binds the state and its government, while the regulations that bind the public require separate legislation.

Functional Dimensions of State Administrative Law

In terms of its functions, state administrative law can be divided into three categories: normative, instrumental, and assurance. Philipus M. Hadjon posits that these three functions are interrelated.[45] The normative function encom-

44 I. Nyoman Gede Remaja, *Hukum Administrasi Negara, Singaraja: Fakultas Hukum Universitas Panji Sakti* (Singaraja: Universitas Panji Sakti, 2017).

45 Philipus M. Hadjon, *Pemerintahan Menurut Hukum, Surabaya, Universitas Airlangga* (Surabaya: Yuridika, 1992)

passes the establishment of rules regarding the authority to govern. In its operationalization, it necessitates an instrumental function to establish benchmarks for the utilization of such authority. Conversely, the assurance function is reflected in the manner in which the exercise of power provides legal protection guarantees for society.

Normative Function

A comprehensive investigation of state administrative law norms necessitates a detailed examination of legislative regulations. The roadmap is not solely reliant on the content of legal rules and regulations. Rather, a combination of various rules and decisions of congress or the state administrative court (TUN) is required, which collectively constitutes state administrative law. In general, legal provisions related to state administrative law are merely general norms requiring further details to be delegated to implementing rules, or "terugtred." This term is used to describe the legislative retreat action for several reasons.[46] Firstly, state administrative law (TUN) has a broad scope of coverage, while formal laws have comprehensive limitations on regulation. TUN legal norms must be adapted to accommodate various changes and developments over time. Those responsible for formulating laws are constrained if the developments in question are entirely contained within a formal regulation. From a technical standpoint, laws necessitate the implementation of supplementary rules providing detailed guidelines for interpreting the general content of the law. This is evidenced by the enactment of regulations or decisions at the lower levels of state administrative law, such as in presidential decrees and ministerial regulations.

All governmental actions must be conducted in accordance with the legality principle. The government's initial objective is to ascertain the legality of its actions with regard to the law, with the aim of establishing a basis for action. In the event that the government is unable to identify a basis for its actions within the relevant legislation, it is then at liberty to exercise its discretionary authority, or *freies ermessen*.[47]

Nevertheless, the utilization of *freies ermessen* is constrained by clear limitations to ensure that the government's freedom to act does not exceed its inherent powers. At the level of discretion, ethical considerations are necessary to ensure that the government's actions are aligned with the principles of justice and fairness. Sjachran Basah posits that the exercise of discretion must be based on moral accountability to God and the limits of the legal hierarchy.[48]

46 S. F. Marbun and Deno Kamelus, *Dimensi-Dimensi Pemikiran Hukum Administrasi Negara* (Jakarta: UII Press, 2001).

47 Ali Abdul Wahid, "Kedudukan Hukum Administrasi Negara Dalam Tata Hukum Indonesia," *Jurnal Sosial Dan Humanis Sains (JSHS)* 2, no. 1 (2017).

48 Basah, Sjachran. *Eksistensi Dan Tolak Ukur Badan Peradilan Administrasi Di Indonesia* (Bandung: Alumni, 1989).

The limits of the legal hierarchy in this regard are twofold. The upper limit concerns the consistency of rules at levels lower than those above them. The lower level pertains to the boundaries of citizens' human rights, and the actions of state administrative bodies must not exceed these boundaries. Moreover, according to Basah, discretion must adhere to the General Principles of Good Governance. Consequently, the normative function of state administrative law is to regulate and provide guidelines for government actions to align with the ideals of the rule of law.

Instrumental Function

In fulfilling its instrumental role, the government employs juridical instruments as guidelines that are then applied through specific regulations, decisions, and policies. In countries that adhere to the welfare state model, the delegation of government authority is a logical consequence of this model's complex scope of actions and responsibilities. In order to establish a framework for the exercise of its inherent authority, the government must devise and develop a range of legal instruments that delineate the means by which its governance functions are to be carried out.

Guarantee Function

The guarantee function of state administrative law is defined by the manner in which the law ensures the protection of citizens through state administrative actions. Sjachran Basah posits that the function of state administrative law is operationalized whenever violations occur resulting in harm to citizens' rights. Conversely, state administrative law serves to safeguard the operations of state administration, provided that it adheres to the parameters of applicable legislation. In this capacity, state administrative law addresses disputes between the government and citizens through the judiciary.

These three functions of state administrative law serve as the foundation of its existence, providing a framework for the government to conduct activities in accordance with existing regulations and based on the legality principle. Additionally, general principles are of significant importance when the government exercises discretion. All government operations are subject to clear moral and legal responsibilities. The government must employ legal instruments providing for its actions to comply with formal and material rules and which do not harm citizens.[49]

49 Ali Abdul Wahid, "Kedudukan Hukum Administrasi Negara Dalam Tata Hukum Indonesia," *Jurnal Sosial Dan Humanis Sains (JSHS)* 2, no. 1 (2017).

Paradigmatic Shift in Governmental Administration

Hamzah posits that Law No. 30/2014 on Government Administration represents an effort to improve government administration while emphasizing the state and government's responsibility to provide efficient and affordable public services. This legislation represents a shift in the paradigm of government administration toward a new paradigm of public service that has evolved in line with the era of increasing information transparency for citizens. As a consequence of this development, the nature and scope of government duties have become more complex. The far-reaching implications of Law No. 30/2014 extend to the administrative and judicial systems. This legislation also serves as a framework for safeguarding the legal rights of citizens utilizing public services and provides a novel legal foundation for administrative courts in the adjudication of state administrative disputes.[50]

Nevertheless, Law No. 30/2014, which underscores the significance of public participation, necessitates the formulation of more precise regulations on government administration in its implementation. This, in turn, requires adjustments in administrative and judicial procedures to ensure harmonization with Law No. 30/2014. Barnes presents a historical and comparative analysis of the transformation of the government administration paradigm into three generations: the judicial, the legislative, and the administrative.[51] According to Barnes, the judicial model, as the inaugural generation, emerged from traditional administrative and regulatory models whose fundamental structure has remained relatively stable since the 19th century and into the future. The legislative model, representing the second generation, is distinguished by its emphasis on rule-making by legislative and executive bodies. In contrast to the collaborative dialogue between citizens and institutions characterizing the first model, the second model regards public participation as a defensive right. In contrast, the administrative model, representing the third generation, adheres to democratic principles in all fields, including public policy. Accordingly, this third-generation model represents the optimal paradigm for the development of contemporary society. It is particularly well-suited to the government administration law, which emphasizes citizen participation and protection, and aligns with the conduct of government officials.

50 M. Guntur Hamzah, "Paradigma Baru Penyelenggaraan Pemerintahan Berdasarkan Undang-Undang Administrasi Pemerintahan (Kaitannya Dengan Perkembangan Hukum Acara Peratun)," in *Makalah Yang Disampaikan Pada Seminar Sehari Dalam Rangka HUT Peradilan Tata Usaha Negara Ke-26, Yang Diselenggarakan Di Hotel Mercure, Jakarta*, vol. 26, 2016, https://ptun-jakarta.go.id/wp-content/uploads/file/makalah_narasumber_hut_peratun_2017/prof_dr_m_guntur_hamzah_sh/Makalah%20Prof.%20Dr.%20M.%20Guntur%20Hamzah.pdf.

51 Javier Barnes, "Towards a Third Generation of Administrative Procedure," in *Comparative Administrative Law* (Cheltenham: Edward Elgar Publishing, 2010), https://doi.org/10.4337/9781849808101.00030.

Law No. 30/2014 represents a new foundation and material legal framework for state administrative courts. It has altered the absolute competence of the courts, including several points in the administrative judicial procedures. One aspect of Law No. 30/2014 that has implications for the expansion of administrative judicial authority is Article 21. This article stipulates that the court is empowered to accept, examine, and decide on the presence or absence of elements of the abuse of authority by government officials, a competence that was not applicable before the enactment of this law. In this context, the administrative courts are responsible for determining whether government officials have abused their authority, including in cases of corruption.

The scope of the concept previously regulated in Law No. 5/1986, as amended by Law No. 9/2004, and then Law No. 51/2009 on the state administrative court, has expanded following the enactment of Law No. 30/2014 on Government Administration. The expansion encompasses the definition of state administrative decisions as outlined in Article 87 of Law No. 30/2014, the expansion of administrative judicial competence as stipulated in Article 1, point (8) of Law No. 30/2014, the authority of administrative courts encompassing state administrative decisions, and the factual actions of state administrative officials. There has been a paradigm shift regarding the silent actions of administrative officials from negative fictitious to positive fictious as stated in Article 53 of Law No. 30/2014. This shift entails the competence of administrative courts to hear post-administrative action lawsuits by superior officials, with a tiered process of internal examination of government agencies, and legalizing decisions through electronic forms. In accordance with the principle of *lex posterior derogate legi priori*, several provisions in Law No. 51/2009 on the Administrative Court and its amendments are no longer applicable in light of Law No. 30/2014 on Government Administration and will not be applied by administrative court judges.

Conclusion

With the integration of state administration into the private lives of citizens, there is a renewed aim is to fulfill the function of managing citizens' welfare. This necessitates a system of administrative law that provides a legal basis for the state to implement the system and serves as the justification for the state's activities in attempting to regulate private matters. Each term or phrase associated with state administrative law has different variations in each country. The Netherlands uses the terms, *administratifrecht*, or *bestuursrecht*, which means, "the environment of power," or an administration separated from the legislative and judicial environments. France uses the term, *droit administratif*, which means "free administrative law." England uses the phrase "administrative law," which is similar to the term used in Germany: *verwaltung recht*.

The diversity in the use of different terminology also applies to the Indonesian context. Indonesian experts use various phrases. Prodjodikoro uses the phrase, "hukum tata usaha pemerintahan," or "government administrative law," while

Djulal Husein prefers to use the phrase, "hukum tata usaha negara," or "state administrative law."[52] The use of the phrase, "hukum administrasi negara," was first introduced by Utrecht, although initially, "hukum tata usaha Indonesia," and then later, "hukum tata usaha negara Indonesia," were the words used.[53] The phrase, "hukum administrasi negara," is inseparable from the joint agreement reached during the joint faculty staff meeting from law faculties across Indonesia in March 1973 in Cirebon.[54] This agreement was based on the idea that state administrative law is broader and more suitable for the legal climate in Indonesia's development.[55]

The fundamental concept of state administrative law is now divided into three general concepts. Firstly, the American concept is based on the definition of administrative law that emphasizes the regulation of government power and actions, including laws governing the review of administrative practices. United States definitions rely on the administrative process outlined in the Administrative Procedure Act of 1946, which focuses on formal law rather than on regulation and public administration.

Secondly, there is the English concept of administrative law as pioneered by A. V. Dicey.[56] Dicey's English definition posits that administrative law represents a form of legal discrimination perpetrated by the government against the people. However, this English concept lacks a clear focus on either substantive or formal law. As a result, modern English administrative law has gradually moved away from Dicey's interpretation and has shifted instead toward the concept pioneered by Ivor Jennings, who related administrative law to issues of state administration. The fundamental distinction between the English and American concepts lies in their respective emphases. The American concept is primarily concerned with the administrative process, whereas the English concept places greater emphasis on the exercise of power. This implies that English administrative law is concerned with the concept of *ultra vires*, which has implications for the utilization of regulatory functions in public administration. The evolution of English legal concepts has unfolded in a systematic manner. Currently, English administrative law is focused on the concept of the public service, with an approach to public service rights that encompasses both physical and psychological elements. The physical element pertains to

52 Wirjono Prodjodikoro, *Asas-Asas Ilmu Negara Dan Politik* (Bandung: PT. Eresco, 1971).

53 Ernst Utrecht, *Pengantar Hukum Tatausaha Negara Indonesia* (Jakarta: NV Bali Buku Indonesia, 1957).

54 Yos Johan Utama, *Hukum Administrasi Negara, Universitas Terbuka* (Tangerang Selatan: Tangerang Selatan, 2018).

55 W. Riawan Tjandra, *Hukum Administrasi Negara* (Jakarta: Sinar Grafika, 2021); Nur Asyiah, *Hukum Administrasi Negara* (Deepublish, 2018).

56 Albert Venn Dicey, *The Law of the Constitution*, vol. 1 (Oxford: Oxford University Press, 2013); Albert Venn Dicey, *Introduction to the Study of the Law of the Constitution* (London: Macmillan, 1956).

the availability of resources, whereas the psychological element concerns the behaviors or actions of administrative officials.

The third concept is that of the French, which was first developed by J. Laubadere.[57] He posits that administrative law is a branch of internal public law that governs the organization and activities of administration. The specifics of this concept encompass the organization of state administration, the examination of administrative activities, the instruments of action, and the patterns of litigation or administrative court control.[58]

The concept of state administrative law in France, which was aso adopted by the Netherlands and thereby influenced adoption of the administrative law system in Indonesia, is of considerable significance. This is due to Indonesia's legal system being based on the Dutch legal system, as Indonesia was previously a Dutch colony. The French concept of state administrative law encompasses almost all aspects of the original concept, including both formal and material elements. These include administrative processes, or the administrative developmental changes over time in certain regulations, supervision, and administrative justice. Consequently, France has established a specialized administrative judiciary.

The role of state administrative law in protecting human rights in Indonesia isessential to understanding and acknowledging the influence of a community of international actors, particularly institutions like the World Bank, which provided support to the domestic economy around 1992. The World Bank underscored the necessity for developing countries receiving assistance to foster the establishment of effective governance. Good governance subsequently spread to the fields of national and international governance and state law. Over time, the concepts in the principles of good governance have evolved in conjunction with the twin goals of economic development and preservation of the rule of law, with the ultimate objective of establishing a connection between the administrative law system and human rights. Indeed, these newly reenvisioned principles of good governance have been established on the basis of protecting human rights. The formation of legislation has been identified as a key contributing factor influencing the establishment of essential human rights protection going forward.

References

Amirin, Tatang M. *Pokok-Pokok Teori Sistem*. Denpasar: Rajawali, 1989.

Anand, Gopesh, Eric C. Larson, and Joseph T. Mahoney. "Thomas Kuhn on Paradigms." *Production and Operations Management* 29, no. 7 (2020): 1650–57. https://doi.org/10.1111/poms.13188

57 André de Laubadère, "B. Droit Administratif," *Revue Internationale de Droit Comparé* 16, no. 4 (1964): 771–73.

58 Horace B. Jacobini, *An Introduction to Comparative Administrative Law* (New York: Oceana Publications, 1991).

Arauf, Muhammad, and H. B. Gusliana. "Penerapan Ganti Rugi Terhadap Warga Masyarakat Akibat Perbuatan Melanggar Hukum Pemerintah (Onrechtmatige Overheidsdaad) Melalui Peradilan Tata Usaha Negara." *Riau Law Journal* 7, no. 2 (2019): 231–47. https://doi.org/10.30652/rlj.v7i2.8083

Asyiah, Nur. *Hukum Administrasi Negara*. Yogyakarta: Deepublish, 2018.

Atmosudirdjo, S. Prajudi. *Hukum Administrasi Negara*. Jakarta: Ghalia Indonesia, 1981.

Barnes, Javier. "Towards a Third Generation of Administrative Procedure." In *Comparative Administrative Law*. Cheltenham: Edward Elgar Publishing, 2010. https://doi.org/10.4337/9781849808101.00030

Barzelay, Michael. *Breaking through Bureaucracy: A New Vision for Managing in Government*. Berkeley: University of California Press, 1992. https://doi.org/10.1525/9780520912496

Basah, Sjachran. *Eksistensi Dan Tolak Ukur Badan Peradilan Administrasi Di Indonesia*. Bandung: Alumni, 1989.

Caiden, Gerald E. *Administrative Reform Comes of Age*. Vol. 28. Berlin: Walter de Gruyter GmbH & Co KG, 2014.

Davis, Kenneth Culp. "Behavioral Science and Administrative Law." *Journal of Legal Education* 17, no. 2 (1964): 137–54. https://www.jstor.org/stable/42891618

Denhardt, Janet Vinzant. *The New Public Service, Expanded Edition: Serving, Not Steering*. New York: ME Sharpe, 2007.

Denhardt, Robert B., and Janet Vinzant Denhardt. "The New Public Service: Serving Rather Than Steering." *Public Administration Review* 60, no. 6 (2000): 549–59. https://doi.org/10.1111/0033-3352.00117

Dicey, Albert Venn. *Introduction to the Study of the Law of the Constitution*. London: Macmillan, 1956.

Dicey, Albert Venn. *The Law of the Constitution*. Vol. 1. Oxford: Oxford University Press, 2013.

Edwards, Raymond. "An Elaboration of the Administrative Theory of the 14 Principles of Management by Henri Fayol." *International Journal for Empirical Education and Research* 1, no. 1 (2018): 41–51. https://doi.org/10.35935/edr/21.5241

Ewan, Ferlie, Andrew Pettigrew, Lynn Ashburner, and Louise Fitzgerald. "The New Public Management in Action." *Long Range Planning* 30, no. 1 (1997): 145. https://doi.org/10.1016/S0024-6301(97)86612-5

Friedman, Lawrence M. "Legal Culture and Social Development." *Law and Society Review* (1969): 29–44. https://doi.org/10.2307/3052760

Garson, G. David, and E. Samuel Overman. *Public Management Research in the United States*. New York: Praeger, 1983.

Gaus, John M. "Trends in the Theory of Public Administration." *Public Administration Review* 10, no. 3 (1950): 161–68. https://doi.org/10.2307/972811

Ginsburg, Tom. "The Judicialization of Administrative Governance: Causes, Consequences and Limits." In *Administrative Law and Governance in Asia*, 11–30. London: Routledge, 2008. https://doi.org/10.4324/9780203888681.

Ginsburg, Tom, and Albert H. Y. Chen. "Administrative Law and Governance in Asia." In *Comparative Perspectives*. London: Routledge, 2009. https://doi.org/10.4324/9780203888681.

Goodnow, Frank J. *Politics and Administration: A Study in Government*. London: Routledge, 2017. https://doi.org/10.4324/9781351308281.

Gulick, Luther, and Lyndall Urwick. *Papers on the Science of Administration*. London: Routledge, 2004. https://doi.org/10.4324/9780203509241.

Hadjon, Philipus M. *Pemerintahan Menurut Hukum. Surabaya, Universitas Airlangga.* Surabaya: Yuridika, 1992.

Hadjon, Philipus M., and R. Sri Soemantri Marto Soewgnjo. *Pengantar Hukum Administrasi Negara Indonesia. Surabaya: Yuridika.* Surabaya: Yuridika, 2002.

Hamzah, M. Guntur. "Paradigma Baru Penyelenggaraan Pemerintahan Berdasarkan Undang-Undang Administrasi Pemerintahan (Kaitannya Dengan Perkembangan Hukum Acara Peratun)." In *Makalah Yang Disampaikan Pada Seminar Sehari Dalam Rangka HUT Peradilan Tata Usaha Negara Ke-26, Yang Diselenggarakan Di Hotel Mercure, Jakarta*, vol. 26, 2016. https://ptun-jakarta.go.id/wp-content/uploads/file/makalah_narasumber_hut_peratun_2017/prof_dr_m_guntur_hamzah_sh/Makalah%20Prof.%20Dr.%20M.%20Guntur%20Hamzah.pdf

Hood, Christopher. "A Public Management for All Seasons?" *Public Administration* 69, no. 1 (1991): 3–19. https://doi.org/10.1111/j.1467-9299.1991.tb00779.x

Jacobini, Horace B. *An Introduction to Comparative Administrative Law.* New York: Oceana Publications, 1991.

Jurdi, Fajlurrahman. *Pengantar Hukum Administrasi Negara.* Jakarta Timur: Prenada Media, 2023.

Keban, Yeremias T. *Dimensi Strategis Administrasi Publik Konsep, Teori, Dan Isu Edisi Kedua.* Yogyakarta: Gaya Media, 2008.

Keban, Yeremias T. *Enam Dimensi Strategis Administrasi Publik: Konsep, Teori Dan Isu.* Yogyakarta: Gava Media, 2004.

Laubadère, André de. "B. Droit Administratif." *Revue Internationale de Droit Comparé* 16, no. 4 (1964): 771–73. https://www.persee.fr/doc/ridc_0035-3337_1964_num_16_4_14029

Marbun, S. F., and Deno Kamelus. *Dimensi-Dimensi Pemikiran Hukum Administrasi Negara.* Jakarta: UII Press, 2001.

Marx, Fritz Morstein. *Elements of Public Administration.* New York: Prentice-Hall, 1946.

Munaf, Yusri. *Hukum Administrasi Negara.* Pekanbaru: Marpoyan Tujuh, 2016.

Osborne, David, and Ted Gaebler. *Reinventing Government: The Five Strategies for Reinventing Government.* New York: Penguin, 1993. https://doi.org/10.2307/3381012

Prins, W. F., and R. Kosim Adisapoetra. *Pengantar Ilmu Hukum Administrasi Negara, Cet.* V. Jakarta: PT. Pradnya Paramita, 1993.

Prodjodikoro, Wirjono. *Asas-Asas Ilmu Negara Dan Politik.* Bandung: PT. Eresco, 1971.

Razy, Fakhruddin. *Buku Ajar Hukum Administrasi Negara.* Purwokerto Selatan: Pena Persada, 2020. https://doi.org/10.31237/osf.io/ug8hm

Remaja, I Nyoman Gede. *Hukum Administrasi Negara. Singaraja: Fakultas Hukum Universitas Panji Sakti.* Singaraja: Universitas Panji Sakti, 2017.

Schiller, Jim. "Indonesia: Living with Uncertainty." *Policy, Organisation and Society* 18, no. 1 (1999): 123–39. https://doi.org/10.1080/10349952.1999.11876713

Simon, Herbert A. *Administrative Behavior: A Study of Decision-Making Processes in Administrative Organizations.* 4th ed. New York: The Free Press, 1997.

Storing, Herbert J. "Leonard D. White and the Study of Public Administration." *Public Administration Review* (1965): 38–51. https://doi.org/10.2307/974006

Sumanto, Hetifah Sj. *Inovasi, Partisipasi Dan Good* Governance. Jakarta: Yayasan Obor Indonesia, 2006.

Susanto, Sri Nurhari. "Komponen, Konsep Dan Pendekatan Hukum Administrasi Negara." *Administrative Law & Governance Journal* 4, no. 1 (2021): 144–57. https://ejournal2.undip.ac.id/index.php/alj/article/view/11280
Tjandra, W. Riawan. *Hukum Administrasi Negara*. Jakarta: Sinar Grafika, 2021.
Utama, Yos Johan. *Hukum Administrasi Negara*. Tangerang Selatan: Universitas Terbuka, 2018.
Utomo, Warsito. *Administrasi Publik Baru Indonesia: Perubahan Paradigma Dari Administrasi Negara Ke Administrasi Publik*. Yogyakarta: Pustaka Pelajar, 2009.
Utrecht, Ernst. *Pengantar Hukum Tatausaha Negara Indonesia*. Jakarta: NV Bali Buku Indonesia, 1957.
Wahid, Ali Abdul. "Kedudukan Hukum Administrasi Negara Dalam Tata Hukum Indonesia." *Jurnal Sosial Dan Humanis Sains (JSHS)* 2, no. 1 (2017). https://www.jurnal.saburai.id/index.php/jshs/article/view/104
White, Leonard D. "Public Administration Under the Federalists." *Boston University Law Review* 24 (1944): 144.
Willoughby, William Franklin. *Principles of Public Administration: With Special Reference to the National and State Governments of the United States*. Baltimore, MD: Johns Hopkins Press, 1927.

2 Scope of State Administrative Law

Introduction to Scope and Jurisprudential Principles of State Administrative Law

Administrative law scholars have engaged in lengthy debates regarding the position of administrative law as a science. This discourse has persisted since the 1930s, with proponents and opponents presenting divergent views.[1] Critics of this notion address government administration, essentially arguing for a strict separation of powers distinct from the constitution. Moreover, proponents of government administration contend that administrative bodies often execute tasks that appear to contravene constitutional principles. Goodnow posits that the principle of the separation of powers is challenging to operationalize amidst the exigencies of modern government administration.[2] It is imperative to acknowledge that contemporary political necessities demand a degree of alignment in implementing state objectives to prevent political paralysis. The administrative process emerges from the inadequacy of a simplistic separation of powers in addressing complex contemporary issues.[3]

Hamburger presents a more stringent critique, asserting that administrative law constitutes a form of constitutional violation.[4] This perspective characterizes the constitution as fundamentally anti-administrative. According to this view, administrative institutions lack constitutional legitimacy in their integration of legislative, executive, and judicial powers through various regulations that bind personal actions and establish adjudicative bodies involving government regulations.[5]

1 Gillian E. Metzger, "1930s Redux: The Administrative State Under Seige," *Harvard Law Review* 131 (2017): 1.
2 Frank J. Goodnow, *Politics and Administration: A Study in Government* (London: Routledge, 2017).
3 James M. Landis, "Perspectives on the Administrative Process," *Administrative Law Review* (1961): 66–74, https://www.jstor.org/stable/40708383.
4 Philip Hamburger, *Is Administrative Law Unlawful?* (Chicago: University of Chicago Press, 2014).
5 Gary Lawson, "The Rise and Rise of the Administrative State," *Harvard Law Review* 107, no. 6 (1994): 1231–54.

DOI: 10.4324/9781003518563-2

However, scholars who align with the government administration perspective assert that administrative law is ***not*** inherently problematic within the context of legal studies. This view is predicated on the separation of powers delineated in the constitution, which differs from the separation of administrative functions such as rule formulation and adjudication not explicitly regulated in the constitution.[6] According to this perspective, administrative law utilizes the authority of congress and society to oversee and constrain politicized decision-making through judicial review.[7]

Mashaw posits that the centralization of power within executive bodies serves as a foundation for congress to implement open-ended regulations, a process he views as intrinsically linked to the formation of the republic.[8] This perspective suggests that the delegation of power to the executive branch is not merely a practical necessity but a fundamental aspect of the American constitutional system. In a parallel vein, Lessig and Sunstein advance the argument that the constitution has effectively segregated administrative power from the executive branch.[9] They further contend that this separation extends to the relationship between administrative institutions and presidential control. This interpretation challenges the notion of a unitary executive and suggests a more nuanced understanding of the distribution of powers within the federal government.

While the debate concerning administrative law as a constitutional or non-constitutional science persists, Wurman posits that this discourse necessitates a more profound analysis of the fundamental premises underlying administrative law.[10] Wurman contends that administrative law as a disciplinemust recognize the scope of its own powers, withits primary function being toexecute the laws established by congress. He further elucidates this concept through an examination of the inherent complexity of governmental power, which defies simplistic classification.

Wurman particularly emphasizes the dual nature of power when public organizations design and formulate rules that bind individuals. This scenario, he argues, exemplifies a dualism of executive and legislative functions and-serves to bridge the understanding that power is ambiguously situated, while

6 Gillian E Metzger, "1930s Redux: The Administrative State Under Seige," *Harvard Law Review* 131 (2017): 1.

7 Mark Tushnet, "New Institutional Mechanisms for Making Constitutional Law," 2015, https://doi.org/10.2139/ssrn.2589178; Mark V. Tushnet, Mark A. Graber, and Sanford Levinson, *The Oxford Handbook of the US Constitution* (Oxford: Oxford University Press, 2015).

8 Jerry L. Mashaw, *Creating the Administrative Constitution: The Lost One Hundred Years of American Administrative Law* (New Haven, CT: Yale University Press, 2012).

9 Lawrence Lessig and Cass R. Sunstein, "The President and the Administration," *Columbia Law Review* 94, no. 1 (1994): 1–123.

10 Ilan Wurman, "Administrative Law Theory and Fundamentals: An Integrated Approach," *Harvard Journal of Law & Public Policy Per Curiam* 1 (2021), https://doi.org/10.2139/ssrn.3839666.

simultaneously embodying characteristics of both the legislative and the executive authority.

More specifically, the scope of state administrative law encompasses several aspects.[11] Firstly, it ensures the coherence of public policy implementation, focusing on the alignment between policy formulation and evaluation. In this context, state administrative law guarantees a transparent, participatory process free from conflicts of interest. Secondly, it protects human rights, including access to services, participation, and justice. Thirdly, administrative law necessitates the establishment of clear procedures to ensure its effective enforcement. Fourthly, administrative law mandates transparency in decision-making processes and government accountability, aiming to foster a responsive and transparent governance structure that respects citizens' rights. This comprehensive framework emphasizes the multifaceted role of state administrative law in modern governance. It not only serves as a regulatory mechanism but also as a guardian of democratic principles and human rights. These four aspects crystallize in the concept of human rights and state administrative acts.

Human Rights in the Context of State Administrative Law

Human rights find their genesis in natural law theory,[12] which posits that every individual possesses inalienable rights inherent to their humanity. These rights transcend boundaries of gender, language, nationality, or culture. Grotius, as the progenitor of this theory, laid the groundwork for subsequent thinkers, notably John Locke, whose contributions catalyzed the tumultuous rights revolutions in England, the United States, and France during the 17th and 18th centuries.[13] In *The Second Treatise of Civil Government and a Letter Concerning Toleration*, both Locke and modern Welsh historian J.W. Gough, in his accompanying historical commentary, have assertedthat individuals possess a social contract that the state must not infringe upon.[14] Locke and Gough argue that if rulers neglect their obligations related to this social contract, citizens retain the right to overthrow and replace the government.

Edmund Burke opposed the doctrine ofhuman rights predicated on Locke's natural rights theory.[15] Burke's argument stemmed from his perception of

11 F. C. Susila Adiyanta, "Hukum Dan Studi Penelitian Empiris: Penggunaan Metode Survey Sebagai Instrumen Penelitian Hukum Empiris," *Administrative Law and Governance Journal* 2, no. 4 (2019): 697–709.

12 Ralph McInerny, "Natural Law and Human Rights," *American Journal of Jurisprudence* 36 (1991): 1.

13 Knud Haakonssen, "Hugo Grotius and the History of Political Thought," in *Grotius and Law* (London: Routledge, 2017), 69–95.

14 John Locke and John Wiedhofft Gough, "The Second Treatise on Civil Government and a Letter Concerning Toleration," *Philosophy* 23, no. 85 (1948), 178–179.

15 Edmund Burke, *Reflections on the Revolution in France (1790)* (New York: Everyman's Library, 1986).

human nature as fundamentally irrational and emotional, particularly in the context of the French Revolution, which he viewed as precipitating dangerous societal upheaval. Similarly, Jeremy Bentham contended that the natural rights theory was inherently unverifiable and its truthfulness unconfirmable. Notwithstanding these critiques, the natural rights theory precipitated the emergence of human rights on the international stage. The United Nations (UN) has played a pivotal role in bridging the internationalization of these ideas through the promulgation of the International Bill of Human Rights.[16]

The universality of human rights encompasses the concept that every individual possesses legitimacy in defining freedom and benefit, as articulated in the Universal Declaration of Human Rights. This principle has gained widespread political and legal acceptance across various nations. The Universal Declaration reflects general moral intuitions, including freedom of expression, religious or ethnic equality, and gender equality. In the pre-World War II era, Francisco de Vitoria (1486–1546) recognized that all individuals should be treated with dignity, regardless of their status as foreigners or locals. Consequently, efforts were made to establish legal mechanisms, such as, "International Human Rights Law," to protect foreigners and uphold other humanitarian aspects. These include the following:

1. Human Rights and Traditional International Law

The initial scope of international law was primarily confined to mediating diplomatic relations between sovereign states. Within this framework, individuals were subjected to the rules and authorities of their respective states, with states exercising discretion in prioritizing individual interests. However, the emergence of the principle of, "protection of foreign nationals" marked a significant shift whichenabled individuals whose fundamental rights were being violated by state authorities or governments to pursue claims against the offending state authority.

2. Humanitarian Intervention

Introduced by Hugo Grotius in the 19th century, humanitarian intervention grants states the right to intervene militarily to protect citizens if they are mistreated.

3. Abolition of Slavery System

The opposition to slavery practices was initially included in the 1814 Treaty of Paris Peace by Britain and France. In the 20th century, the international struggle against slavery continued, with the League of Nations forming the Slavery Convention in 1926, which initially strongly opposed slavery in the former

16 James Pomeroy Hendrick, *An International Bill of Human Rights*, vol. 3055 (Washington, D.C: Department of State, 1948).

colonies of Turkey and Germany. The 1926 Convention also served as the basis for implementing the prohibition of slavery practices, and was amended in 1953 to include points related to modern-day slavery.

4. International Red Cross

Formed in the 19th century, the International Committee of the Red Cross is an organization that aims to provide protection and good treatment to war victims and prisoners of war as outlined in the Geneva Convention. The Red Cross also spearheaded international humanitarian law.

5. League of Nations (LN)

The League of Nations was established through the Treaty of Versailles with the aim of achieving international security and peace. The League has had many notable achievements, including establishing a system of mandates in which former colonies of Turkey and Germany, the defeated parties in the war, were placed under the guardianship of the victorious states. The League was officially dissolved on April 18, 1946, and the United Nations was formed in its place.

As previously explained, if individuals are the objects of international law, they become subjects of international law, holding rights and obligations over time. Additionally, there are international legal norms that emerged after World War II, which include the following:

a. Modern International Human Rights

This places individuals, as "right-holders," in a legal position to have their rights guaranteed internationally, with states acting as "duty-holders." The relationship between rights-holders and "duty-holders" governs obligations which are accommodated and regulated through monitoring and complaint mechanisms related to human rights.

b. The United Nations Charter

The United Nations Charter explicitly includes provisions regarding the protection of human rights. For example, in Article 1, paragraph 3, it states that member parties must, "promote and encourage respect for human rights and fundamental freedoms for all without distinction as to race, sex, language, or religion." The UN Charter popularized the internationalization of human rights and legally binds its members.

c. International Bill of Human Rights

The UN promulgated the Universal Declaration to set general standards forhuman rights protection internationally. The Declaration generally consists of the Universal Declaration of Human Rights, the International Covenant on Civil and Political Rights, and the International Covenant on Economic, Social, and Cultural Rights. The Declaration also gives rise to various international treaties related to human rights.

Human rights internationally are founded on principles such as equality and non-discrimination. The principle of equality grantsevery individual entitlement to equal treatment under the same circumstances. Moreover, the principle of non-discrimination addresses disparity in treatment under identical circumstances. Discrimination is divided into two categories: direct and indirect. Karel Vasak, a French jurist, further elucidated the development of human rights, conceptualizing it in relation to the tripartite motto of the French Revolution: "liberty, equality, and fraternity." This framework delineates the following three generations of human rights:

1. First Generation Civil and Political Rights: This generation of rights emerged in response to the absolute rule of monarchs during the 17th and 18th centuries, when those in proximity to the sovereign were accorded special or privileged rights. The general populace demanded the right to live and develop their lives free from arbitrary power.
2. Second Generation Economic, Social, and Cultural Rights: This generation of rights is associated with the principle of equality and resulted inpeople demanding their rights related to employment and the fulfillment of basic needs.
3. Third Generation Collective or Solidarity Rights: This generation of rights is marked by the development of the principle of fraternity and expanded beyond individual rights to encompass group rights as well, including cultural identity rights and environmental rights.

Human Rights Framework in Indonesia

An analysis of state governance in Indonesia through the lens of *Rechtstaat* and the rule of law principles reveals the following several key aspects of the 1945 Constitution:

1. Human Rights Protection: The Constitution affirms recognition and protection of human rights in Chapter XA, Articles 28A-28J.
2. Separation of Powers: The constitution delineates executive (the president), legislative (the DPR, DPD, and MPR), and judicial (the supreme court, the judicial commission, and the constitutional court) functions. Additional institutions like the Supreme Audit Agency and the Bank Indonesia exist outside the classic *trias politica* model.
3. Administrative Judiciary: The Peradilan Tata Usaha Negara (PTUN) or administrative court, under the supreme court, handles cases of legal violations by the government (Article 24, paragraph 2).

The abovementioned constitutional structure demonstrates Indonesia's adherence to *Rechtstaat* principles, while simultaneously showing how Indonesia has adapted to specific national contexts and needs.

The rule of law in Indonesian law is evident in the following areas:

1. Legal Supremacy:

- Legal supremacy is emphasized in the 1945 Constitution's preamble in the use of terms or phrases like, "justice," "fair," and "social justice."
- Constitutionalism is explicitly stated in the preamble.
- A pre-amendment explanation (now removed) clarified Indonesia as a *Rechtstaat*, not solely as a *Machtstaat*.

2. Equality Before the Law:

- Article 27(1): All citizens are equal before the law and government.
- Article 28D(1): Every person is entitled to legal certainty and equal treatment.
- Article 28I(1): There is a right to be recognized as a person before the law which is inalienable.

3. Constitution Based on Human Rights:

- Chapter XA, Articles 28A-28J guarantee human rights.

Following on from this argument, both *Rechtstaat* and the rule of law indicators in Indonesia aim to uphold human rights. Indonesia's methodology for human rights protection within the domain of state administrative law was substantially shaped by international interventions, notably the World Bank's economic support initiative of 1992.[17] The World Bank's good governance paradigm, delineated by transparent policy formulation, a professional bureaucratic apparatus, robust legislative frameworks, and active civil society engagement, became inextricably linked with human rights principles. The efficacious implementation of human rights is contingent upon an efficient governmental bureaucracy that facilitates public participation in legislative processes, thereby reflecting accountability and reverence for cultural pluralism. This symbiotic relationship manifests primarily through legislative formulation, with human rights serving as an operational instrument for the actualization of legal state principles.

17 Rahayu Rahayu, "Dampak Globalisasi Terhadap Perkembangan Kesadaran Penghormatan Hak Asasi Manusia Di Indonesia," *Masalah-Masalah Hukum* 39, no. 4 (2010): 302–11; Fikri Hadi, "Negara Hukum Dan Hak Asasi Manusia Di Indonesia," *Wijaya Putra Law Review* 1, no. 2 (2022): 170–88.

In the wake of the New Order regime's dissolution, concerns pertaining to human rights and demands for governmental praxis reform gained increasing salience. Two antithetical perspectives emerged, in which:

1. Reformists advocated for the augmentation of human rights protections, deeming extant measures inadequate.
2. Conservatives posited that current legislative frameworks sufficiently safeguarded rights and expressed trepidation that comprehensive reforms would alter Indonesia's foundational ethos.

This discourse exemplified the dichotomy between the exigency for reform and the entrenched legacy of the New Order's veneration of the constitution, underscoring Indonesia's complex transition from authoritarian governance to democratic rule. The dialectic surrounding human rights in post-1998 Indonesia reflected multifaceted political dynamics. Parliamentary discord regarding constitutional amendments emanated from divergent interpretations of human rights principles, influenced by the founding fathers' 1945 deliberations and also by apprehensions regarding the investigation of antecedent transgressions implicating pro-New Order elites.[18]

The 2000 MPR Annual Session successfully incorporated human rights into the constitution, expanding Article 28 with Chapter XA (Articles 28A-28J). However, Article 28J(2) allows for lawful restrictions on individual rights to protect citizens' freedoms and meet societal demands, emphasizing a balanced approach to human rights implementation in Indonesia's evolving democracy. Article 28J(2) of the Indonesian constitution permits human rights restrictions based on moral and religious considerations, reflecting the Pancasila state's unique character. This approach, rooted in the principles of, a "Just and Civilized Humanity" and the, "Belief in the One and Only God," forms the philosophical foundation of Indonesian governance.[19]

The concept of harmony between government and people, central to Indonesia's legal framework, is based on the principle of *gotong royong* (communal work). This principle emphasizes kinship values and seeks to maintain a harmonious relationship between the state and its citizens.[20] This approach aims to balance individual rights with societal obligations, adapting human rights to Indonesia's living law. While prioritizing deliberation for dispute resolution, the judicial system serves as a last resort for human rights protection.[21]

18 Suparman Marzuki, "Politik Hukum HAM Di Indonesia," *Disampaikan Dalam Pelatihan HAM Dasar Dosen Hukum HAM Se-Indonesia, Singgasana Hotel Surabaya* 6, no. 2 (2011): 10–13.

19 Kuntjoro Purbopranoto, *Hak-Hak Azasi Manusia Dan Pancasila* (Jakarta: Pradnya Paramita, 1979).

20 Philipus M Hadjon, "Pengantar Hukum Administrasi Indonesia (Introduction to the Indonesian Administrative Law)" (Yogyakarta: Gadjah Mada University Press, 2002).

21 Dewi Yustiana, *Hukum Administrasi Negara* (Surabaya: Penerbit CV. Mitra Sumber Rejeki, 2019).

The Indonesian model thus presents a unique blend of universal human rights principles and indigenous values, reflecting its individual cultural and historical context.[22]

However, problematic legislation can hinder implementation of the law, provoking public rejection, impeding social development, and compromising human rights enforcement. Factors contributing to poor legislation include: inadequate scientific support; low-quality legal drafting; insufficient infrastructure; and unfavorable political configurations. The principles of participation, transparency, and accountability are crucial for effective legislation. However, Indonesia has not fully implemented these principles, particularly in terms of public influence on policy outcomes (e.g. the degrees of citizens' power). This shortfall in good governance practices ultimately threatens the establishment and enforcement of human rights in Indonesia. This situation highlights the complex interplay between international influences, domestic governance practices, and human rights protection in Indonesia's evolving legal and administrative framework.

Juridical Analysis of State Administrative Acts

Zaelani articulates a significant distinction between, "administrative acts," and, "government acts," despite their frequent interchangeable usage.[23] Administrative acts are conceptualized as measures aimed at addressing administrative infractions committed by state officials. In contrast, government acts encompass a broader spectrum of activities undertaken by state officials, in which they leverage their authority to achieve effective governance and optimal public service delivery.[24] This notion of government can be interpreted in both broad and narrow contexts. Prodjodikoro articulates a comprehensive view of government, encompassing functions pertaining to Indonesian state affairs in which state institutions adhere to legal frameworks.[25] Moreover, the narrow interpretation confines the government to executive institutions. Purbopranoto posits that the government, in its broader sense, encompasses

22 Rosiady H. Sayuti et al., "Impact of COVID-19 Pandemic on the Existence of Social Solidarity: Evidence from Rural-Urban Communities in Lombok Island, Indonesia," *Frontiers in Sociology* 8 (2023): 1164837; Teresia Noiman Derung, "Gotong Royong Dan Indonesia," *Sapa: Jurnal Kateketik Dan Pastoral* 4, no. 1 (2019): 5–13; Sri Widayati, *Gotong Royong* (Semarang: Alprin, 2020).

23 Muhammad Aziz Zaelani, "Perbuatan Administrasi Negara," in *Hukum Administrasi Negara*, ed. Anik Iftitah (Banten: Sada Kurnia Pustaka, 2023), 116–30.

24 Bambang Arwanto, "Perlindungan Hukum Bagi Rakyat Akibat Tindakan Faktual Pemerintah," *Jurnal Yuridika* 31, no. 3 (2016); Dwi Suryanti et al., "Unfolding the Landscape of Conflict: UN Volunteer Organisations and Violence Against Women," *JSEAHR* 7 (2023): 21.

25 Wirjono Prodjodikoro, *Asas-Asas Ilmu Negara Dan Politik* (Bandung: PT. Eresco, 1971).

all state actions aimed at managing citizens' welfare and the state's interests.[26] Irrespective of the breadth of this interpretation, the government bears certain duties and obligations to execute state tasks predicated on legal foundations.[27] This conceptualization implies that governmental recognition is contingent upon the fulfillment of government duties and obligations within the national sphere.

Scholarly perspectives on government acts exhibit a degree of uniformity, with some emphasizing adherence to the law, and others accentuating initiatives lacking explicit legal regulation. Utrecht contends that law-based government acts stem from the power and authority vested in executive institutions to discharge state duties.[28] Furthermore, Van Vollenhoven argues that government acts may constitute direct acts or initiatives responding to emergent situations and needs, without necessitating superior directives.[29] However, such governmental initiatives are underpinned by a responsibility to serve the public's interests.

Remaja offers another theoretical framework, positing that government acts, or *bestuurshandelingen*, are instrumental acts performed by the governmental apparatus, *bestuursorgaan,* in the execution of governmental functions, or *bestuursfunctie*.[30] This explication of government and state administrative acts emphasizes the multifaceted nature of governmental authority and its manifestation in practical governance, balancing legal adherence with responsive initiative.

Furthermore, the state administrative acts are characterized by the following key attributes:[31]

1. Comprehensive General Nature: These actions tend to have wide-ranging implications and applicability.
2. Universality: While potentially subject to bias, state administrative acts serve as mechanisms for addressing projected future issues. This forward-looking orientation accentuates the role of state administrative acts in proactive governance.

26 Kuntjoro Purbopranoto, *Perkembangan Hukum Administrasi Indonesia* (Jakarta: Bina Cipta, 1981).

27 M. Zaenul Muttaqin, *Public Administration and Epistemology: Experience, Power, and Agency: Arthur J. Sementelli* (New York and London: Routledge, 2021), Vii, 200. (Taylor & Francis, 2023).

28 Ernst Utrecht, *Pengantar Hukum Tatausaha Negara Indonesia* (Jakarta: NV Bali Buku Indonesia, 1957).

29 Cornelis Van Vollenhoven, *Van Vollenhoven on Indonesian Adat Law*, ed. J F Holleman (Berlin: Springer, 2013).

30 I Nyoman Gede Remaja, *Hukum Administrasi Negara, Singaraja: Fakultas Hukum Universitas Panji Sakti* (Singaraja: Universitas Panji Sakti, 2017).

31 Kartika Widya Utama, "Surat Keputusan Tata Usaha Negara Yang Bersifat Fiktif Positif," *Notarius* 8, no. 2 (2015): 141–251.

3. Corrective Nature: This characteristic is manifested through provisions for procedural review and enables the rectification of administrative acts. This ensures that any administrative missteps or errors can be addressed and corrected, thereby maintaining the integrity of the administrative process.

This delineation of characteristics illuminates the complex nature of state administrative acts, highlighting their dual role in both addressing current administrative issues and anticipating future challenges. The corrective aspect, in particular, emphasizes the importance of accountability and adaptability in administrative processes.

The classification of state administrative acts based on their function provides a comprehensive framework for understanding the complex nature of governmental operations. This bifurcation into two crucial dimensions offers valuable insights into the interplay between individual authority and institutional responsibilities within the state apparatus. Firstly, administrative acts in exercising authority focus on the competence to act, representing a general authority to perform legal acts. As Gandara notes, while this competence is universally applicable under Article 1329 of the civil code, it becomes specific when applied to certain individuals for particular legal acts.[32] The specificity of competence to act is manifested through the following:

- Delineation of action types
- Clarification of authority granting purposes
- Absence of general provisions

Ilmar emphasizes that legal acts create binding consequences for the actor.[33] This principle accentuates the need for legal system protection for subjects lacking full awareness of their actions' implications, leading to the establishment of a causal relationship between competence to act and the age of majority. Secondly, administrative acts in performing functions and orders encompass the execution of governmental duties in specific fields to achieve national objectives. This dimension highlights the role of government agencies in executing daily state tasks, positioning the government dependently in terms of state accountability. The dependent nature of the government is limited to executing the state's daily tasks according to prescribed procedures and authority. This classification further elucidates the complex interplay between individual authority and institutional functions within the governmental framework. It also emphasizes the importance of clearly defined competencies and hierarchical structures to ensureeffective and accountable governance. The classification of state administrative acts based on purpose and/or object

32 Moh Gandara, "Kewenangan Atribusi, Delegasi Dan Mandat," *Khazanah Hukum* 2, no. 3 (2020): 92–99.

33 Aminuddin Ilmar, *Hukum Tata Pemerintahan* (Jakarta: Prenada Media, 2014).

provides further insight into the multifaceted nature of governmental operations. This framework, as outlined by Putra, delineates the following three primary categories of government administrative acts:[34]

1. Issuing regulations
2. Issuing decisions
3. Performing material acts

This tripartite categorization illuminates the diverse ways in which administrative bodies exercise their authority and fulfill their mandates. It encompasses both the creation of regulatory frameworks and the implementation of specific actions.

Moreover, the analysis of government acts in performing functions reveals the following three key components:

- Regulations encompassing provisions related to duties and assignments
- Executors embodying the state's forms and functions in public service
- Evaluation of state fulfillment

Additionally, official orders or instructions from superiors are subordinate to actions to be taken or avoided. This aspect highlights the hierarchical nature of governmental operations and the importance of clear lines of authority and responsibility. This bifurcation of state administrative acts, considering both the function and the purpose and/or object, elucidates the complex interplay between individual authority and institutional functions within the governmental framework. It emphasizes the importance of clearly defined competencies and hierarchical structures to ensure effective and accountable governance.

However, some legal scholars propose an expanded four-category system: legislative enactment; adjudicative decision-making; civil litigation engagement; and discretionary policy formulation.[35] This expanded model offers a more nuanced understanding of administrative authority, recognizing both the implementation and creation of regulatory frameworks. It particularly emphasizes discretionary policy-making, highlighting administrative bodies' adaptability to emerging challenges. This comprehensive approach better captures the multifaceted nature of contemporary governance, acknowledging the

34 Erlanda Juliansyah Putra, "Pengelolaan Kepegawaian Pada Era Otonomi Daerah," *Kanun Jurnal Ilmu Hukum* 17, no. 1 (2015): 37–60.

35 Shannon Rosemary Bernadika and Frederick Appiah Afriyie, "Legitimacy of Proof of Letters in the Era of the E-Litigation Proof System in the State Administrative Court," *Indonesian State Law Review (ISLRev)* 6, no. 1 (2023): 221–252; Fakhruddin Razy, *Buku Ajar Hukum Administrasi Negara* (Purwokerto Selatan: Pena Persada, 2020); Rahayu Rahayu, "Dampak Globalisasi Terhadap Perkembangan Kesadaran Penghormatan Hak Asasi Manusia Di Indonesia," *Masalah-Masalah Hukum* 39, no. 4 (2010): 302–11.

complex interplay between competing interests, evolving societal needs, and intricate legal structures.

Legislation serves as a governmental tool for addressing societal issues, with government-originated legislation categorized as regulation—an extension of delegated legislative power. This framework enables the creation of subordinate or technical regulations to support executive functions.[36] While higher-level products can distinguish between legislation and delegated regulations, confusion arises among various regulatory types in Indonesia. The current hierarchical classification proves inadequate, necessitating a more comprehensive analysis encompassing content, authority sources, regulatory scope, and legislation types.

This nuanced approach is not yet integrated into Indonesia's legislative nomenclature, which has led to regulatory conflicts. A prime example is the marginalization of regional regulations by ministerial regulations based on a perceived hierarchical position.[37]

To address these issues, legislative synchronization efforts are crucial, particularly for quasi-regulatory types that do not fit neatly within the existing hierarchical classification. Theaim is to create a more coherent regulatory framework, reducing conflicts and enhancing system efficacy. This situation highlights the complex interplay between governmental authority levels and the need for a more nuanced understanding of legislative processes that go beyond simple hierarchical classifications.

The State Administrative Decrees (KTUN) represent the primary government administrative's instrument. Law No. 30 of 2014 on Government Administration significantly expanded KTUN's scope beyond its previous definition in Law No. 5/1986 and Law No. 51/2009. The new definition broadens KTUN to include any written determination issued by a government agency or official in governance administration, encompassing material acts and factual KTUN acts. State administrative acts involving civil acts prioritize the public interest within civil law principles. The law now accommodates factual KTUN acts in governmental functions, which extends beyond formal aspects. Policy-making based on discretionary authority is the final classification of state administrative acts. Soimin distinguishes between subjective and objective administrative freedoms.[38] Administrative discretion includes interpretion (the discretion of government agencies to interpret laws), consideration (the discretion to choose between legal options under certain conditions),

36 H. R. Ridwan, "Pertanggungjawaban Publik Pemerintah Dalam Perspektif Hukum Administrasi Negara," *Jurnal Hukum Ius Quia Iustum* 10, no. 22 (2003): 27–38.

37 H. R. Ridwan, *Hukum Administrasi Negara* (Jakarta: Raja Grafindo Persada, 2006).

38 Soimin Soimin, "Pelembagaan Program-Program Pemerintah Dalam Suatu Tinjauan Hukum Administrasi Negara," *Edulaw: Journal of Islamic Law and Jurisprudance* 6, no. 1 (2024): 70–82.

and policy-making (the authority granted by legislators to exercise power by inventorying while while considering various interests).

Hamdi defines policy as a decision addressing specific problems, encompassing recommended actions for various entities within environments containing obstacles and opportunities.[39] While public policy is etymologically identical to government or state policy, its nomenclature is adjusted based on purpose, form, and function. This expanded understanding of state administrative acts reflects the complex nature of modern governance andemphasizes the need for flexibility and discretion in addressing diverse societal needs while maintaining legal and administrative integrity.

Fundamental Principles Governing State Administrative Acts

Ridwan identifies the following two fundamental pillars governing state administrative acts:[40]

1. The Principle of Legality: Codified in Article 5 of Law No. 30/2014, this principle requires government administration to be based on: a) Legality principles; b) Human rights protection; and c) Asas Umum Pemerintahan yang Baik (AUPB), or the Principles of Good Governance.

Government acts must align with the authority derived from the following three sources:

a) Attribution: Constitutional framers and lawmakers grant authority to state bodies, institutions, or officials. For example, the doctrine of attribution is fundamental to the law-formulation powers attributed to the president and the DPR.
b) Delegation: Authority transfers between state entities, which includes certain responsibilities. An example of this is would be the DPD's approval authority for regional deputy head candidates.
c) Mandate: Authority transfers within the governmental hierarchy, in which responsibility remains with the entity or individual holding the mandate.

This tripartite classification of the sources of authority sources highlights the complexity of power distribution in state administration and emphasizes the need for a more nuanced understanding to ensure legitimacy and accountability in government acts.

The principle of legality, as codified in Law No. 30/2014 and expounded upon by Ridwan, forms a foundational element in ensuring the legal and

39 Muchlis Hamdi, *Kebijakan Publik: Proses, Analisis, Dan Partisipasi* (Bogor: Ghalia Indonesia, 2014).
40 H. R. Ridwan, *Hukum Administrasi Negara* (Jakarta: Rajawali Press, 2018).

ethical soundness of government acts. The legality principle integrates human rights protection and good governance, and aims to balance administrative efficiency with individual rights protection to promote transparent, accountable governance. The legality of government acts remains contentious in modern administrative law due to the complex interplay between legal basis, societal legitimacy, and administrative discretion. One argument emphasizes the necessity of societal legitimization, even for those acts which lack an explicit legal foundation, which highlights the tension between formal legality and social acceptance.

In state administration, the law is viewed as a body of written rules outlining systematic procedures for government agencies. Legitimacy, however, extends tosocietal acceptance and the perceived justness of administrative acts. The concept of discretionary power further complicates the state administrative law landscape. Under certain circumstances, the government may act without explicit legal basis inexercising its discretion. This practice, while sometimes necessary, challenges the principle of legality and the fundamental tenet of government adherence to the law in a rule-of-law state. The tension between legal certainty and governance flexibility represents a key challenge in modern administrative law. This dilemma highlights the need to balance adherence to established rules with the practical demands of governance, which may require actions not explicitly covered by existing legislation. This ongoing debate reflects the dynamic nature of administrative law and the continuous effort to reconcile formal legality with effective governance and societal expectations. As Jimly Asshiddiqie notes, this situation also calls for a nuanced understanding of legality that accommodates both strict legal adherence and governance flexibility.[41] Hadjon argues that the government can exercise discretion in fulfilling public interest duties under certain conditions, in the absence of explicit public law regulation governing these actions. Government actions must remain legally grounded, as actors operate on behalf of a law-bound sovereign government.Government actions must also have a legal basis due to existing legal accountability mechanisms.[42] These constraints accentuate the delicate balance between administrative flexibility and legal accountability in governmental discretion.

2. The Principles of Good Governance (AUPB): As outlined by Ridwan, these principles position the state to serve as a duty-bearing organization in public law.[43] Public legal entities operate through: a) Delegation of

41 Jimly Asshiddiqie, *Omnibus Law Dan Penerapannya Di Indonesia* (Jakarta: Konstitusi Press, 2020).

42 Philipus Hadjon, *Hukum Administrasi Dan Good Governance* (Jakarta: Universitas Trisakti, 2010).

43 H. R. Ridwan, *Hukum Administrasi Negara* (Jakarta: Rajawali Press, 2018).

authority; b) Implementation of functions; and c) Issuance of instructions to agencies.

Government acts involve the following three key elements: the legal entity, the agency, and the official. The interrelationship between these elements is dynamic, manifesting in various forms of authority, function execution, and instructions. Ridwan notes that there is a parallelism which becomes evident in the context of public body funding used by government agencies.

The framework of state administrative acts necessitates a nuanced understanding of administrative authority, which must balance flexibility with accountability to ensure effective and principled governance. In exercising their authority, functions, and instructions, individual legal entities, agencies, and officials may deviate from their mandates and createpublic losses. Common deviations include the abuse of authority and arbitrary acts. Arbitrary acts occur when actions lack procedural legality in jurisdiction or fail to comply with implementing rules, rendering them unaccountable. The AUPB now serves as a normative legal basis for government administration. As a consequence:

1. Government decisions and acts must be AUPB-based.
2. State organizers must inform the public about planned actions, including their reasons, methods, and objectives.
3. All government acts must be announced, with mechanisms varying based on importance and objectives.

Administrative acts are classified as having either general or individual applicability. This classification emphasizes the importance of transparency, accountability, and adherence to good governance principles in state administrative acts and acknowledges the challenge of maintaining these standards in practice.

Legal Prerequisites for State Administrative Acts

State administrative acts encompass actions undertaken by state officials and/or public legal entities that are derived from state legal regulations and serve public or state interests. Kansil delineates two fundamental requisites that underpin the legitimacy of an administrative act.[44]

The primary requisite of validity constitutes a condition for the formal legal efficacy of an administrative act. This validity condition is typically established when an authorized administrative official appends his or her signature to the act. However, practical instances exist in which actions precede ratification. In such cases, retroactive ratification may be employed, conferring legal material effect on the previously executed action. This practice frequently engenders protests, often culminating in administrative disputes. Unratified

44 C. S. T. Kansil, *Hukum Administrasi Negara* (Jakarta: PT. Pradnya Paramita, 2005).

administrative acts may be deemed illegal, jeopardizing legal certainty and potentially fostering arbitrary governance. A novel mechanism has emerged precluding retroactive administrative acts except in exigent circumstances. This principle asserts that an action's validity commences from its effective origination date, prohibiting retroactivity while permitting retroactive effects.

The secondary requisite of opposability must also be satisfied. This condition determines the initiation of an administrative act's enforcement, particularly concerning its susceptibility to challenge or opposition by affected members of the public. In light of this requirement, an administrative act may only be enforced or take effect from the moment it is announced, adhering to procedures and forms of proclamation established by legal regulations. The commencement of enforcement signifies the act's coercive force upon the populace.

Discretionary Powers in State Administration

In the realm of legal jurisprudence, the concept of, "discretion," embodies a nuanced and multifaceted significance. This term denotes the latitude in decision-making accorded to authorized entities, predicated on individual reasoning within specific contexts. However, from the perspective of aspirational legal frameworks, this conception diverges from the draft of government administrative legislation in Indonesia, which construes discretion as the prerogative of governmental bodies, officials, and other juridical entities to select and execute legal acts within the governmental purview.

The terminological variance of discretion across different jurisdictions is noteworthy, manifesting as, *discretionair*, in French, "discretion," in English, and, *freies ermessen*, in German.[45]

Indonesian legal scholars proffer diverse interpretations of discretion. Indroharto posits that discretion constitutes an authority that does not mandate governmental bodies or officials to exercise their power based on specific circumstances, provided they do not contravene binding regulations.[46] Sjachran Basah conceptualizes discretion as the liberty to act on personal initiative, with the caveat that such state administrative acts must align with legal precepts or, in the Indonesian context, the Pancasila legal state.[47] Halim Koentjoro emphasizes that state discretion represents the freedom of executive governmental administrative acts in addressing urgent issues, particularly in the absence of specific regulatory frameworks.[48]

45 S. Prajudi Atmosudirdjo, *Hukum Administrasi Negara* (Bogor: Ghalia Indonesia, 1981).

46 Indroharto, *Usaha Memahami Undang-Undang Tentang Peradilan Tata Usaha Negara* (Jakarta: Pustaka Sinar Harapan, 1991).

47 Sjachran Basah, *Eksistensi Dan Tolak Ukur Badan Peradilan Administrasi Di Indonesia* (Bandung: Alumni, 1989).

48 Diana Halim Koentjoro, *Hukum Administrasi Negara* (Bogor: Ghalia Indonesia, 2004).

These scholarly perspectives emphasize discretion as a critical and fundamental phenomenon in public policy implementation. Discretion serves a dual purpose: it affords the executive branch freedom to act in regulatory lacunae while simultaneously aiming to optimize public outcomes.[49] This conceptualization aligns with Prajudi Atmosudirjo's assertion that discretion is essential in complementing the legality principle, which mandates that all state administrative acts must be grounded in legal provisions. This viewpoint stems from the recognition that not all quotidian administrative positions are explicitly codified in the law.[50] This understanding also harmonizes with the legislative principle elucidating rules and exceptions, thereby acknowledging the necessity for discretionary acts which adhere to the broader framework of governmental administration and legal compliance.

The conceptual evolution of discretionary powers vested in state administrative agencies and officials can be traced to the seminal works on the separation of powers initially propounded by John Locke and subsequently refined by Montesquieu. The doctrine of the separation of powers is fundamentally predicated on a normative distribution of authority which is designed to preclude the concentration of power within a single institution or entity and thereby safeguard against the emergence of absolutism.

John Locke, in his seminal work, *Two Treaties of Civil Government*, laid the foundational framework for a theory of the separation of powers.[51] Locke's model delineated three distinct spheres of power: the legislative, the executive, and the federative. The legislative branch formed the law, the executive branch implemented the law, and the federative branch managed inter-state relations.

Montesquieu further developed upon Locke's theoretical construct byproposing a tripartite division of governmental power: the executive, the legislative, and the judiciary.[52] Montesquieu's conception emphasized the necessity for these three branches to maintain functional and organizational autonomy.[53] However, the subsequent emergence of the welfare state paradigm and

49 Esmi Warassih, *Pranata Hukum Sebuah Telaah Sosiologis, Suryandaru Utama* (Semarang: PT Suryandaru Utama, 2005).

50 S Prajudi Atmosudirdjo, *Hukum Administrasi Negara* (Bogor: Ghalia Indonesia, 1981).

51 John Locke, *Two Treatises on Civil Government*, vol. 9 (G. Routledge and Sons, Limited, 1887).

52 Fajrul Ilmy Darussalam and Andi Batara Indra, "Kedaulatan Rakyat Dalam Pemikiran Filsafat Politik Montesquieu," *Jurnal Politik Profetik* 9, no. 2 (2021): 189–204; Ruhenda Ruhenda et al., "Tinjauan Trias Politika Terhadap Terbentuknya Sistem Politik Dan Pemerintahan Di Indonesia," *Journal of Governance and Social Policy* 1, no. 2 (2020): 58–69.

53 Annisa Zahra et al., "Teori Pemisahan Kekuasaan Trias Politica Dalam Pemikiran Filsafat Hukum Montesquieu," *Praxis: Jurnal Filsafat Terapan* 1, no. 01 (2022), 1–25; Anne M. Cohler, Basia Carolyn Miller, and Harold Samuel Stone, *Montesquieu: The Spirit of the Laws* (Cambridge: Cambridge University Press, 1989); David Lowenthal, "Montesquieu and the Classics: Republican Government in the Spirit of the Laws," in *Charles-Louis de Secondat, Baron de Montesquieu* (Londnon: Routledge, 2017), 187–216, https://doi.org/10.4324/9781315095813-10.

concomitant demands for universal public welfare necessitated an expansion of executive responsibilities. This evolution compelled governments to transcend Montesquieu's initial conceptualization of the executive function, which was primarily limited to execution of the law. The executive branch subsequently assumed partial legislative responsibilities in drafting laws and regulations, and in some jurisdictions, such as in Indonesia, even acquired quasi-judicial functions in specific domains like tax dispute resolution.[54]

The interpretation of the separation of powers has thus evolved from a strict segregation to a more nuanced division of powers. This contemporary understanding acknowledges the distinct nature and function of the three governmental branches while also recognizing the imperative for interbranch cooperation to ensure effective governance. Modern constitutional law theory has further refined this concept, introducing more complex interrelationships between the different branches of state power. This evolution has given rise to the system of checks and balances, which is designed to equilibrate and oversee the interactions between various centers of power in state governance.[55]

Doctrinal Perspectives on Separation and Division of Powers

The distinction between the concepts of the separation of powers and the evolution into a division of powers, while nuanced, can be elucidated through Sunny's perspicacious framework.[56] Sunny's conceptual differentiation provides a cogent basis for understanding and applying both concepts of power division.

Sunny posits a dichotomy between the separation of powers in a material sense and the division of powers in a formal sense. The material interpretation of the separation of powers explicitly pertains to the delineation of tasks among state institutions. Moreover, the formal conception of the division of powers is characterized by implicit implementation. The division of powers does not aim for the complete delegation of tasks to disparate institutions; rather, it adheres to constitutional precepts.

In the Indonesian context, the evolution of these concepts has manifested in the amendments to the 1945 Constitution, specifically in Chapter III (executive power), Chapter VII (legislative power), and Chapter IX (judicial power). Prior to these amendments, the 1945 Constitution emphasized a formal, rather than material, interpretation of power. Sovereignty was vested in the populace and exercised *in toto* by the People's Consultative Assembly (MPR), which represented the apex of power acting on behalf of the citizenry.

54 Hans Kelsen, *General Theory of Law and State* (London: Routledge, 2017).

55 Zulkarnain Ridlwan, "Cita Demokrasi Indonesia Dalam Politik Hukum Pengawasan Dewan Perwakilan Rakyat Terhadap Pemerintah," *Jurnal Konstitusi* 12, no. 2 (2015): 305–27.

56 Ismail Sunny, *Pembagian Kekuasaan Negara, Cet. 1* (Jakarta: Departemen Penerangan RI, 1962).

Despite its preeminent status, the MPR delegated certain powers to subordinate state institutions.

During the New Order regime (1970-1998), the 1945 Constitution adopted the doctrine of the division of powers. This era was characterized by the subordination of judicial power, with the judiciary and supreme court functioning more as projections of statutory law rather than as arbiters of justice and the law.

The post-amendment period witnessed a paradigm shift in the positioning of state institutions, transitioning from a hierarchical structure to an egalitarian structure. These constitutional amendments facilitated the introduction of a system of checks and balances in the exercise of state functions, marking a significant evolution in Indonesia's governance framework. In the absence of legislation that provides clear direction on urgent events, the government may take necessary action to address the situation. In light of the necessity for a responsive approach, it is evident that legal-political discretion, which affords the government with the flexibility to devise rules, is a crucial instrument.

Some researchers have posited that discretion serves to bridge the government's authority to address specific urgent events legally and morally, with several prerequisites. These prerequisites include a prohibition against contravening the prevailing positive legal system,[57] a mandate to act inthe public interest,[58] and a requirement to utilize discretion as an option to fill certain gaps and weaknesses in the application of the legality principle, without disregarding the law entirely.[59] In light of these prerequisites, it is evident that the government must strive to achieve its goals in a morally and legally responsible manner.

The historical and constitutional foundations of Indonesian law reflect a sophisticated amalgamation of two fundamental principles: the rule of law and the welfare state. This dual foundation provides the basis for the acceptance of discretionary power within the political constitution. The principle of the rule of law, enshrined in Article 1(3) of the 1945 Constitution following its amendment, establishes a framework of governance predicated on legal supremacy. Concurrently, the principle of the welfare state, articulated in paragraph IV of the preamble to the 1945 Constitution, emphasizes the state's commitment to societal well-being. These principles collectively form

57 Amrah Muslimin, *Beberapa Asas Dan Pengertian Pokok Tentang Administrasi Dan Hukum Administrasi* (Bandung: Pb. Alumni, 1985).

58 I Gusti Ayu Apsari Hadi, "Pertanggungjawaban Pejabat Pemerintahan Dalam Tindakan Diskresi Pasca Berlakunya Undang-Undang No. 30 Tahun 2014 Tentang Administrasi Pemerintahan," *Kertha Patrika* 39, no. 01 (2017): 33–46.

59 Lutfil Ansori, "Diskresi Dan Pertanggungjawaban Pemerintah Dalam Penyelenggaraan Pemerintahan," *Jurnal Yuridis* 2, no. 1 (2015): 135–50; Julista Mustamu, "Diskresi Dan Tanggungjawab Administrasi Pemerintahan," *Jurnal Sasi* 17, no. 2 (2011), https://doi.org/10.47268/sasi.v17i2.349.

the constitutional bedrock upon which the concept of political discretion is constructed and legitimized.

The legality principle, a cornerstone of the rule of law, mandates that all governmental acts must be grounded in existing legal frameworks. This principle serves the following dual purpose:

1. It provides explicit guarantees and limitations on the freedom of legal subjects, thereby delineating the boundaries of permissible action.
2. It safeguards state administrative acts against arbitrary power and potential abuse, ensuring that governmental authority is exercised within prescribed legal parameters.

The legality principle also operates on the maxim that no action is prohibited in the absence of an explicit legal provision proscribing such action. This concept aligns with the ideas propounded by Von Feuerbach, who posited that the formulation of legal rules must encompass a comprehensive spectrum of actions, prohibitions, and corresponding criminal provisions.[60]

Von Feuerbach's approach to legal codification emphasizes the need for clarity and specificity in legal provisions. Feuerbach's perspective suggests that the law should not only delineate prohibited actions but also explicate the consequences of contravening these prohibitions. Such an approach aims to provide a clear and predictable legal framework and enhance the rule of law by ensuring that individuals and state actors alike can anticipate the legal ramifications of their actions.

The concept of discretion in Indonesian law presents a nuanced interaction with the legality principle, revealing the complex nature of governance in situations that deviate from the law. This interaction highlights the limitations of strict legal adherence and the necessity for flexible administrative action in certain circumstances. The legality principle, while fundamental to the rule of law, demonstrates inherent limitations in providing comprehensive, precise, and unambiguous directives for governmental acts across all potential scenarios. In response to this limitation, the legitimacy of discretionary power is derived not from the legality principle itself, but from a broader legal framework. This distinction is crucial, as it acknowledges that state administrative acts may sometimes deviate from general patterns or average situations in order to address specific, unforeseen circumstances.[61]

The use of discretion in this context emerges in response to align certain considerations with the principles of justice. Discretion serves to guide certain

60 Tatjana Hörnle, "Foundational Texts: PJA Von Feuerbach and His Textbook of the Common Penal Law (1801)," 2014, https://doi.org/10.1093/acprof:oso/9780199673612.003.0007.

61 Krishna D. Darumurti, *Diskresi: Kajian Teori Hukum Dengan Postscript Dan Apendiks* (Yogyakarta: Genta Publishing, 2016).

actions that may diverge from strict legal interpretations. This conceptualization of discretion defines it as a necessary tool for responsive and effective governance, particularly in situations where rigid adherence to existing legal provisions might lead to suboptimal or unjust outcomes.

The legal framework for discretion in Indonesia has evolved through the following key legislative acts:

1. Law No. 5/1974 on the Basic Principles of Regional Government
2. Law No. 5/1986 on the Administrative Court (PTUN)
3. Law No. 30/2014 on Government Administration

Law No. 30/2014, in particular, provides a comprehensive framework for the exercise of discretion. Article 22 of this law delineates the purposes of discretion, which include, facilitating government administration, addressing legal weaknesses and deficiencies, providing legal certainty for governmental acts, and overcoming governmental stagnation in certain situations for the common good.

Furthermore, Article 23 of the same law outlines the scope of discretionary power, encompassing the regulations that provide options for decision-making action in the absence of written regulations governing a particular matter, or where there is incompleteness in the existing regulations and governmental stagnation affecting broader interests. The outputs of discretionary actions can take various forms, including in policy regulations, decisions, instructions, circulars, and other official announcements

Theoretical Distinctions Between Free and Bound Discretion

In the realm of administrative law, the concept of discretion is bifurcated into two distinct categories: free discretion and bound discretion. This differentiation provides a nuanced understanding of the scope and limitations of administrative decision-making power. Free discretion operates within a paradigm in which legislation establishes broad parameters for governmental acts. Within these expansive boundaries, the relevant administrative body retains substantial autonomy in decision-making, constrained primarily by the obligation not to transgress established legal parameters. This model of discretion facilitates flexibility in addressing complex or unforeseen situations, allowing administrators to adapt to evolving circumstances. In addition, bound discretion presents a more structured and constrained decision-making process, characterized by more specific legal directives and limited administrative latitude. The law delineates several specific alternatives from which the state administration must select. While this approach limits the range of possible actions, it still allows for some degree of administrative judgment in choosing the most appropriate option.

Discretion may be used as a way to address essential issues in number of circumstances.[62] Firstly, the issue must involve the public interest (national and state, community, and development interests). Secondly, the issue may be sudden or beyond the planned scope. Thirdly, there is an absence of legislation containing the resolution of specific issues, thus giving the state administration the freedom to resolve siutations based on its own initiative. Fourthly, the procedures cannot be resolved according to regular administration and are, therefore, less effective. Fifthly, there exists a situation that may cause harm to the public interest if the issue is not resolved immediately. These situations collectively justify the transfer of certain legislative powers to the executive branch, enabling it to be more responsive and efficient governance. However, it is crucial to note that this transfer of power does not equate to a shift in supremacy from the legislative branch to the executive branch.[63] The fundamental purpose of discretion is to facilitate public service delivery in situations where legal provisions are unclear or inadequate.

Theoretically, discretion provides a way to correct various weaknesses in legalistic approaches which give rise to legality. Although the legality principle is primarily applied in criminal law, it intersects with state administrative law when state officials commit unlawful acts. This intersection can be seen in Law No. 31/1999 Concerning the Eradication of Corruption Crimes (corruption law), later revised through Law No. 20/2001. In this case, state administrative acts are criminalized with the formulation that they, "may harm the state finances or the state economy," in Article 2 paragraph (1). This formulation focuses too much on state loss without further considering discretion that is beneficial for the public interest. The use of the term, "may," in corruption law falls under the criminal law statutes. even if the corrupt act has not actually in fact been committed and creates room for multiple interpretations by law enforcement agencies. Courts regard such policy products as open to the potential for criminal prosecution, which should ideally be administered through a judicial review mechanism. As a result, bureaucratic officials fear exercising discretion due to the deadlock outlined in the law. In 2006, Dawud Djatmiko filed a judicial review challenging use of the word "may" in this Article, through Case No. 003/PUU-IV/2005, but the constitutional court did not grant attention to the term.

62 Saut P. Panjaitan, "Makna Dan Peranan Freies Ermessen Dalam Hukum Administrasi Negara," *Unisia* 10 (1991): 53–60.

63 Siti Soetami, *Hukum Administrasi Negara* (Semarang: Badan Penerbit Universitas Diponegoro, 2000).

Case Study: Application of State Administrative Law in Human Rights Jurisprudence

Human rights remain a significant challenge for Indonesian administrative justice, particularly concerning freedom of expression on the Internet. These restrictions on digital human rights often disproportionately affect individuals from minority groups and certain professions. Notably, human rights violations in Papua have consistently drawn the attention of international organizations such as Amnesty International.[64] Papua, in particular, continues to be a focal point for various human rights concerns. The following case exemplifies how governmental actions may exceed discretionary authority by imposing undue limitations on digital human rights.

The Jakarta State Administrative Court Decision No. 230/G/TF/2019/PTUN-JKT exemplifies a judicial resolution of unlawful governmental acts in Indonesia. This case, which garnered significant attention, stemmed from the central government's imposition of internet access restrictions in the Papua and West Papua provinces.[65] The restrictions, affecting 29 regencies and municipalities, commenced on August 19, 2019, initially manifesting as access deceleration before escalating to a comprehensive cessation of internet data services.

In response to government acts, two civil society organizations—the Alliance of Independent Journalists (AJI) and the Southeast Asia Freedom of Expression Network (SafeNet)—initiated legal proceedings against the president and the ministry of communication and information technology (Kemenkominfo) in the Jakarta State Administrative Court. This legal act positioned the president and Kemenkominfo as co-defendants in a case that would scrutinize the legality and justification of the government's internet restriction policy.

The government proposed that the internet access restriction was a strategic measure to suppress the dissemination of misinformation in Papua. The government's rationale for this act was based on Article 40 of Law No. 19/2016 on Electronic Information and Transactions (ITE), which is purported to be aimed at safeguarding public order. Moreover, Kemenkominfo argued that this measure constituted a discretionary action, justified by the absence of specific legal provisions regarding internet access termination procedures. In support of this argument, Kemenkominfo invoked Articles 22-23

64 M Hafizh Nabiyyin and Stivani Ismawira Sinambela, "Peran Amnesty International Pada Pembatasan Kebebasan Berekspresi Human Rights Defender Di Indonesia: Studi Kasus Veronica Koman," *Papua Journal of Diplomacy and International Relations* 3, no. 1 (2023): 1–18.

65 Kelvin Chandra and Tundjung Herning Sitabuana, "Kebijakan Negara Melakukan Pembatasan Internet Di Papua Dan Papua Barat Dalam Putusan Nomor 230/G/Tf/2019/PTUN-JKT Melalui Perspektif Hak Asasi Manusia," *Jurnal Syntax Transformation* 3, no. 10 (2022): 1353–60; Yusuf Syibly Ramadhan and Adis Imam Munandar, "Policy Analysis of Restriction of Internet Access in The Region of Papua in 2019 in A National Security Perspective," *JKMP (Jurnal Kebijakan Dan Manajemen Publik)* 9, no. 1 (2021): 44–55.

of Law No. 30/2014 on Government Administration. The judges articulated a more constrained view of governmental discretion, however, grounding their interpretation in the normative framework established by Article 49 paragraph (2b) of the Information and Electronic Transactions (ITE) Law. The court's interpretation narrowly construes the government's power to restrict access, limiting such power solely to content that contravenes legal norms. Significantly, the ruling explicitly precludes the implementation of wholesale network termination.

The judicial panel elucidated that Article 40 of the ITE law must be interpreted in light of limitations imposed by Article 49, paragraph (2b). Furthermore, the judicial panel refuted the government's discretion argument, clarifying that discretionary powers under Article 22 paragraph (2b) of Law No. 30/2014 on Government Administration must fulfill cumulative objectives rather than alternative ones. The judges suggested that the government could have referenced the existing regulations governing emergencies, such as Government Regulation in Lieu of Law No. 23/1959, thus invalidating claims of a legal vacuum.

Consequently, the court categorized Kemenkominfo's acts as unlawful and characterized them as a violation of digital human rights. This ruling demonstrates the administrative court's application of a holistic concept of administrative justice. The court's legal reasoning in this case reflects a commitment to upholding moral principles that prioritize individual access rights for the greater societal good.

Conclusion

Scholars of state administrative law have engaged in extensive debates regarding the position of administrative legal science since the 1930s, with both proponents and opponents. Critics of the view that state administrative law is a scientific discipline point to governmental administration, arguing that the separation of powers differs from constitutional provisions. However, state administrative law's position within the Indonesian legal system has eventually been accepted due to its focus on discretion and the administration of government systems.

The scope of state administrative law in this context is divided into three parts: human rights, discretion, and state administrative acts. The historical background of human rights adoption in Indonesia's state administrative law is noteworthy. The protection of human rights in Indonesian administrative law is inextricably linked to international intervention, notably from the World Bank, which supported the domestic economy in the early 1990s. The World Bank emphasized that developing countries receiving aid should embed good governance principles into their governance systems. This concept subsequently permeated governance science and state law, evolving to connect development, legal supremacy, and human rights. Thus, the acceptance of good governance became instrumental in Indonesia's legal system upholding human rights, with legislation formation playing a crucial role in establishing human rights protection. State administrative acts, based on their functions, are categorized into acts of authority and acts based on orders. Acts based on general authority are characterized by the administrator's capacity to perform legal acts, while acts based on orders embody governmental duties in specific fields aimed at achieving national objectives.

Regarding discretion, state administrative law conceptualizes two forms: free discretion and bound discretion. Free discretion posits that the law establishes boundaries for government action, leaving decision-making choices to government bodies within these boundaries. Moreover, bound discretion involves the law providing several alternative decisions, allowing the state administration to select from these options. Several aspects are inherent in discretion as a means to address essential issues.

The concept of the rule of law emerged from historical social struggles against the absolutism of monarchical power. State administrative law, as a component of legal science, faces several challenges in its application, particularly concerning actors, biases, and the principle of the separation of powers. A lack of expertise in state administrative law impacts the robust application of values based in justice and derived from sociological factors and legal facts. Bijal Shah's research indicates that this deficiency in expertise contributes to weak accountability chains in the executive branch, particularly as it relates to immigration enforcement agencies and environmental regulations.[66]

Arguments in this regard point to the professional background of some state administrative law practitioners, who do not always originate from the legal profession. Additionally, some members of dispute resolution bodies tend to interpret the content of general and complex rules subjectively. There is also concern that some administrative court members may be employed by multiple interested agencies, potentially leading to bias. These weaknesses are compounded by time constraints, insufficient resources, and a lack of experts capable of analyzing information related to the social system.[67] Strong multi-stakeholder involvement is not aligned with the ability to sift through information outside of formal rules. Wagner calls this failure of information analysis a, "filter failure," relating to the inadequate commitment to process information within the legal system. Finally, delegating authority to administrative authorities can potentially violate both the principle of the separation of powers and the law. Consequently, Bijal Shah suggests expanding administrative discretion to oversee potentially harmful political content in administrative institutions.[68]

66 Bijal Shah, "Judicial Administration," *UC Irvine Law Review* 11 (2020): 1119; Bijal Shah, "Administrative Subordination," *Boston College Law School Legal Studies Research Paper*, 2023, https://papers.ssrn.com/sol3/papers.cfm?abstract_id=4392123.

67 Wendy E. Wagner, "Administrative Law, Filter Failure, and Information Capture," *Duke Law Journal* 59 (2009): 1321.

68 Bijal Shah, "Judicial Administration," *UC Irvine Law Review* 11 (2020): 1119.

References

Adiyanta, F. C. Susila. "Hukum Dan Studi Penelitian Empiris: Penggunaan Metode Survey Sebagai Instrumen Penelitian Hukum Empiris." *Administrative Law and Governance Journal* 2, no. 4 (2019): 697–709. https://doi.org/10.14710/alj.v2i4.697-709

Ansori, Lutfil. "Diskresi Dan Pertanggungjawaban Pemerintah Dalam Penyelenggaraan Pemerintahan." *Jurnal Yuridis* 2, no. 1 (2015): 135–50. https://ejournal.upnvj.ac.id/Yuridis/article/view/165

Arwanto, Bambang. "Perlindungan Hukum Bagi Rakyat Akibat Tindakan Faktual Pemerintah." *Jurnal Yuridika* 31, no. 3 (2016). https://doi.org/10.20473/ydk.v31i3.4857

Asshiddiqie, Jimly. *Omnibus Law Dan Penerapannya Di Indonesia*. Jakarta: Konstitusi Press, 2020.

Atmosudirdjo, S. Prajudi. *Hukum Administrasi Negara*. Bogor: Ghalia Indonesia, 1981.

Basah, Sjachran. *Eksistensi Dan Tolak Ukur Badan Peradilan Administrasi Di Indonesia*. Bandung: Alumni, 1989.

Bernadika, Shannon Rosemary, and Frederick Appiah Afriyie. "Legitimacy of Proof of Letters in the Era of the E-Litigation Proof System in the State Administrative Court." *Indonesian State Law Review (ISLRev)* 6, no. 1 (2023). https://doi.org/10.15294/islrev.v6i1.68236

Burke, Edmund. *Reflections on the Revolution in France (1790)*. New York: Everyman's Library, 1986.

Chandra, Kelvin, and Tundjung Herning Sitabuana. "Kebijakan Negara Mmelakukan Pembatasan Internet Di Papua Dan Papua Barat Dalam Putusan Nomor 230/G/Tf/2019/PTUN-JKT Melalui Perspektif Hak Asasi Manusia." *Jurnal Syntax Transformation* 3, no. 10 (2022): 1353–60. https://doi.org/10.46799/jst.v3i10.621

Cohler, Anne M., Basia Carolyn Miller, and Harold Samuel Stone. *Montesquieu: The Spirit of the Laws*. Cambridge: Cambridge University Press, 1989.

Darumurti, Krishna D. *Diskresi: Kajian Teori Hukum Dengan Postscript Dan Apendiks*. Yogyakarta: Genta Publishing, 2016.

Darussalam, Fajrul Ilmy, and Andi Batara Indra. "Kedaulatan Rakyat Dalam Pemikiran Filsafat Politik Montesquieu." *Jurnal Politik Profetik* 9, no. 2 (2021): 189–204. https://doi.org/10.24252/profetik.v9i2a2

Derung, Teresia Noiman. "Gotong Royong Dan Indonesia." *Sapa: Jurnal Kateketik Dan Pastoral* 4, no. 1 (2019): 5–13. https://doi.org/10.53544/sapa.v4i1.62

Gandara, Moh. "Kewenangan Atribusi, Delegasi Dan Mandat." *Khazanah Hukum* 2, no. 3 (2020): 92–99. https://doi.org/10.15575/kh.v2i3.8187

Goodnow, Frank J. *Politics and Administration: A Study in Government*. London: Routledge, 2017. https://doi.org/10.4324/9781351308281

Haakonssen, Knud. "Hugo Grotius and the History of Political Thought." In *Grotius and Law*, 69–95. London: Routledge, 2017. https://doi.org/10.4324/9781315093376-3

Hadi, Fikri. "Negara Hukum Dan Hak Asasi Manusia Di Indonesia." *Wijaya Putra Law Review* 1, no. 2 (2022): 170–88. https://doi.org/10.38156/wplr.v1i2.79

Hadi, I. Gusti Ayu Apsari. "Pertanggungjawaban Pejabat Pemerintahan Dalam Tindakan Diskresi Pasca Berlakunya Undang-Undang No. 30 Tahun 2014 Tentang

Administrasi Pemerintahan." *Kertha Patrika* 39, no. 01 (2017): 33–46. https://doi.org/10.24843/KP.2017.v39.i01.p03
Hadjon, Philipus M. *Hukum Administrasi Dan Good Governance*. Jakarta: Universitas Trisakti, 2010.
Hadjon, Philipus M. *Pengantar Hukum Administrasi Indonesia (Introduction to the Indonesian Administrative Law)*. Yogyakarta: Gadjah Mada University Press, 2002.
Hamburger, Philip. *Is Administrative Law Unlawful?* Chicago: University of Chicago Press, 2014. https://doi.org/10.7208/chicago/9780226116457.001.0001
Hamdi, Muchlis. *Kebijakan Publik: Proses, Analisis, Dan Partisipasi*. Bogor: Ghalia Indonesia, 2014.
Hendrick, James Pomeroy. *An International Bill of Human Rights*. Vol. 3055. Washington, D.C: Department of State, 1948.
Hörnle, Tatjana. "Foundational Texts: PJA Von Feuerbach and His Textbook of the Common Penal Law (1801)." 2014. https://doi.org/10.1093/acprof:oso/9780199673612.003.0007
Ilmar, Aminuddin. *Hukum Tata Pemerintahan*. Jakarta: Prenada Media, 2014.
Indroharto. *Usaha Memahami Undang-Undang Tentang Peradilan Tata Usaha Negara*. Jakarta: Pustaka Sinar Harapan, 1991.
Kansil, C. S. T. *Hukum Administrasi Negara*. Jakarta: PT. Pradnya Paramita, 2005.
Kelsen, Hans. *General Theory of Law and State*. Londnon: Routledge, 2017. https://doi.org/10.4324/9780203790960
Koentjoro, Diana Halim. *Hukum Administrasi Negara*. Bogor: Ghalia Indonesia, 2004.
Landis, James M. "Perspectives on the Administrative Process." *Administrative Law Review* (1961): 66–74. https://www.jstor.org/stable/40708383
Lawson, Gary. "The Rise and Rise of the Administrative State." *Harvard Law Review* 107, no. 6 (1994): 1231–54. https://doi.org/10.2307/1341842
Lessig, Lawrence, and Cass R. Sunstein. "The President and the Administration." *Columbia Law Review* 94, no. 1 (1994): 1–123. https://doi.org/10.2307/1123119
Locke, John. *Two Treatises on Civil Government*. Vol. 9. G. Routledge and Sons, Limited, 1887.
Locke, John, and John Wiedhofft Gough. *The Second Treatise on Civil Government and a Letter Concerning Toleration*. Oxford: Basil Blackwell, 1948.
Lowenthal, David. "Montesquieu and the Classics: Republican Government in the Spirit of the Laws." In *Charles-Louis de Secondat, Baron de Montesquieu*, 187–216. London: Routledge, 2017. https://doi.org/10.4324/9781315095813-10
Marzuki, Suparman. *Politik Hukum HAM di Indonesia*. Jakarta: Erlangga, 2014.
Mashaw, Jerry L. *Creating the Administrative Constitution: The Lost One Hundred Years of American Administrative Law*. New Haven, CT: Yale University Press, 2012.
McInerny, Ralph. "Natural Law and Human Rights." *American Journal of Jurisprudence* 36 (1991): 1. https://doi.org/10.1093/ajj/36.1.1
Metzger, Gillian E. "1930s Redux: The Administrative State Under Seige." *Harvard Law Review* 131 (2017): 1. https://harvardlawreview.org/print/vol-131/1930s-redux-the-administrative-state-under-siege/
Muslimin, Amrah. *Beberapa Asas Dan Pengertian Pokok Tentang Administrasi Dan Hukum Administrasi*. Bandung: Pb. Alumni, 1985.

Mustamu, Julista. "Diskresi Dan Tanggungjawab Administrasi Pemerintahan." *Jurnal Sasi* 17, no. 2 (2011). https://doi.org/10.47268/sasi.v17i2.349

Muttaqin, M. Zaenul. *Public Administration and Epistemology: Experience, Power, and Agency: Arthur J. Sementelli*, Vii, 200. New York and London: Routledge, 2021. Taylor & Francis, 2023. https://doi.org/10.1080/10841806.2022.2112455

Nabiyyin, M. Hafizh, and Stivani Ismawira Sinambela. "Peran Amnesty International Pada Pembatasan Kebebasan Berekspresi Human Rights Defender Di Indonesia: Studi Kasus Veronica Koman." *Papua Journal of Diplomacy and International Relations* 3, no. 1 (2023): 1–18. https://ejournal.uncen.ac.id/index.php/PJDIR/article/view/2464/2256

Panjaitan, Saut P. "Makna Dan Peranan Freies Ermessen Dalam Hukum Administrasi Negara." *Unisia*, no. 10 (1991): 53–60. https://doi.org/10.20885/unisia.vol11.iss10.art4

Prodjodikoro, Wirjono. *Asas-Asas Ilmu Negara Dan Politik*. Bandung: PT. Eresco, 1971.

Purbopranoto, Kuntjoro. *Hak-Hak Azasi Manusia Dan Pancasila*. Jakarta: Pradnya Paramita, 1979.

Purbopranoto, Kuntjoro. *Perkembangan Hukum Administrasi Indonesia*. Jakarta: Bina Cipta, 1981.

Putra, Erlanda Juliansyah. "Pengelolaan Kepegawaian Pada Era Otonomi Daerah." *Kanun Jurnal Ilmu Hukum* 17, no. 1 (2015): 37–60. https://jurnal.usk.ac.id/kanun/article/view/6052

Rahayu, Rahayu. "Dampak Globalisasi Terhadap Perkembangan Kesadaran Penghormatan Hak Asasi Manusia Di Indonesia." *Masalah-Masalah Hukum* 39, no. 4 (2010): 302–11. https://ejournal.undip.ac.id/index.php/mmh/article/view/11588

Ramadhan, Yusuf Syibly, and Adis Imam Munandar. "Policy Analysis of Restriction of Internet Access in The Region of Papua in 2019 in A National Security Perspective." *JKMP (Jurnal Kebijakan Dan Manajemen Publik)* 9, no. 1 (2021): 44–55. https://doi.org/10.21070/jkmp.v9i1.1566

Razy, Fakhruddin. *Buku Ajar Hukum Administrasi Negara*. Purwokerto Selatan: Pena Persada, 2020. https://doi.org/10.31237/osf.io/ug8hm

Remaja, I Nyoman Gede. *Hukum Administrasi Negara. Singaraja: Fakultas Hukum Universitas Panji Sakti*. Singaraja: Universitas Panji Sakti, 2017.

Ridlwan, Zulkarnain. "Cita Demokrasi Indonesia Dalam Politik Hukum Pengawasan Dewan Perwakilan Rakyat Terhadap Pemerintah." *Jurnal Konstitusi* 12, no. 2 (2015): 305–27. https://doi.org/10.31078/jk1226

Ridwan, H. R. *Hukum Administrasi Negara*. Jakarta: Raja Grafindo Persada, 2006.

Ridwan, H. R. *Hukum Administrasi Negara*. Jakarta: Rajawali Press, 2018.

Ridwan, H. R. "Pertanggungjawaban Publik Pemerintah Dalam Perspektif Hukum Administrasi Negara." *Jurnal Hukum Ius Quia Iustum* 10, no. 22 (2003): 27–38. https://doi.org/10.20885/iustum.vol10.iss22.art3

Ruhenda, Ruhenda, Heldi Heldi, Hasan Mustapa, and Muhammad Andi Septiadi. "Tinjauan Trias Politika Terhadap Terbentuknya Sistem Politik Dan Pemerintahan Di Indonesia." *Journal of Governance and Social Policy* 1, no. 2 (2020): 58–69. https://doi.org/10.24815/gaspol.v1i2.18221

Sayuti, Rosiady H., Moh Taqiuddin, Azhari Evendi, Siti Aisyah Hidayati, and M. Zaenul Muttaqin. "Impact of COVID-19 Pandemic on the Existence of Social Solidarity:

Evidence from Rural-Urban Communities in Lombok Island, Indonesia." *Frontiers in Sociology* 8 (2023): 1164837. https://doi.org/10.3389/fsoc.2023.1164837

Sementelli, Arthur. *Public Administration and Epistemology: Experience, Power, and Agency*. London: Routledge, 2020. https://doi.org/10.4324/9781003006053

Shah, Bijal. "Administrative Subordination." *Boston College Law School Legal Studies Research Paper*, 2023. https://papers.ssrn.com/sol3/papers.cfm?abstract_id=4392123

Shah, Bijal. "Judicial Administration." *UC Irvine Law Review* 11 (2020): 1119. https://scholarship.law.uci.edu/ucilr/vol11/iss4/9/

Soetami, Siti. *Hukum Administrasi Negara*. Semarang: Badan Penerbit Universitas Diponegoro, 2000.

Soimin, Soimin. "Pelembagaan Program-Program Pemerintah Dalam Suatu Tinjauan Hukum Administrasi Negara." *Edulaw: Journal of Islamic Law and Jurisprudance* 6, no. 1 (2024): 70–82. https://journal.bungabangsacirebon.ac.id/index.php/edulaw/article/view/2040

Sunny, Ismail. *Pembagian Kekuasaan Negara, Cet. 1*. Jakarta: Departemen Penerangan RI, 1962.

Suryanti, Dwi, Made Selly, M. Zaenul Muttaqin, and Sukron Makmun. "Unfolding the Landscape of Conflict: UN Volunteer Organisations and Violence Against Women." *JSEAHR* 7 (2023): 21. https://doi.org/10.19184/jseahr.v7i1.30517

Tushnet, Mark V. "New Institutional Mechanisms for Making Constitutional Law." 2015. https://doi.org/10.2139/ssrn.2589178

Tushnet, Mark V., Mark A. Graber, and Sanford Levinson. *The Oxford Handbook of the US Constitution*. Oxford: Oxford University Press, 2015. https://doi.org/10.1093/oxfordhb/9780190245757.001.0001

Utama, Kartika Widya. "Surat Keputusan Tata Usaha Negara Yang Bersifat Fiktif Positif." *Notarius* 8, no. 2 (2015): 141–251. https://ejournal.undip.ac.id/index.php/notarius/article/view/10259

Utrecht, Ernst. *Pengantar Hukum Tatausaha Negara Indonesia*. Jakarta: NV Bali Buku Indonesia, 1957.

Vollenhoven, Cornelis Van. *Van Vollenhoven on Indonesian Adat Law*. Edited by J. F. Holleman. Berlin: Springer, 2013.

Wagner, Wendy E. "Administrative Law, Filter Failure, and Information Capture." *Duke Law Journal* 59 (2009): 1321. https://scholarship.law.duke.edu/dlj/vol59/iss7/2/

Warassih, Esmi. *Pranata Hukum Sebuah Telaah Sosiologis. Suryandaru Utama*. Semarang: PT Suryandaru Utama, 2005.

Widayati, Sri. *Gotong Royong*. Semarang: Alprin, 2020.

Wurman, Ilan. "Administrative Law Theory and Fundamentals: An Integrated Approach." *Harvard Journal of Law & Public Policy Per Curiam* 1 (2021). https://doi.org/10.2139/ssrn.3839666

Yustiana, Dewi. *Hukum Administrasi Negara*. Surabaya: Penerbit CV. Mitra Sumber Rejeki, 2019.

Zaelani, Muhammad Aziz. "Perbuatan Administrasi Negara." In *Hukum Administrasi Negara*, edited by Anik Iftitah, 116–30. Banten: Sada Kurnia Pustaka, 2023.

Zahra, Annisa, Christian Alam Tegar Charisma, Muhammad Afir Ridho Azaby, and Siti Nurul Fadilah. "Teori Pemisahan Kekuasaan Trias Politica Dalam Pemikiran Filsafat Hukum Montesquieu." *Praxis: Jurnal Filsafat Terapan* 1, no. 01 (2022). https://journal.forikami.com/index.php/praxis/article/view/533/292

3 Administrative Law in Southeast Asia

Introduction

State administrative law, a subdiscipline examining judicial roles, has predominantly focused on East Asian studies within the Asian context.[1] Ginsburg posits that East Asian nations pioneered development regimes implementing state systems rooted in domestic political culture rather than in market forces.[2] This regional approach to state administrative law reflects traditional systems that prioritize policy over judicial mechanisms, thereby affording government officials substantial discretionary power. However, recent decades have witnessed significant transformations in state administrative law across Asia, particularly in Southeast Asia.

The judicial domain has experienced an increased emphasis on judges' roles.[3] This shift delineates judges' involvement in critical policy formulation, a function previously confined to government bureaucracies, politicians, and private entities.[4] Furthermore, the scope of government policy formulation has expanded to encompass procedural aspects, integrating the judiciary within a novel social framework.

This analysis examines state administrative law issues within Southeast Asia, focusing on five countries to provide a comprehensive overview of evolving administrative law systems. While research on state administrative law in national contexts has burgeoned over the past three decades, scholarly

1 Tom Ginsburg and Albert H. Y. Chen, "Administrative Law and Governance in Asia," in *Comparative Perspectives*, 2009. https://doi.org/10.4324/9780203888681

2 Tom Ginsburg, "The Judicialization of Administrative Governance: Causes, Consequences and Limits," in *Administrative Law and Governance in Asia*, edited By Tom Ginsburg, Albert H.Y. Chen. (London: Routledge, 2008), 11–30.

3 Rachel Sieder, Line Schjolden, and Alan Angell, *The Judicialization of Politics in Latin America* (Berlin: Springer, 2005); Roberto Gargarella, Pilar Domingo, and Theunis Roux, *Courts and Social Transformation in New Democracies: An Institutional Voice for the Poor?* (London: Routledge, 2017).

4 Torbjörn Vallinder and C. Neal Tate, *Global Expansion of Judicial Power* (New York: New York University Press, 1997).

DOI: 10.4324/9781003518563-3

attention has predominantly centered on European and American jurisdictions.[5] Moreover, studies on Southeast Asian state administrative law have primarily emphasized constitutional law aspects.[6] Recent literature reviews reveal a dearth of research on state administrative law in Southeast Asia, attributed to limited collaboration among researchers in this field.[7] The current research imperative lies in stimulating interest in state administrative law studies, as citizens are more likely to interact directly with government entities in their daily lives—interactions that intersect with state administrative law rather than with other legal disciplines.[8] Therefore, the primary objective of this chapter is to advance the study of state administrative law in Southeast Asian countries, thereby catalyzing further discourse on state administrative law and its practical applications.

Administrative Law in Vietnam

Administrative law in Vietnam has adopted the Soviet legal system, with slight adjustments to local culture since the 1960s.[9] This localization practice is manifested through neo-Confucian moral values that encourage harsh punishment for rule violations. Meanwhile, the basis of administrative law concepts leans on socialist values. In its development, adjustments have been made to integrate centralism democracy for state economic governance, with neo-Confucian moral values guiding the state's relationship with citizens.[10] At the micro level, the encouragement of interaction between officials and citizens is seen as a superior spectrum compared to the law, as it often happens that the technical substance of the rules is deemed not as important amidst the flexible demands of the local community.

At the macro level, the discourse of neoliberalism emerges, with the administrative system becoming a crucial instrument for asserting the separation

5 Alec Stone, *The Birth of Judicial Politics in France: The Constitutional Council in Comparative Perspective* (Seattle, WA: University of Washington, 1990); Tom Ginsburg, "The Judicialization of Administrative Governance: Causes, Consequences and Limits." in *Administrative Law and Governance in Asia* (London: Routledge, 2008), 11–30.

6 Wandi Ardiansyah et al., "Bibliometric Analysis and Visualization of State Administrative Law in Scopus Database from 2017–2021," *Cogent Social Sciences* 10, no. 1 (2024), https://doi.org/https://doi.org/10.1080/23311886.2024.2310935.

7 Wandi Ardiansyah et al., "Bibliometric Analysis and Visualization of State Administrative Law in Scopus Database from 2017–2021," *Cogent Social Sciences* 10, no. 1 (2024), https://doi.org/https://doi.org/10.1080/23311886.2024.2310935.

8 Ran Hirschl, *Towards Juristocracy: The Origins and Consequences of the New Constitutionalism* (Cambridge: Harvard University Press, 2009); Tom Ginsburg et al., "Judicial Review in New Democracies: Constitutional Courts in Asian Cases," *NTU Law Review* 3 (2008): 143.

9 John Gillespie, "The Juridification of Administrative Complaints and Review in Vietnam," in *Administrative Law and Governance in Asia*, edited By Tom Ginsburg, Albert H.Y. Chen. (London: Routledge, 2008), 215–39.

10 Thanh Hung Pham et al., "The Impact of Quality of Public Administration on Local Economic Growth in Vietnam," *Journal of Risk and Financial Management* 15, no. 4 (2022): 158.

between the public and private spheres through power. However, judicial institutions also provide space for corporations to gain control over the state. After several decades, socialist discretion faces rejection from government elites. Their rejection is directed toward an administrative system that emphasizes flexibility and grants more freedom for businesses to obtain official permits.

Pressure for administrative reform emerged alongside conflicts in all Vietnamese rural areas, presenting various challenges in the use of violence. The 7th National Congress of the Communist Party of Vietnam agreed to adopt constitutional values in 1991, drawing from Gorbachev's Soviet thinking that used the law to command, and used the constitutional function to limit and oversee state administration. Operating in the background, party elites insisted on party authority over the state and citizens. Eventually, in 2005, the Vietnamese party emphasized the urgency of administrative reform, including law and justice.[11] Most attention was focused on the urgency for executive institutions to implement public accountability and expand the role of lawyers in creating channels for social justice.[12]

In its development, the private sector responded to numerous rule changes and extensive government interventions, encouraging circles of corruption among government officialswhich led to administrative challenges in Vietnam. Domestic companies' demand for legal-based interactions coincided with the growing complexity of the economy. Entrepreneurs believed that their relationship with the state required certain legal guarantees.[13] The deregulation of company law in 1991 indirectly facilitated market access at the domestic level and even led to a wave of mergers and domestic investments. This law shifted the legal framework for domestic businesses to engage in transactions and expand business networks through rational law and administration.[14] The push for deregulation provided opportunities for entrepreneurs to avoid vulnerability to government officials, who might abuse their responsibilities regarding business permits. In other words, companies relied on a private legal framework rather than deal directly with state administrators on a more personal level.

11 Martin Painter, "Public Administration Reform in Vietnam: Problems and Prospects," *Public Administration and Development* 23, no. 3 (2003): 259–71; Truong Xuan Do and Quang Truong, "The Changing Face of Public Sector Management in Vietnam," in *The Changing Face of Vietnamese Management* (Routledge, 2009), 187–220.

12 John Gillespie, "The Juridification of Administrative Complaints and Review in Vietnam," in *Administrative Law and Governance in Asia*, edited By Tom Ginsburg, Albert H.Y. Chen. (London: Routledge, 2008), 215–39.

13 Alec Stone Sweet, *Governing with Judges: Constitutional Politics in Europe* (Oxford: Oxford University Press, 2000).

14 Sunita Kikeri, Thomas John Kenyon, and Vincent Palmade, *Reforming the Investment Climate: Lessons for Practitioners*, vol. 3986 (Washington, DC: World Bank Publications, 2006), https://doi.org/10.1596/978-0-8213-6837-4; Philip Abott et al., "Trade and Development in Vietnam: Exploring Investment Linkages," 2008, https://mpra.ub.uni-muenchen.de/29382/2/MPRA_paper_29382.pdf

However, entrepreneurs still secured their positions and long-term relationships with state regulators to expand their business networks and accrue profits.[15] An example of this happened during the negotiations between computer entrepreneurs in Ho Chi Minh City and the market in Hanoi. These negotiations involved leniency in tax payments to local officials in Hanoi. While local officials have the authority to adjust central regulations and use context-based solutions,central regulations become alternative guiding sources and normative exogenous sources in policy-making. For the local officials, state administrative management is not explicitly stated in the legal text; consequently, personal bargaining with the business world becomes a viable business alternative at the local level. This certainly facilitates the goals of specific local business networks. Moreover, bureaucrats perform functions that are not yet defined in formal regulations and administrative processes. A similar situation also applies to state-owned enterprises, which are often resolved through political channels with regulators rather than through legal processes.

After the 1997 economic crisis, the rationalization of state administration toward national governments in Asia intensified and was driven by international bodies. It was believed that regional economic development would occur if a country employed rational governance in its administration. Underlying this was the assumption that rational governance hides the international mission to intervene in developing countries in the Asian region. Vietnam only ratified bilateral trade agreements with the United States four years later, in 2001, and joined the WTO in 2007. However, the main argument for rational governance is the thorough reform of bureaucracy throughtransparency, accountability, corruption resolution, and optimization of oversight functions. These reforms transformed the state administration system based on the rule of law. Foreign investors also championed this push for reform. The main goal of this foreign push for reform was to support the rule of law, placing foreign companies at the local level on an equal footing before the law.

In terms of administrative complaints, the main strength of Vietnam's administrative law is its formal and informal complaints systems.[16] There are three main areas of complaints related to government actions, including land and housing administration, implementation of court decisions, and general administrative matters like licensing. Land and housing administration are the dominant areas for complaints, comprising 60% of the annual complaint figure. The law guides the formal complaint mechanism through Complaints of 2004 and the Law on Administrative Procedure of 1996. Meanwhile, informal complaints are made through parties that have the political power to pursue such complaints, such as village chiefs, party officials, and legislative bodies.

15 John Gillespie, "The Juridification of Administrative Complaints and Review in Vietnam," in *Administrative Law and Governance in Asia*, edited By Tom Ginsburg, Albert H.Y. Chen. (London: Routledge, 2008), 215–39.

16 John Gillespie, "The Juridification of Administrative Complaints and Review in Vietnam," in *Administrative Law and Governance in Asia*, edited By Tom Ginsburg, Albert H.Y. Chen. (London: Routledge, 2008), 215–39.

However, formal administrative complaints face several challenges, including the lack of clarity in technical and procedural aspects of the complaint process, narrow reviews, and the complexity of dispute resolution methods. The technically biased complaint mechanisms contribute to the limited enforcement of the law for thousands of complainants each year. Additionally, administrative violations are often narrowly interpreted in specific areas without extension to other related fields.[17] For example, the establishment of a company may not extend to complex business licensing under the authority of the ministry of planning and investment.

The increasing social demand for administrative justice in Vietnam is not new. Since 1996, administrative courts have received dozens of case reports, increasing to thousands of complaints yearly. However, the limited enforcement of decisions remains a notable issue in all administrative cases.[18] What this emphasizes is that the main obstacle in administrative justice is the citizens' overwhelming lack of hope for fairness. Another obstacle lies in the prohibition of group lawsuits, which poses a risk of court litigation. The relationships established between bureaucratic officials and companies further complicate administrative justice affairs.

Most of the jurisdictional authority of administrative justice pertains to business violations. However, the review of reports of human rights violations is not within the jurisdiction of administrative courts. In reality, the judicial reform of 2001 created a paradox with the initial goal of sterilizing the courts from the grip of local governments.[19] Local authorities still play a role and intervene in the judicial process, including pressuring the courts to make the final decisions. However, the supreme court compels judges to act delicately in administrative cases involving the government so as to avoid repercussions.[20]

Administrative Law in the Philippines

The Philippines, a key country in this study, has a unique state administrative law system heavily influenced by its long history as a United States colony.

17 John Gillespie, "The Juridification of Administrative Complaints and Review in Vietnam," in *Administrative Law and Governance in Asia*, edited By Tom Ginsburg, Albert H.Y. Chen. (London: Routledge, 2008), 215–39.

18 John Gillespie, "The Juridification of Administrative Complaints and Review in Vietnam," in *Administrative Law and Governance in Asia*, edited By Tom Ginsburg, Albert H.Y. Chen. (London: Routledge, 2008), 215–39.

19 Dat T Bui, "Due-Process-Evading Justice: The Case of Vietnam," *International Journal of Law, Crime and Justice* 63 (2020): 100426; Tran Quoc Hung, Huang Yong Peng, and Nguyen Thi Lien, "Significance of Judicial Independence in the Law Governed by the Rule of Law in Vietnam," *International Journal of Criminal Justice Sciences* 16, no. 2 (2021); Penelope Nicholson and Nguyen Hung Quang, "The Vietnamese Judiciary: The Politics of Appointment and Promotion," *Pacific Rim Law & Policy Journal | Law Reviews and Journals* 14 (2005): 1.

20 Nguyen Thi Hong Nhung, Huynh Thi Nam Hai, and Luu Minh Sang, "E-Court in Resolving Civil Cases-Foreign Experiences and Recommendations for Vietnam," *Science & Technology Development Journal: Economics-Law & Management* 5, no. 3 (2021): 1733–40.

This American-influenced framework distinguishes the Philippines from other Southeast Asian countries and highlights the lasting impact of colonial legacies on postcolonial administrative systems. Pangalangan notes that the country's legal foundations still strongly reflect American legalistic preferences.[21] This is evident in the use of legal formalism that often prioritizes governmental power over principles of justice. Consequently, Philippine state administrative law inherently incorporates significant legal discretion in policy-making, even when applying seemingly objective standards.

The Philippines has undergone four major changes in constitutional law.[22] These changes are historically related to the Philippines' history as a colony of Spain, the United States, and Japan. The first change was the 1899 Malolos Constitution, which emerged from the Philippine People's Revolution against Spanish colonization.[23] The second change was the 1935 Constitution, which represented a shift to a government model replicating that of the United States.[24] This Constitution established presidential elections held every four years. The third constitutional change was the 1973 Constitution, which was spearheaded by Ferdinand Marcos.[25] This Constitution transformed the 1935 Constitution from a presidential to a parliamentary system. However, this Constitution drew scrutiny due to suspicions that it was designed to facilitate authoritarian rule. The 1987 Constitution was the fourth constitutional change. It was championed by Corazon Aquino following Marcos' regime.[26] Aquino formed the Philippine Constitutional Commission to establish the 1987 Constitution through a referendum. The content of the new constitution includes the formation of Philippine representation in the executive, the

21 Raul C. Pangalangan, "'Government by Judiciary' in the Philippines: Ideological and Doctrinal Framework," in *Administrative Law and Governance in Asia* (Oxfordshire, London: Routledge, 2008), 323–38.

22 Dante Gatmaytan, "Constitutional Change as Suspect Projects: The Philippines," *Journal of Comparative Law* 14 (2019): 139; Araceli Baviera, "Politics and the Recent Constitutional Changes in the Philippines," *Philippine Law Journal* 57 (1982): 226; Surin Maisrikrod, "Changing Forms of Democracy in Asia? Some Observations on the Thai and Philippine Constitutions," *Asian Studies Review* 23, no. 3 (1999): 355–73.

23 Joseph G. Deluna, *Analysis of the 5 Constitution of the Philippines and Its Implication to the Economical, and Social Indicators of Development* (Technological University of the Philippines, 2021); Filomeno V. Aguilar, "Church-State Relations in the 1899 Malolos Constitution: Filipinization and Visions of National Community," *Southeast Asian Studies* 4, no. 2 (2015): 279–311.

24 Adam Burns, *The Foundations of the Modern Philippine State: Imperial Rule and the American Constitutional Tradition in the Philippine Islands, 1898–1935* (Oxford: Oxford University Press, 2019); Emmanuel S. de Dios, "(DP 2002-03) Welfare and Nationalism in the 1935 Philippine Constitution," *UPSE Discussion Papers*, 2010. https://econ.upd.edu.ph/dp/index.php/dp/article/view/35

25 Jean Grossholtz, "Philippines 1973: Whither Marcos?," *Asian Survey* 14, no. 1 (1974): 101–12.

26 Dante B. Gatmaytan, "Judicial Review and Emergencies in Post-Marcos Philippines," *Constitutionalism under Extreme Conditions: Law, Emergency, Exception* (2020): 41–62.

bicameral legislative, and the judiciary branches.[27] Aquino reverted from the parliamentary system to a presidential system and extended the presidential term to six years from aprevious term of four years.

Pangalangan elucidates the multifaceted doctrinal evolution of judicialization in the Philippines.[28] This evolution encompasses the codification of policy objectives and substantive norms, which encapsulate various guiding principles. Firstly, the democratization process is prioritized, with fundamental societal norms and values being enshrined in the constitution. The government systematically codifies state responsibilities, predicated on these guiding principles, making them into statutory law. The constitution distinctively emphasizes protectionist and static economic theories, delineating them from articles on national economy and patrimony. The constitution further incorporates affirmative action institutions within articles on social justice and human rights, encompassing the right to health, sustainable ecology, education, and notably, a national economy sovereign to Philippine citizens. Pangalangan posits that the framers of the Philippine constitution were appointees rather than electees chosen on merit or competence. This assertion is grounded in the political compromises inherent in democratic countries, where the constitution is intrinsically linked to congressional authority and welfare state policies.

Secondly, economic protectionism happens when the law functions as a means to advance Philippine nationalist ideologies. The goal of protectionism is to isolate foreign control in the domestic economy. This is manifested in the initial policy of codifying the charter's first special treatment for citizens. The state is responsible for ensuring Philippine labor absorption, optimizing domestic natural resources and raw materials, and ensuring domestic products are competitive. Thirdly, there are specific social justice clauses as a consequence of these redistributive claims. Historically, redistributive claims have been recognized in constitutional law under the umbrella of social justice. This was first constitutionalized by the government in the 1935 Constitution during the US occupation, which opted for a welfare state over one that is more *laissez-faire.* The task of the constitution framers was to provide a legal doctrine to reform affirmative action and preferential treatment. Pangalangan notes that any identification of the constitution with vulnerable groups, such as what happens in agrarian reform policies, is subject to the principles of social justice on one side and to a free market on the other side. However, constitutional clauses tend to act as dominant agents in legitimate communal actions. The constitution's content, which always uses the phrase, "The State shall," indicates an excessive reliance on formal state mechanisms and a disregard

27 Surabhi Chopra, "The Constitution of the Philippines and Transformative Constitutionalism," *Global Constitutionalism* 10, no. 2 (2021): 307–30.

28 Raul C. Pangalangan, "'Government by Judiciary' in the Philippines: Ideological and Doctrinal Framework," in *Administrative Law and Governance in Asia* (Oxfordshire, London: Routledge, 2008), 323–38.

for collective forces acting outside the law. The expansion of judicial power characterizes the second aspect of the doctrinal evolution of Philippine judicialization. This is marked by the judiciary's responsibility to resolve disputes fairly, especially when the issues are controversial, and the judiciary has extensive responsibility for nonjudicial decisions of government agencies. However, government agencies often use open discretion by ignoring objective protection, allowing judges to use their discretion and rely upon the wisdom of previous decision-makers. This expansion of judicial power alters the balance of the separation of powers set forth in the constitution, which then informs the adjustment of review language.

Fourthly, the alignment of law enforcement with directive principles is a direct consequence of the aforementioned principles. Pangalangan observes that the supreme court plays a pivotal role in this process. When the supreme court formulates normative statements, the courts are able to enforce them directly, without the necessity of legislative implementation. This argument is based on the assumption that there are common substantive standards, such as balanced ecological rights and the right to health, which can be integrated with corrective procedures that encourage courts to enter uncharted territory, namely the making of social and economic policies. It is possible for legislative and executive institutions, as policy-makers, to expand the fundamental values of ecological and health rights if they are not specifically included in the rules.

Fifthly, there is a strengthening of personal action rights. This is exemplified by the supreme court's relaxation of the application requirements. This has the effect of enhancing a citizen's ability to file tax claims in a more comprehensive manner and to gain access to information regarding the government's judicialization. Pangalangan offers a constructive critique of the current state of democracy in the Philippines. The lofty norms set forth in Philippine legal codes are frequently violated in practice. Consequently, if the judicial process is not committed to prioritizing public norms, other mechanisms aligned with the idea of decision-making based on the law should be delegated to institutions that do not have conflicts of interest. Nevertheless, with regard to state administrative law, there is room for improvement in Philippine democracy. The incorporation of moral preferences and policies into the 1987 Constitution suggests a lack of confidence in the ability of the next legislative body to act in the public interest. Moreover, the constitution's fetishism will impede the society's political capacity and lead to erosion of the state's moral responsibility.[29]

29 Richard D. Parker, "Here, the People Rule: A Constitutional Populist Manifesto," *Valparaiso University Law Review* 27 (1992): 531.

Administrative Law in Thailand

Thailand has adopted a constitutional monarchy system of government. Thailand's system changed in 1932, replacing the absolute monarchy with a constitutional monarchy. The constitutional monarchy system provides more freedom to the monarchy within certain limits stipulated in the constitution. However, in practice, this constitutional monarchy system has shown signs of deviating from its intended purpose. People feel that this system tends to lean toward an absolute monarchy. The practice of absolute monarchy is characterized by the enactment of the *Lesè Majesté* law, which is used by authorities to prevent insults toward or criticisms of the king by the public. As a result, the ideal democratic practice does not facilitate the opening of public participation.

From a legal perspective, Thailand's legal system still reflects elements of the continental European legal system, or *Rechtsstaat*, and the Anglo-Saxon, or rule-of-law principles.[30] Despite being under monarchy rule, Thailand is a role model for democracy. Courts in Thailand include the constitutional court, the court of justice, the administrative courts, and the military courts. One notable aspect of Thailand's governance is that despite having a monarchy system of government, it implements the separation of powers, dividing authority among the executive, the judiciary, and the legislature. The executive branch comprises two clusters: the king and the prime minister. As the head of state, the king exercises legislative power through the parliament, executive power through the cabinet, and judicial power through the courts. The succession of the head of state is determined by criteria outlined in the 1924 Palace Law of Succession, stipulating that the head of state be a male and also a Buddhist. The king acts as the upholder of rights and justice in various aspects of societal life, including in religious, social, and cultural matters. The second executive cluster includes the prime minister, who plays a central role as the one responsible for most national policy formulations. The prime minister serves as the head of the cabinet, overseeing subdivisions such as the budget bureau, the national security council, the judiciary council, socioeconomic bodies, the investment promotion board, the civil service commission, and other subdivisions related to national policy formulation. Additionally, the prime minister oversees 20 ministries. As for the legislative branch, Thailand has a bicameral parliament, the *Rathasapha*, consisting of the Senate and the House of Representatives. The speaker of the House of Representatives serves as the president of the national assembly, while the Senate's speaker serves as the vice president of the national assembly. The main functions of the national assembly include disseminating laws, overseeing state administration, and approving or rejecting administrative programs. The House of Representatives was formed after the 1932 revolution when the People's Party ousted the

30 Peter Leyland, "The Emergence of Administrative Justice in Thailand under the 1997 Constitution," in *Administrative Law and Governance in Asia*, edited By Tom Ginsburg, Albert H.Y. Chen. (London: Routledge, 2008), 240–66.

absolute monarchy and established a constitutional monarchy. The House of Representatives in Thailand, beyond its primary legislative function, exercises oversight of state administration. In conjunction with the Senate, it deliberates on matters of national significance, including constitutional issues and critical governmental procedures. The Senate's mandate encompasses several key functions: ratifying legislation originating from the House of Representatives, conducting oversight of state administration, nominating candidates for judicial appointments, and initiating proceedings for the removal of public officials implicated in corruption. The judicial branch of Thailand, distinct from the legislative bodies, adjudicates legal disputes and upholds the rule of law within the state.

In addition to employing the separation of powers in the government structure, Thailand has a separate administrative judiciary. This judiciary was established by the Administrative Court Act of Thailand in 1999, or the Act on Establishment of Administrative Court and Administrative Court Procedure B.E.2542 (1999). The administrative courts aim to examine, adjudicate, and settle disputes related to administrative acts that violate regulations.[31] Thailand's administrative judiciary is a historical artefact of the 1997 Constitution, reflecting optimistic progress similar to the French administrative court system. The 1997 Constitution follows the administrative court system as a branch of the regular court system.[32] These courts have the authority to follow up on complaints by imposing sanctions on official government bodies. The administrative judiciary was legally established in 1999 through the law on establishing administrative courts and the procedures for administrative court proceedings, and it began operating two years later.[33] The optimistic progress of Thailand's administrative judiciary is marked by the division of administrative courts into two hierarchies. The central administrative court has jurisdiction over Bangkok and its surrounding provinces, while the regional administrative court oversees trials at the regional level. The Supreme Administrative Court is responsible for the appellate review of judgments from the central administrative court and adjudicates various issues related to the central government's acts. Leyland illustrates this with cases involving decisions by the royal government and the council of ministers, which can be tried by the Central Supreme Administrative Court.

Leyland further explains that Thailand's administrative judiciary has had a clear system for recruiting judges from the outset. The Judicial Commission of the Administrative Court (JCAC) is tasked with selecting prospective judges

31 Peter Leyland, "The Emergence of Administrative Justice in Thailand under the 1997 Constitution," in *Administrative Law and Governance in Asia* (Oxfordshire, London: Routledge, 2008), 240–66.

32 Andrew Harding and Peter Leyland, "The Constitutional Courts of Thailand and Indonesia: Two Case Studies from South East Asia," *Journal of Comparative Law* 3 (2008): 118.

33 Peter Leyland, "The Emergence of Administrative Justice in Thailand under the 1997 Constitution," in *Administrative Law and Governance in Asia* (Oxfordshire, London: Routledge, 2008), 240–66.

who are appointed based on criteria including that a candiate be over 35 years old and meet other specific requirements. This professionalism is also manifested in decision-making. Thailand's administrative court rulings that annul officials' decisions are promulgated through the official government gazette. When the court renders a judgment imposing monetary obligations or compensation in kind, it possesses the authority to execute such judgments against the defendant's assets. Moreover, the court may enforce judgments mandating specific performance or injunctive relief by applying civil procedure law *mutatis mutandis*. During administrative proceedings, the court is empowered to impose sanctions on defendant officials who disregard judicial orders. These sanctions may include contempt of court penalties, disciplinary measures, and referral to the prime minister. With the extensive authority of Thailand's administrative courts, there are instances where administrative oversight duties overlap with the role of the ombudsman. Applicants can directly petition the court if there is evidence of maladministration involving dereliction of duty.[34]

State Administrative Law in Malaysia

After the arrival of British colonizers (1800–1940), particularly in the 19th century, there were changes in the region's political landscape, governance systems, and state administration (bureaucracy).[35] This occurred as Britain began intervening in the bureaucratic affairs of Malay states and introducing new bureaucratic forms in the Malay Peninsula. This condition persisted until Malaya achieved independence with a newly adopted bureaucratic structure known as the system of the separation of powers. Through the system of the separation of powers, the body responsible for legislation (parliament) solely focused on lawmaking and did not involve itself in the judiciary, which was carried out by the courts, nor did it interfere in the jurisdiction of the bureaucratic body. The bureaucratic sphere was not allowed to intermingle with the judicial or legislative jurisdictions. In the context of present-day Malaysia, this concept of a separation of powers can be observed through three main branches of government: the bureaucratic body (the executive) handles state bureaucracy, the legislative body (the legislature) formulates laws, and the judicial body (the judiciary) administers justice and legal proceedings.

Bureaucratic reform has been underway in Malaysia since the country's independence in 1957.[36] Independence and bureaucratic reform have involved

34 Peter Leyland, "The Emergence of Administrative Justice in Thailand under the 1997 Constitution," in *Administrative Law and Governance in Asia* (Oxfordshire, London: Routledge, 2008), 240–66.

35 Sridevi Thambapillay, "Recent Developments in Judicial Review of Administrative Action in Malaysia: A Shift from Grounds Based on Common Law Principles to the Federal Constitution," 2007. https://eprints.um.edu.my/13505/1/RECENT_DEVELOPMENTS_IN_JUDICIAL.pdf

36 Hong-Hai Lim, "Improving Administrative Performance in Malaysia: The More Difficult next Steps in Reform," *Policy and Society* 26, no. 2 (2007): 33–59.

a continuous effort to ensure that governance developments progress in line with the changing times, as the inherited colonial systems have become inadequate to address developmental challenges and high demand for services from the public. However, bureaucratic reform in Malaysia emphasizes restructuring the bureaucratic role as the engine of growth within the state bureaucracy.[37]

The legal system of Malaysia comprises laws that have emerged from three significant periods in Malaysian history: from the Sultanate of Malacca, the spread of Islam to Southeast Asia, and subsequently, the absorption of the legal culture of British colonial governance, which introduced constitutional governance and the Anglo-Saxon legal system.[38] Anglo-Saxon or common law is a legal system developed in England in the 11th century. Common law is often referred to as, "unwritten law," but this is not entirely accurate, because within the common law there are also written sources of law (the statutes). The sources of law in the common law system include the judicial decisions, customs, written regulations, laws, and administrative regulations of the state. The sources in the common law system are judicial decisions, and it is through these decisions that legal principles are formed and become generally binding rules. In addition to judicial decisions, the common law system also recognizes local customs, written legislative regulations, and state administrative regulations. The common law system's sources of customary law, legislative, and administrative regulations are not systematically organized in a hierarchy as they are in the civil law.[39] In the common law system, judges have a broader authority to interpret existing regulations and make decisions by creating new legal principles that guide other judges in adjudicating similar cases.

The administration of Malaysia is divided into three structures: (1) the federal government in Kuala Lumpur; (2) the state governments; and (3) the local government authorities. The federal government has authority in several areas, including in finance, national maritime and land matters, and in matters pertaining to domestic security, education, and social welfare. The state governments regulate authority regarding religious matters. This allows states like Kelantan to implement Islamic law as the formal law.

As a country adhering to the common law system, Malaysia has ties to the common law system practiced in England. However, a significant addition to Malaysia's public law system is that it also relates to the federal constitution. Fundamental rights are well articulated in this written constitution, so that when the state, through its institutions, takes adverse action against an individual's fundamental rights, the state will always be subject to constitutional scrutiny, including rules limiting those fundamental rights. Administrative courts

37 Hasnah Hussin and Mardiana Nordin, *Pengajian Malaysia* (Selangor: Oxford Fajar, 2007).

38 Andrew Harding, *Law, Government and the Constitution in Malaysia*, vol. 1 (Leiden: Brill, 2024).

39 Andrew Harding and Peter Leyland, "The Constitutional Courts of Thailand and Indonesia: Two Case Studies from South East Asia," *Journal of Comparative Law* 3 (2008): 118.

consider individual rights and freedoms based on the objectives contained in the regulations. The proportionality of administrative courts is adjusted in line with institutional choices regarding fundamental rights, although the discretion of legislative and administrative bodies has been expanding.

Chuan illustrates a case involving the registrar of societies and the minister rejecting an application for the registration of a political party at the national level.[40] The high court conducts a constitutional review of this decision. This illustration affirms the significant responsibility of the reviewing authority in assessing the legality of anapplicant's petition according to administrative law. The court has the authority to annul the actions of state institutions according to considerations of objectivity, justice, and the proportionality of decision-making objectives.

In the field of employment, the court provides procedural justice for the protection of employees who have issues with a particular company. The doctrine of proportionality is inherent in the broad consideration and interpretation of the word, "Life" in Article 5(1) of the federal constitution. The expansion of this form of court jurisdiction is also revealed through the inclusion of the right of terminated employees to know the reasons behind administrative decisions involving their employment.

However, Chuan argues that Malaysian public law reverted to its restrictive, pre-1996 ethos with a more narrow and limited interpretation of human rights issues.[41] He illustrates this with the case of Beatrice Fernandes, who filed a lawsuit against her dismissal as a flight attendant with Malaysian Airline System (MAS). The basis of the appeal to the Malaysian High Court of Appeal was Article 8(1) of the federal constitution, which stipulates equality before the law. The high court ruled that the applicant failed to provide evidence that Malaysian Airline System, as a public authority, fell within the administrative law. In short, the applicant's lawsuit did not meet the criteria of the rational classification doctrine.

However, the Schedule to the Courts of Judicature Act 1964, particularly in its first paragraph, includes the protection of fundamental rights, yet excludes complaints about threats to the safety of foreigners. In both cases, the high court disregarded the importance of protecting the applicants' fundamental rights and instead focused more on procedural aspects. In other words, the federal court must shift away from an anti-human rights paradigm and instead initiate the development of the public law system amidst the dynamic changes in society.

40 Gan Ching Chuan, "Administrative Law and Judicialized Governance in Malaysia: The Indian Connection," in *Administrative Law and Governance in Asia*, edited By Tom Ginsburg, Albert H.Y. Chen. (Oxfordshire, London: Routledge, 2008), 267–96.

41 Gan Ching Chuan, "Administrative Law and Judicialized Governance in Malaysia: The Indian Connection," in *Administrative Law and Governance in Asia*, edited By Tom Ginsburg, Albert H.Y. Chen. (Oxfordshire, London: Routledge, 2008), 267–96.

Administrative Law in Singapore

As one of the countries in Southeast Asia that has quickly transformed its state power post-colonization, Singapore has enjoyed considerable success in economic development and ought to be commended highly for its strategic governmental management.[42] Singapore's development is inseparable from its economic model, which fosters innovation in industry and exports. Support for governmental authority in both areas is also bolstered by social instruments and focused coordination for development goals. However, Singapore's distinctiveness in administrative law is relatively underdeveloped.[43] This is influenced by the limited role of the judiciary in regulatory management. Meanwhile, legislative delegation is widely delegated to the executive branch. Consequently, the role of the Singaporean administrative judiciary must align with national economic development goals.

The primary objective of regulation is to facilitate national objectives, and the role of the courts is limited to ensuring a conducive business environment. In the realm of regulation, courts rarely have the responsibility to monitor executive actions. Similarly, in the judicial field, the role of the courts is merely to ensure that the delegation of authority from parliament to the executive is in accordance with the law. The rule of law in commercial and other economic fields will always be upheld, even though the WTO has emphasized the importance of administrative processes in rules management. Historically, Singapore's separation from Malaysia in 1965 dealt a severe blow to the national economy, including imports in the industrial sector. The only remaining option was to initiate export-oriented industrialization to forestall widespread poverty. The United Nations recommended that Singapore industrialize, creating an indirect yet significant catalyst forpolitically active, disciplined workforce strategies, developing industries suited to geographical conditions, and foreign investment and international corporate opportunities. The first of these strategies was manifested primarily by recruiting civil servants in line with national development goals. Stringent selection processes and broad bureaucratic powers directly closed the gap for corrupt practices. Thus, ideal civil servants and an administrative system aligned with national politics helped to minimize legal challenges in administrative actions.[44]

Legal bodies serve as a preferred means of implementing economic development and socioeconomic programs. The executive branch holds broad authority in policy formulation, while legal bodies operate under this executive authority. All legal bodies cover various crucial socioeconomic domains.

42 CHNG Kenny, "Form and Substance in Singapore Constitutional and Administrative Law," *Asian Journal of Comparative Law* 15, no. 2 (2020): 363–84.

43 Jolene Lin, "The Judicialization of Governance: The Case of Singapore," in *Administrative Law and Governance in Asia*, edited by Yeo Tiong Min, Hans Tjio, Tang Hang Wu. (London: Routledge, 2008), 297–322.

44 Thio Li-ann, "The Theory and Practice of Judicial Review of Administrative Action in Singapore," edited by Yeo Tiong Min, Hans Tjio, Tang Hang Wu. (The Adelphi: Singapore Academic of Law, 2011), 2006–10.

Therefore, from an administrative law perspective, legal bodies actively participate in executing some executive functions in regulatory functions.

Singaporean law has a strong foundation in English law due to the history of British colonization. The legal system in Singapore, in general, differs significantly from the western legal model, which emphasizes rights and individualism. English administrative law, on the other hand, developed without a written constitution. In Singapore, the law tends to be duty and regulation-based and has a written constitution that clarifies the limits of legislative power. Because its role is to promote the creation of a pro-industryeconomic environment, the law is appreciated only for its utility and function in facilitating these goals. Similarly, regarding administrative law, the limited role of judicial bodies demonstrates the government's dominance in development strategies. Singaporean administrative law tends to be conservative, meaning in practice there is little elaboration on principles and issues in judicial review stemming from creative elaboration.

Unlike civil law systems, the Singaporean administrative justice system is not separate from public organizations. Mechanically, petitioners typically lodge their complaints through legal procedures first for administrative matters. This is stipulated in the Administrative Procedure Act. If this avenue is unavailable, petitioners may resort to judicial review at a higher level, namely the supreme court as the court of supervisory jurisdiction. This judicial process mandates obligations on the high court per the laws of the Supreme Court of Singapore.

Jolene Lin explains that certain provisions regarding judicial review aim to consider the content of provisions that are "possible" within primary legislation, which grants the government the authority to implement secondary regulations.[45] The analysis of secondary legislation opens the door for the application of *ultra vires* in judicial review. Pragmatically, the Singaporean parliament designs various supporting clauses to expand the role of administrative bodies in formulating regulations. This inevitably raises essential issues, as delegation through legislation is challenging to control. Administrative bodies might justify their extensive authority based on parliamentary directives.

The role of administrative courts in Singapore highlights their limitations in oversight functions and interpreting the rule of law.[46] Additionally, the court's role in legal interpretation is demarcated from decision-making. Decisions regarding the rights of disputing parties are delegated to administrative bodies. In short, the courts do not have the authority to go beyond interpreting the law.

45 Jolene Lin, "The Judicialization of Governance: The Case of Singapore," in *Administrative Law and Governance in Asia*, edited By Tom Ginsburg, Albert H.Y. Chen. (London: Routledge, 2008), 297–322.

46 R. Cotterell, "Judicial Review and Legal Theory," in *Administrative Law and Government Action*, ed. G. Richardson and H. Genn (Oxford: Clarendon Press, 1994).

Lin illustrates this through the case of *Galstaun*, in which private land acquired by the state under the Land Acquisition Act was challenged as illegal. Through their legal counsel, the owners contested the provisions of Section 5(1) of the Act, arguing that part of the land released was not for public use. However, the court dismissed the suit, stating that public interest was determined solely from within the government's purview. A similar case involved Teng Fuh Holdings Pte Ltd., which was challenged in 2005 for not using the acquired land for public purposes for over two decades. The court ruled that the significant delay from the time of the property's release led the appellate court to reject the petitioner's claim. Based on these case illustrations, the courts, which ideally should resolve such matters, did not implement ther role. Instead, from this perspective, the judiciary does not engage in policy-making actions.

Chee Siok Chin's case illustrates a similar situation to the two previously mentioned cases. Chin's lawsuit pertained to the rights of expression and freedom of assembly in public spaces stipulated in Article 14(1) of Singapore's constitution. The lawsuit was directed to the minister of home affairs and the police. The case originated from the dissolution and arrest of protesters in front of the Central Provident Fund (CPF) building, which is a case demanding financial accountability and transparency. However, the court dismissed the lawsuit, reasoning that the protest tarnished the public integrity of government institutions. This case demonstrates how Singapore's administrative courts often disregard the principle of proportionality, instead showing a tendency to uphold the decisions of authorities rather than reform them through the court's judgments.

This background can be traced to the patron-client relationship between the state and its citizens. Indeed, since its independence, the government of Singapore has legitimized its authority through a succession of well-performing political objectives ensuring housing, employment, and food security. The success in achieving these goals has implicitly and latently accumulated government power in the control of economic activities. This integration of government and the economy has impacted the entire development process.[47] The extensive power of the executive has led to several side effects, including the weak role of the administrative judiciary in monitoring administrative acts and the weak participation of the public due to numerous legal factors including, the long durations and high costs associated with legal efforts. Citizens, as clients, often only channel their aspirations through simple means via their local parliament. This inferiority in position is also evident in an environmental impact analysis. The lack of information disseminated among the public regarding policy-making in this area contributes to the public's reluctance to

47 S. Sudo, "Regional Governance and East and Southeast Asia: Towards the Regulatory State?," *Japanese Journal of Political Science* 4, no. 2 (2003).

question and complain about the effectiveness and oversight of government actions.

At this point, administrative law in Singapore is merely an instrument that paves the way for investment and maintains investor confidence for economic sustainability. Both administrative law and the law in general have limited roles in the Singaporean governance system, which is dominated by the executive and complemented by other legal bodies, leaving the executive virtually unchallenged at the parliamentary level.

Reflections on State Administrative Law in Southeast Asian Countries

The administrative legal frameworks of Southeast Asian nations exhibit significant commonalities, predominantly stemming from their shared colonial legacies. The administrative law systems in Malaysia and Singapore are derivatives of the common law tradition, whereas the systems in Vietnam, Thailand, the Philippines, and Indonesia reflect civil law influences.[48] While these jurisdictions generally adhere to the tripartite separation of powers doctrine, the relative authority of each branch may vary contextually.

This comparative analysis examines the administrative law systems of select Southeast Asian nations. Malaysia and Singapore, as exemplars of common law jurisdictions in the region, inherited their legal systems from British colonial rule.[49] Malaysia's federal structure delineates power between central and state governments. Notably, Malaysia lacks a specialized administrative court, with administrative disputes falling under the purview of the general courts.[50] Singapore, like Malaysia, adopted the common law system due to British colonial influence.[51] However, Singapore's governance structure is more centralized, befitting its city-state status. Singapore's administrative system is

48 Y. A. A. Tan Sri Dato'Abdul Hamid, "Administration of Justice in Malaysia," *The Denning Law Journal* 2, no. 1 (1987): 1–22; Kevin Tan, *The Singapore Legal System* (Singapore: NUS Press, 1999); James Chin, "History and Context of Public Administration in Malaysia," in *Public Administration in Southeast Asia* (London: Routledge, 2017), 141–54, https://doi.org/10.4324/9781315089287-7; Karin Buhmann, "Reforms of Administrative Law in the PRC and Vietnam: The Possible Role of the Legal Tradition," *Nordic Journal of International Law* 72, no. 2 (2003): 253–90; Peter Leyland, "Droit Administratif Thai Style: A Comparative Analysis of the Administrative Courts in Thailand," *Australian Journal of Asian Law* 8, no. 2 (2006): 121–54; Stewart Fenwick, "Administrative Law and Judicial Review in Indonesia: The Search for Accountability," in *Administrative Law and Governance in Asia*, edited By Tom Ginsburg, Albert H.Y. Chen. (London: Routledge, 2008), 339–68.

49 Andrew Harding, *Law, Government and the Constitution in Malaysia*, vol. 1 (Leiden: Brill, 2024).

50 Andrew Harding, *Law, Government and the Constitution in Malaysia*, vol. 1 (Leiden: Brill, 2024).

51 Kevin Y. L. Tan, *The Constitution of Singapore: A Contextual Analysis* (London: Bloomsbury Publishing, 2015).

renowned for its efficient and effective implementation of good governance principles, particularly in anti-corruption measures.

In contrast, Vietnam's legal system is rooted in the socialist tradition, influenced by the Soviet model.[52] The Vietnamese governance structure is characterized by a single-party system dominated by the Communist Party of Vietnam, which has resulted in a more centralized administrative framework compared to its regional counterparts. The Philippines presents a unique case because it employs a mixed legal system that incorporates elements of both civil and common law.[53] Its governmental structure closely resembles that of the United States by featuring a presidential system. Thailand, by contrast, adheres to a civil law system, influenced by continental European jurisprudence.[54] The Thai governance structure is predicated on a constitutional monarchy, with the monarch serving as head of state. It is worth noting that Thailand's administrative law development has been significantly shaped not only by its colonial history but also by the country's constitutional amendments and military interventions.

Indonesia, akin to Vietnam and Thailand, follows a civil law system, and has been primarily influenced by Dutch legal traditions.[55] The Indonesian governance model is characterized by extensive regional autonomy. Despite the existence of specialized state administrative courts for adjudicating administrative disputes, Indonesia's administrative justice system faces both internal challenges, such as evolving jurisdictional competencies, and external pressures, including the expansion of administrative discretion and its potential correlation with public sector corruption.

Conclusion

This chapter aims to describe the historical background and development of state administrative law in several Southeast Asian countries. The commonality of Southeast Asian countries as former colonies shapes the administrative law landscape in this region, with their similarities and differences. This chapter has been motivated by concerns regarding the study of state administrative law in these Southeast Asian countries.

Firstly, the focus on state administrative law has traditionally been limited to European and American countries.[56] Secondly, most studies of state admin-

52 Mark Sidel, *Law and Society in Vietnam: The Transition from Socialism in Comparative Perspective* (Cambridge: Cambridge University Press, 2008).

53 Raul C. Pangalangan, *Philippine Materials in International Law*, vol. 11 (Leiden: Brill, 2021).

54 Andrew Harding and Peter Leyland, *The Constitutional System of Thailand: A Contextual Analysis* (London: Bloomsbury Publishing, 2011).

55 Adriaan Bedner, *Administrative Courts in Indonesia: A Socio-Legal Study*, vol. 6 (Leiden: Martinus Nijhoff Publishers, 2001).

56 Alec Stone, *The Birth of Judicial Politics in France: The Constitutional Council in Comparative Perspective* (Seattle, WA: University of Washington, 1990).

istrative law in countries in the Southeast Asian region have focused more on constitutional law.[57] Recent literature studies indicate a lack of attention from state administrative law researchers in Southeast Asia due to limited collaboration among researchers focusing on this field.

However, there is a current urgency to draw attention to state administrative law studies, because citizens, in their routine affairs, have tended to encounter government actions directly related to state administrative law more often than in other legal disciplines.[58] Therefore, the main prospect in prioritizing state administrative law studies in Southeast Asian countries is to foster further discussions on state administrative law and its applications.

Quah, in his writings, explains that Asian countries combating corruption face challenges due to dependence on corrupt political leadership and officials, including the anti-corruption institutions themselves.[59] Based on his measurements, Quah demonstrates that the Philippines has only 31.3% control over corruption, followed by Vietnam at 34.1%, Indonesia at 38.0%, and Thailand at 39.4%. Meanwhile, Malaysia and Singapore demonstrate optimal control over corruption, with Malaysia achieving 62.5% control and Singapore reaching a significant 99.5% control. This indicates that Indonesia requires a more effective judicial system and control mechanisms to confront corruption.

Dressel and Bonoan posit that a weak judicial system is the outcome of interventions by elitist and populist groups.[60] As Dressel demonstrates, populism in the Philippines and Indonesia shows how executive elite legitimacy over judicial institutions leads to a more progressive power vacuum in various forms, such as in the amending of the laws, including anti-corruption laws in Indonesia, causing democratic values to be eroded or replaced during the struggles involving populist groups.[61]

Recent judicial decisions reflect a complex interplay between populist tendencies and the state administrative law of Indonesia, particularly evident in cases concerning national strategic projects. Decisions such as PTUN Semarang No. 68/G/PU/2021/PTUN.SMG and Supreme Court Decision No. 482 K/TUN/2021 rejected the lawsuit of Wadas residents seeking the annulment or invalidation of Governor's Decree No. 590/20 of 2021. Of particular note is

57 Wandi Ardiansyah et al., "Bibliometric Analysis and Visualization of State Administrative Law in Scopus Database from 2017–2021," *Cogent Social Sciences* 10, no. 1 (2024), https://doi.org/https://doi.org/10.1080/23311886.2024.2310935.

58 Ran Hirschl, *Towards Juristocracy: The Origins and Consequences of the New Constitutionalism* (Cambridge: Harvard University Press, 2009).

59 Jon S. T. Quah, "Breaking the Cycle of Failure in Combating Corruption in Asian Countries," *Public Administration and Policy* 24, no. 2 (2021): 125–38.

60 Björn Dressel and Cristina Regina Bonoan, "Courts and Authoritarian Populism in Asia: Reflections from Indonesia and the Philippines," *Law & Policy*, 2024.

61 Björn Dressel and Cristina Regina Bonoan, "Courts and Authoritarian Populism in Asia: Reflections from Indonesia and the Philippines," *Law & Policy* (2024), https://doi.org/10.1111/lapo.12240.

the legal reasoning in PTUN Semarang No. 68/G/PU/2021/PTUN.SMG, in which the judicial panel scrutinized Article 21 paragraph (6) of Presidential Regulation (Perpres) No. 58/2017 on Accelerating the Implementation of National Strategic Projects. This regulation served as the legal basis for the Governor of Central Java's issuance of Decree No. 50/20 of 2021. The court's analysis ultimately affirmed the legal validity of this regulatory framework.[62]

The supreme court's cassation panel, through Decision No. 482 K/TUN/2021, affirmed the lower court's ruling. In its *ratio decidendi*, the panel concluded that the *judex factie* decision did not contravene applicable laws or regulations. However, this decision raises significant concerns regarding the hierarchical integrity of Indonesia's legal system and the efficacy of administrative justice. In this case, the judges appear to have overlooked the fundamental principle that presidential regulations, as delegated legislation, are inherently subordinate to primary legislation. Additionally, by prioritizing parameters derived solely from executive or delegated regulations over those established in primary legislation, the court potentially undermined the essence of state administrative law. This decision potentially exposes a systemic weakness in Indonesia's administrative justice system, particularly in cases involving high-level executive actions.

References

Abott, Philip, Kathryn Boys, Finn Tarp, and Pham Lan Huong. "Trade and Development in Vietnam: Exploring Investment Linkages," 2008. https://mpra.ub.uni-muenchen.de/29382/2/MPRA_paper_29382.pdf

Aguilar, Filomeno V. "Church-State Relations in the 1899 Malolos Constitution: Filipinization and Visions of National Community." *Southeast Asian Studies* 4, no. 2 (2015): 279–311. https://archium.ateneo.edu/cgi/viewcontent.cgi?article=1003&context=history-faculty-pubs

Ardiansyah, Wandi, Suparto, M. Rafi, and Pahmi Amri. "Bibliometric Analysis and Visualization of State Administrative Law in Scopus Database from 2017–2021." *Cogent Social Sciences* 10, no. 1 (2024). https://doi.org/10.1080/23311886.2024.2310935.

Baviera, Araceli. "Politics and the Recent Constitutional Changes in the Philippines." *Philippine Law Journal* 57 (1982): 226.

Bedner, Adriaan. *Administrative Courts in Indonesia: A Socio-Legal Study*. Vol. 6. Leiden: Martinus Nijhoff Publishers, 2001. https://doi.org/10.1163/9789004481992

Buhmann, Karin. "Reforms of Administrative Law in the PRC and Vietnam: The Possible Role of the Legal Tradition." *Nordic Journal of International Law* 72, no. 2 (2003): 253–90. https://doi.org/10.1163/157181003322560574

62 Adam Wahyu Nugroho and Ika Agustin Kurniawati, "Penyelesaian Kasus Wadas Di Jawa Tengah Oleh Pemerintah Melalui Putusan MA No. 482 KTUN," *Jurnal Mediasi* 3, no. 1 (2024): 45–65.

Bui, Dat T. "Due-Process-Evading Justice: The Case of Vietnam." *International Journal of Law, Crime and Justice* 63 (2020): 100426. https://doi.org/10.1016/j.ijlcj.2020.100426

Burns, Adam. *The Foundations of the Modern Philippine State: Imperial Rule and the American Constitutional Tradition in the Philippine Islands, 1898–1935*. Oxford: Oxford University Press, 2019. https://doi.org/10.1093/jahist/jaz262

Chin, James. "History and Context of Public Administration in Malaysia." In *Public Administration in Southeast Asia*, 141–54. London: Routledge, 2017. https://doi.org/10.4324/9781315089287-7

Chopra, Surabhi. "The Constitution of the Philippines and Transformative Constitutionalism." *Global Constitutionalism* 10, no. 2 (2021): 307–30. https://doi.org/10.1017/S2045381721000174

Chuan, Gan Ching. "Administrative Law and Judicialized Governance in Malaysia: The Indian Connection." In *Administrative Law and Governance in Asia*, edited By Tom Ginsburg, Albert H.Y. Chen. 267–96. London: Routledge, 2008.

Cotterell, R. "Judicial Review and Legal Theory." In *Administrative Law and Government Action*, edited by G. Richardson and H. Genn. Oxford: Clarendon Press, 1994.

Deluna, Joseph G. *Analysis of The 5 Constitution of The Philippines and its Implication to the Economical, and Social Indicators of Development*. Manila: Technological University of the Philippines, 2021.

Dios, Emmanuel S. de. "(DP 2002-03) Welfare and Nationalism in the 1935 Philippine Constitution." *UPSE Discussion Papers*, 2010. https://econ.upd.edu.ph/dp/index.php/dp/article/view/35

Do, Truong Xuan, and Quang Truong. "The Changing Face of Public Sector Management in Vietnam." In *The Changing Face of Vietnamese Management*, 187–220. London: Routledge, 2009. https://doi.org/10.4324/9780203868409-7

Dressel, Björn, and Cristina Regina Bonoan. "Courts and Authoritarian Populism in Asia: Reflections from Indonesia and the Philippines." *Law & Policy* (2024). https://doi.org/10.1111/lapo.12240

Fenwick, Stewart. "Administrative Law and Judicial Review in Indonesia: The Search for Accountability." In *Administrative Law and Governance in Asia*, edited By Tom Ginsburg, Albert H.Y. Chen. 339–68. London: Routledge, 2008.

Gatmaytan, Dante B. "Constitutional Change as Suspect Projects: The Philippines." *Journal of Comparative Law* 14 (2019): 139. https://heinonline.org/HOL/LandingPage?handle=hein.journals/jrnatila14&div=11&id=&page=

Gatmaytan, Dante B. "Judicial Review and Emergencies in Post-Marcos Philippines." *Constitutionalism under Extreme Conditions: Law, Emergency, Exception* (2020): 41–62. https://doi.org/10.1007/978-3-030-49000-3_4

Gillespie, John. "The Juridification of Administrative Complaints and Review in Vietnam." In *Administrative Law and Governance in Asia*, edited By Tom Ginsburg, Albert H.Y. Chen. 215–39. London: Routledge, 2008.

Ginsburg, Tom. "The Judicialization of Administrative Governance: Causes, Consequences and Limits." In *Administrative Law and Governance in Asia*, 11–30. London: Routledge, 2008. https://doi.org/10.4324/9780203888681

Ginsburg, Tom, and Albert H. Y. Chen. "Administrative Law and Governance in Asia." In *Comparative Perspectives*, 2009. https://doi.org/10.4324/9780203888681

Ginsburg, Tom, Jiunn-Rong Yeh, Narufumi Kadomatsu, Hong Sik Cho, Tay-Sheng Wang, Jau-Yuan Hwang, Li-Ju Lee, and Wen-Chen Chang. "Judicial Review in

New Democracies: Constitutional Courts in Asian Cases." *NTU Law Review* 3 (2008): 143.

Grossholtz, Jean. "Philippines 1973: Whither Marcos?" *Asian Survey* 14, no. 1 (1974): 101–12. https://doi.org/10.2307/2642842

Hamid, Y A A Tan Sri Dato'Abdul. "Administration of Justice in Malaysia." *The Denning Law Journal* 2, no. 1 (1987): 1–22. https://doi.org/10.5750/dlj.v2i1.156

Harding, Andrew. *Law, Government and the Constitution in Malaysia*. Vol. 1. Leiden: Brill, 2024.

Harding, Andrew, and Peter Leyland. "The Constitutional Courts of Thailand and Indonesia: Two Case Studies from South East Asia." *Journal of Comparative Law* 3 (2008): 118. https://heinonline.org/HOL/LandingPage?handle=hein.journals/jrnatila3&div=29&id=&page=

Harding, Andrew, and Peter Leyland. *The Constitutional System of Thailand: A Contextual Analysis*. London: Bloomsbury Publishing, 2011.

Hirschl, Ran. *Towards Juristocracy: The Origins and Consequences of the New Constitutionalism*. Cambridge: Harvard University Press, 2009. https://doi.org/10.2307/j.ctv15d81nb

Hung, Tran Quoc, Huang Yong Peng, and Nguyen Thi Lien. "Significance of Judicial Independence in the Law Governed by the Rule of Law in Vietnam." *International Journal of Criminal Justice Sciences* 16, no. 2 (2021). https://ijcjs.com/menu-script/index.php/ijcjs/article/view/53

Hussin, Hasnah, and Mardiana Nordin. *Pengajian Malaysia*. Selangor: Oxford Fajar, 2007.

Kenny, CHNG. "Form and Substance in Singapore Constitutional and Administrative Law." *Asian Journal of Comparative Law* 15, no. 2 (2020): 363–84. https://doi.org/10.1017/asjcl.2021.1

Kikeri, Sunita, Thomas John Kenyon, and Vincent Palmade. *Reforming the Investment Climate: Lessons for Practitioners*. Vol. 3986. Washington, DC: World Bank Publications, 2006. https://doi.org/10.1596/978-0-8213-6837-4

Leyland, Peter. "Droit Administratif Thai Style: A Comparative Analysis of the Administrative Courts in Thailand." *Australian Journal of Asian Law* 8, no. 2 (2006): 121–54. https://doi.org/10.2139/ssrn.1698233

Leyland, Peter. "The Emergence of Administrative Justice in Thailand under the 1997 Constitution." In *Administrative Law and Governance in Asia*, edited by Tom Ginsburg, Albert H.Y. Chen. 240–66. London: Routledge, 2008.

Li-ann, Thio. "The Theory and Practice of Judicial Review of Administrative Action in Singapore.", edited by Yeo Tiong Min, Hans Tjio, Tang Hang Wu. (The Adelphi: Singapore Academy of Law) 2006–10, 2011.

Lim, Hong-Hai. "Improving Administrative Performance in Malaysia: The More Difficult next Steps in Reform." *Policy and Society* 26, no. 2 (2007): 33–59. https://doi.org/10.1016/S1449-4035(07)70107-8

Lin, Jolene. "The Judicialization of Governance: The Case of Singapore." In *Administrative Law and Governance in Asia*, edited by Tom Ginsburg, Albert H.Y. Chen. 297–322. London: Routledge, 2008.

Maisrikrod, Surin. "Changing Forms of Democracy in Asia? Some Observations on the Thai and Philippine Constitutions." *Asian Studies Review* 23, no. 3 (1999): 355–73. https://doi.org/10.1080/10357829908713243

Manullang, Sardjana Orba, Yessy Kusumadewi, Verawati Verawati, Henry Kristian Siburian, Hendro Siburian, and Baren Sipayung. "Problematika Hukum Atas Pembentukan Perubahan Kedua Atas UU KPK." *Journal on Education* 5, no. 2 (2023): 4885–97. https://jonedu.org/index.php/joe/article/view/1223

Nhung, Nguyen Thi Hong, Huynh Thi Nam Hai, and Luu Minh Sang. "E-Court in Resolving Civil Cases-Foreign Experiences and Recommendations for Vietnam." *Science & Technology Development Journal: Economics-Law & Management* 5, no. 3 (2021): 1733–40. https://doi.org/10.32508/stdjelm.v5i3.804

Nicholson, Penelope, and Nguyen Hung Quang. "The Vietnamese Judiciary: The Politics of Appointment and Promotion." *Pacific Rim Law & Policy Journal | Law Reviews and Journals* 14 (2005): 1. https://digitalcommons.law.uw.edu/wilj/vol14/iss1/2/

Nugroho, Adam Wahyu, and Ika Agustin Kurniawati. "Penyelesaian Kasus Wadas Di Jawa Tengah Oleh Pemerintah Melalui Putusan MA No. 482 KTUN." *Jurnal Mediasi* 3, no. 1 (2024): 45–65. https://jurnalilmiah.org/journal/index.php/mediasi/article/view/749

Painter, Martin. "Public Administration Reform in Vietnam: Problems and Prospects." *Public Administration and Development* 23, no. 3 (2003): 259–71. https://doi.org/10.1002/pad.249

Pangalangan, Raul C. "'Government by Judiciary' in the Philippines: Ideological and Doctrinal Framework." In *Administrative Law and Governance in Asia*, edited by Tom Ginsburg, Albert H.Y. Chen. 323–38. London: Routledge, 2008.

Pangalangan, Raul C. *Philippine Materials in International Law*. Vol. 11. Leiden: Brill, 2021.

Parker, Richard D. *Here, the People Rule: A Constitutional Populist Manifesto.* Cambridge: Harvard University Press, 1998.

Pham, Thanh Hung, Thi Thanh Hang Hoang, Eleftherios I Thalassinos, and Hoang Anh Le. "The Impact of Quality of Public Administration on Local Economic Growth in Vietnam." *Journal of Risk and Financial Management* 15, no. 4 (2022): 158. https://doi.org/10.3390/jrfm15040158

Quah, Jon S. T. "Breaking the Cycle of Failure in Combating Corruption in Asian Countries." *Public Administration and Policy* 24, no. 2 (2021): 125–38. https://doi.org/10.1108/PAP-05-2021-0034

Roshady, Mohammad Ezha Fachriza. "Gerakan Koalisi Masyarakat Sipil Antikorupsi Dalam Menolak Agenda Revisi Undang-Undang Nomor 30 Tahun 2002 Tentang Komisi Pemberantasan Tindak Pidana Korupsi Tahun 2019." *Jurnal Ilmu Sosial Indonesia (JISI)* 2, no. 1 (2021): 14–26. https://doi.org/10.15408/jisi.v2i1.22952

Sidel, Mark. *Law and Society in Vietnam: The Transition from Socialism in Comparative Perspective.* Cambridge: Cambridge University Press, 2008. https://doi.org/10.1017/CBO9780511495472

Sieder, Rachel, Line Schjolden, and Alan Angell. *The Judicialization of Politics in Latin America.* Berlin: Springer, 2005. https://doi.org/10.1007/978-1-137-10887-6

Stone, Alec. *The Birth of Judicial Politics in France: The Constitutional Council in Comparative Perspective.* Seattle, WA: University of Washington, 1990.

Sudo, S. "Regional Governance and East and Southeast Asia: Towards the Regulatory State?" *Japanese Journal of Political Science* 4, no. 2 (2003). https://doi.org/10.1017/S1468109903001142

Sweet, Alec Stone. *Governing with Judges: Constitutional Politics in Europe*. Oxford: Oxford University Press, 2000. https://doi.org/10.1093/0198297718.001.0001

Tan, Kevin Y. L. *The Constitution of Singapore: A Contextual Analysis*. London: Bloomsbury Publishing, 2015. https://doi.org/10.5040/9781782258100

Tan, Kevin Y. L. *The Singapore Legal System*. Singapore: NUS Press, 1999.

Thambapillay, Sridevi. "Recent Developments in Judicial Review of Administrative Action in Malaysia: A Shift from Grounds Based on Common Law Principles to the Federal Constitution," 2007. https://eprints.um.edu.my/13505/1/RECENT_DEVELOPMENTS_IN_JUDICIAL.pdf

Vallinder, Torbjörn, and C. Neal Tate. *Global Expansion of Judicial Power*. New York: New York University Press, 1997.

4 State Administrative Law in Indonesia

Introduction

As Sahya postulates, the evolution of state administrative law is inextricably linked to the national legal development system, which encapsulates the state's post-independence mission.[1] Furthermore, state administrative law is connected to the constitutional law system, which serves as the source of political legal values, including Pancasila, the 1945 Constitution, and Garis Besar Haluan Negara (GBHN), or the outline of state policy. Consequently, the investigation and implementation of state administrative law in the Indonesian context necessitates a systematic approach.

The comprehensive material encompassed by state administrative law comprises, firstly, the foundation of good state administration based on the principles of fairness, honesty, efficiency, and effectiveness. Secondly, the functional activities of state administration pertain to the procedures and actions of administrative decision-making, as well as to the methods of fulfilling duties and obligations. Thirdly, the organization, system, and methodology of state administration must be considered. Fourthly, the control, ownership, and utilization of state wealth and accountability procedures must be addressed. Lastly, one must examine the efforts and legal responsibilities of state-owned enterprises concerning personnel administration, including employment.

The scope of state administrative law includes state administrative justice. As the field of state administrative law continues to evolve, it is becoming increasingly evident that this field of law encompasses a multitude of technical areas. Thus, the establishment of the National Legal Development Agency to monitor and analyze state administrative law material on an annual basis is a necessity.

The substance of state administrative law material must reflect the state administrative law system for the law's intent to be realized in the practical life of society and the state. The state administrative law system comprises a complex network of hierarchical positions and organizational units that coordinate

1 Sahya Anggara, *Hukum Administrasi Negara* (Bandung: CV. Pustaka Setia, 2018).

DOI: 10.4324/9781003518563-4

systematically with other organizations. Moreover, this interrelated structure encompasses the functions of officials, including their duties, authorities, and legal responsibilities. In addition to the aforementioned structure, the state administrative law system is equipped with mechanisms that guide state administrative officials in the production of legal products, such as job standard plans and quasi-legislation, which are aligned with the demands of citizens as subjects of the public service.

The state administrative law system is understood to be a subsystem of state law, an aspect of the legal system, and the enforcer of the state administrative system. These interpretations can be understood as the state administrative law system according to the development paths and trends of the government, which in the context of Indonesia refer to the values of Pancasila and the 1945 Constitution. Additionally, the government system is influenced by several factors, including the archipelagic outlook, national legal resilience, economic development, sociocultural factors, and technology.

The primary challenge in state administrative law is the government's litigation strategy in court. The government's authority affords it the ability to act without undue constraints, placing it in a position of privilege relative to ordinary citizens. Therefore, lawsuits against the government must be approached differently than lawsuits against ordinary citizens. Nevertheless, there are circumstances under which lawsuits against the government in civil law may be pursued, including the following:[2]

1) The conceptualization of the state as an institution of power is intrinsically linked to the notion of law as a legitimizing force for authority. This authority manifests through the exercise of power, ostensibly absolving the state from accountability.
2) The concept inherent in the state distinguishes between the state as an authority and the state as a fiscal entity. In its capacity as a sovereign entity, the state is immune from legal action. Nevertheless, as a fiscal entity, citizens are permitted to sue the state.
3) The concept of litigation is based on the fundamental nature of rights. In this context, public law serves to protect a right. In this way, citizens are able to sue the government for the infringement of their rights.
4) The concept places emphasis on the criteria of violated legal interests.
5) The concept is predicated on the premise that the state can be sued for unlawful acts. This concept is not contingent on whether the violated rule pertains to public or civil law. In addition, the concept distinguishes

2 Muhammad Iqbal Ashari, "Theory and Practice of State Administrative Law," *Riwayat: Educational Journal of History and Humanities* 6, no. 3 (2023): 823–30, https://jurnal.usk.ac.id/riwayat/article/view/33562; Miftakhul Ihwan, "Jawade Hafidz Arsyad's Perspective on Corruption in the Perspective of State Administrative Law," *Law Research Review Quarterly* 5, no. 1 (2019): 91–106.

> between the function and the manner in which it is carried out. It is not the function itself that can be sued, but rather the implementation of that function which causes losses.

Furthermore, the fundamental premise that the state and its apparatus are duty-bound, irrespective of the domain (public or civil law), to take into account the norms of ordinary human conduct. Those seeking justice may demand that the state and its instruments act in a manner that is consistent with such behavioral norms. Any behavior that deviates from the norm and causes losses can be the subject of a legal action.

The aforementioned concepts facilitate a comprehensive and nuanced understanding of the state as a legal entity, in which the state has dual roles as a public entity and as a network of roles and enduring work environments. In this context, the government is both a legal entity and a collection of positions representing the legal acts of the state. As a representative of the public legal entity, the government is empowered to initiate civil legal proceedings that, in practice, may potentially conflict with the law. Civil judges may impose sanctions on government actions that contravene the law through mechanisms such as compensation payments and other sanctions in accordance with their judgments. Furthermore, civil judges may issue prohibitions against orders for the government to perform specific actions.

In the Indonesian Civil Code (KUH Perdata), Article 1365 states, "Every unlawful act causing harm to another obliges the person whose fault caused it to make good the harm." However, the interpretation of this provision has evolved in various legal opinions over time, both before and after 1919. Prior to 1919, this provision was narrowly interpreted to include elements such as unlawful acts, the existence of harm, the causal relationship between the unlawful act and the harm, and the perpetrator's fault. After 1919, the criteria for unlawful acts were expanded to include: (1) Interference with the rights of others; (2) Contravention of the legal obligations of the perpetrator; (3) Contravention of morality; (4) Contravention of decency; and (5) The caution that a person should exercise in social interactions with fellow citizens or toward the property of others. This broadened interpretation also impacts the expansion of legal protection for citizens.

The implementation of government legal actions is carried out through unilateral decisions and rulings in the public sphere. This understanding posits that in the implementation of rulings, the government does not rely on external parties. Nevertheless, the government's broad authority to act unilaterally opens the door to potential legal violations against citizens. Therefore, legal protection instruments for citizens to protect against government actions are absolutely necessary. Sjachran Basah identifies the primary focus of legal protection for citizens as the redress of losses resulting from state administrative actions.[3]

The form of legal protection for citizens comprises preventive and punitive protection.[4] Preventive legal protection includes providing opportunities for citizens to raise objections or express specific opinions before the government makes definitive decisions.[5] By its nature, preventive legal protection thus aims to prevent disputes. Preventive legal protection also holds significant meaning for the government's ability to act with discretion. Conversely, punitive protection's mission is resolving disputes through sanctions or penalties.

In Indonesia, legal protection for citizens in response to government legal actions has several possibilities, depending on the legal instruments used by the government. The common legal instruments employed by the government are implemented through legislation and decisions. Legal protection due to the issuance of legislation is pursued through the supreme court via the mechanism of substantive judicial review.

As stipulated in Article 26 of Law No. 14/1970, as revised by Law No. 35/1999 Concerning the Basic Provisions of the Judiciary, Article 31 paragraph (1) of Law No. 14/1985 Concerning the Supreme Court, and Article 5 (2) of MPR Decree No. III/MPR/2000 Concerning Legal Sources and the Sequence of Legislation, the supreme court has the authority to conduct substantive judicial review only over regulations below the level of statutory law.[6] In theory, this role marks one of the rule of law principles regarding the separation of powers. In the context of legal protection, there are criteria for substantively reviewing a regulation, comprising namely whether it contradicts higher regulations and whether it contravenes the public interest.

According to Ridwan H.R., the law is a medium within which values or concepts of justice, truth, and social usefulness are contained. The content of

3 Sjachran Basah, *Eksistensi Dan Tolak Ukur Badan Peradilan Administrasi Di Indonesia* (Bandung: Alumni, 1989).

4 Muhamad Rakhmat, *Hukum Administrasi Negara Indonesia* (Majalengka: Universitas Majalengka, 2014).

5 Patrick Vallerio, "Executive Preview Dalam Sistem Pengawasan Preventif Terhadap Peraturan Daerah," *Jurnal Kewarganegaraan* 7, no. 2 (2023): 2389–95; Syahrul Machmud, "Tindakan Preventif Dan Represif Non-Yustisial Penegakan Hukum Administrasi Oleh Eksekutif," *Jurnal Hukum Media Justitia Nusantara (MJN)* 7, no. 2 (2017): 62–77.

6 Sofyan Jailani, "Independensi Kekuasaan Kehakiman Berdasar Undang-Undang Dasar 1945," *Fiat Justisia: Jurnal Ilmu Hukum* 6, no. 3 (2012), https://doi.org/10.25041/fiatjustisia.v6no3.360; Faridy Faridy, "Menuju Kekuasaan Kehakiman Yang Bebas Dan Mandiri," *HAKAM: Jurnal Kajian Hukum Islam Dan Hukum Ekonomi Islam* 2, no. 2 (2018), https://ejournal.unuja.ac.id/index.php/hakam/article/view/452; H. M. Hambali, "Politik Hukum Undang-Undang Kekuasaan Kehakiman," *Supremasi Hukum: Jurnal Kajian Ilmu Hukum* 1, no. 2 (2012), https://doi.org/10.14421/sh.v1i2.1908; Kevin Angkouw, "Fungsi Mahkamah Agung Sebagai Pengawas Internal Tugas Hakim Dalam Proses Peradilan," *Lex Administratum* 2, no. 2 (2014), https://ejournal.unsrat.ac.id/v3/index.php/administratum/article/view/4746.

the law is abstract.[7] Satjipto Rahardjo posits that law enforcement essentially involves enforcing abstract ideas or concepts. Law enforcement is an effort to transform these ideas into reality.[8] Soerjono Soekanto states that law enforcement is the harmonization of the relationship between values outlined in ordinary norms or value perspectives and actions in a series of value elaborations leading to the final stage of social engineering and control.[9] In this context, law enforcement aims to create, maintain, and preserve the peace of social life.

Concrete law enforcement applies positive law in practice, as the laws should be obeyed. If the essence of law enforcement embodies values or norms containing justice and truth, law enforcement becomes not only the duty of conventional law enforcers but also the duty of every individual. Law enforcement is a process that involves multiple factors. Therefore, the success of law enforcement will be influenced by these factors. Generally, as stated by Soerjono Soekanto, the factors influencing law enforcement include:[10]

1. The law itself
2. Law enforcers (those who form or apply the law)
3. The facilities or resources supporting law enforcement
4. Society (the environment where the law is applied)
5. Culture, which is the result of human creation, intellect, and feelings based on human interactions in social life

These five factors are interconnected in the way they constitute the essence of law enforcement and serve as benchmarks for its effectiveness. Satjipto Rahardjo suggests that for the law to function or play a beneficial role in society, attention must be given to the problems faced, including a careful understanding of the communities targeted for intervention.[11] Further attention is directed toward the values existing within society as a form of social engineering across various sectors of life. At this stage, the values of the selected sectors are determined. Another focus is on hypotheses and selecting the most suitable ones for implementation. Attention is also given to law enforcement mechanisms and measuring their effects. Ten Berge and Spelt mention several aspects that law enforcement needs to consider, including:[12]

1. Regulations should leave no room for differing interpretations.
2. Exceptions should be kept to a minimum.

7 HR Ridwan, *Hukum Administrasi Negara* (Jakarta: Rajawali Press, 2018).
8 Satjipto Rahardjo, *Ilmu Hukum [Legal Studies]* (Bandung: Citra Aditya Bakti, 2014).
9 Soerjono Soekanto, *An Introduction to Sociology* (Jakarta: RajawaliPress, 2012).
10 Soerjono Soekanto, *An Introduction to Sociology* (Jakarta:RajawaliPress, 2012).
11 Satjipto Rahardjo, *Ilmu Hukum [Legal Studies]* (Bandung: Citra Aditya Bakti, 2014).
12 J. B. J. M. ten Berge, N. M. Spelt, and Philipus M. Hadjon, *Pengantar Hukum Perizinan* (Surabaya: Yuridika, 1993).

3. Regulations should be directed toward objectively determinable realities.
4. Regulations should be implementable by those affected by them and by those burdened with enforcement duties.

The administrative law enforcement instruments primarily comprise supervision and sanctions enforcement.[13] Supervision serves as a preventive measure to enforce compliance, while the application of sanctions acts as a punitive measure. In a rule-of-law state, the supervision of government actions is intended to ensure that the government operates in accordance with legal norms and acts as a preventive measure aiming to restore the situation to an original state prior to the violation of legal norms. Legal and policy supervision of government actions in administrative law is designed to provide protection for the populace.

In addition to supervision, sanctions serve as another means of law enforcement. Sanctions are an essential component of every legal regulation. Ten Berge posits that sanctions are at the core of administrative law enforcement.[14] Typically, sanctions are placed at the conclusion of each regulation. In administrative law, the use of administrative sanctions constitutes the exercise of governmental authority, derived from both written and unwritten administrative legal rules. Generally, empowering the government to establish certain administrative legal norms is accompanied by granting the authority to enforce these norms through the application of sanctions against violators. There are at least four elements of sanctions in administrative law which include the following:

1. Sanctions are instruments of power.
2. Sanctions are of a public law nature.
3. Sanctions are used by the government.
4. Sanctions serve as a reaction to non-compliance.

In terms of their targets, two types of sanctions are recognized in administrative law:

1. Reparative sanctions: These are applied in response to norm violations, aimed at restoring the situation to its original state or bringing it into compliance with the law. In other words, they aim to return to the original conditions prior to the violation. Examples include government coercion and imposition of forced fines.
2. Punitive sanctions: These are solely aimed at punishing an offender. An example is the imposition of administrative fines.

13 J. B. J. M. ten Berge, N. M. Spelt, and Philipus M. Hadjon, *Pengantar Hukum Perizinan* (Surabaya: Yuridika, 1993).
14 J. B. J. M. ten Berge, N. M. Spelt, and Philipus M. Hadjon, *Pengantar Hukum Perizinan* (Surabaya: Yuridika, 1993).

Besides these two types, Ten Berge also identifies regressive sanctions, which are applied in response to non-compliance with the provisions contained in issued determinations.[15] These sanctions aim to restore the original legal situation before the determination was issued. Examples of regressive sanctions include withdrawal, modification, and postponement of a determination. Regarding the purpose of applying sanctions, regressive sanctions do not differ significantly from reparative ones. Reparative sanctions are imposed for general violations of administrative legal norms, while regressive sanctions are only imposed for violations of the provisions contained in specific determinations.

Historical Development of Administrative Law in Indonesia

Administrative Law during the Dutch Colonial Period

During Indonesia's Dutch East Indies period, while no specific judiciary existed to adjudicate state administrative disputes, two key pieces of legislation alluded to this issue: the *Indische Staatsregeling* (IS) and the *Reglement op de rechterlijke Organisatie en het beleid der justitie* (RO). Article 134 paragraph (1) of the IS and Article 2 of the RO stipulated that civil disputes fell under the purview of ordinary judges, while the examination and resolution of administrative cases were the prerogative of the administrative institution itself.[16]

Administrative dispute resolution during this period primarily utilized the *administratief beroep* institution, which facilitated internal adjudication within the state administration apparatus. This system mandated that conflicts arising within the administrative sphere be adjudicated by a superior hierarchical body or an independent entity distinct from the original decision-making authority. Article 134, paragraph (2) of the *Indische Staatsregeling* (IS) addressed jurisdictional conflicts between judicial courts and administrative bodies, stipulating that such disputes were to be resolved by the governor-general, with the concurrence of the *Raad van Nederlands-Indie* (Council of the Netherlands Indies), pursuant to procedures established by ordinance. However, it is noteworthy that no such ordinance was ever promulgated during the Dutch colonial period in Indonesia, leaving a regulatory gap in this area.

A fundamental distinction exists between the *administratief Beroep* system and the ordinary administrative judiciary systems.[17] In the *administratief Beroep*, the relevant institution examines both the *doelmatigheid* (expediency)

15 J. B. J. M. ten Berge, N. M. Spelt, and Philipus M. Hadjon, *Pengantar Hukum Perizinan* (Surabaya: Yuridika, 1993).

16 Enrico Simanjuntak, *Hukum Acara Peradilan Tata Usaha Negara: Transformasi & Refleksi* (Jakarta: Sinar Grafika, 2021).

17 Firzhal Arzhi Jiwantara, "Upaya Administratif Dan Penerapannya Dalam Penyelesaian Sengketa Administrasi," *Jatiswara* 34, no. 2 (2019): 131–42, https://doi.org/10.29303/jtsw.v34i2.203; H. M. Laica Marzuki, "Penggunaan Upaya Administratif Dalam Sengketa Tata Usaha Negara," *Jurnal Hukum Dan Pembangunan* 22, no. 2 (1992), https://doi.org/10.21143/jhp.vol22.no2.373.

and *rechtmatigheid* (legality) of a decision, empowering it to replace or amend disputed decisions. Furthermore, in the ordinary administrative judiciary, judges are limited to examining *rechtmatigheid*. While they can annul administrative decisions and impose penalties if the plaintiff prevails, they lack the authority to substitute decisions with new ones. A significant development occurred on January 1, 1916, with the establishment of a special administrative court or *Raad van beroep voor belastingzaken* in Jakarta, based on Ordinance Staatsblad 1915 No. 707. This court held jurisdiction over specific tax-related disputes, with its composition regulated by the regulation on tax cases published in *Staatsblad* 1927 No. 29.

Post-Independence Developments in Administrative Law

Following Indonesia's independence in 1945, the concept of an administrative court continued to evolve, despite the absence of explicit mention in the 1945 Constitution. An initial legislative attempt to address administrative disputes in post-independence Indonesia was embodied in Law No. 9/1948. Article 66 of this statute provisionally vested jurisdiction over administrative matters in the existing judicial hierarchy, stipulating that in the absence of specialized administrative tribunals, the high court and supreme court would adjudicate these cases at the first and second instances, respectively. However, this legislation never entered into force. Concurrently, in 1948, Professor Mr. Wirjono Prodjodikoro, who subsequently served as the chief justice of the supreme court from 1952 to 1966, drafted a comprehensive bill for the establishment of administrative courts. Despite the legal expertise underpinning this initiative and Prodjodikoro's subsequent influential position in the judiciary, the draft legislation failed to secure enactment.[18]

The Provisional Constitution of 1950, which came into effect on August 17th, marked a significant development in Indonesia's approach to administrative dispute resolution. Articles 108 and 142 of this constitution provided a framework for addressing administrative law conflicts.[19] Article 108 stipulated that the resolution of administrative law disputes should be assigned to specialized courts or other competent bodies, with the proviso that such entities maintain guarantees similar to those of justice and truth. Complementing this, Article 142 ensured the continuity of existing regulations, laws, and provisions, unless explicitly revoked or amended under the new constitutional authority. These constitutional provisions presented three potential avenues for the juridical resolution of administrative disputes:

18 Muhamad Rakhmat, *Hukum Administrasi Negara Indonesia* (Majalengka: Universitas Majalengka, 2014).

19 Wirjono Prodjodikoro, *Asas-Asas Ilmu Negara Dan Politik* (Bandung: PT. Eresco, 1971).

1. Resolution of all administrative disputes by civil courts.
2. Establishment of specialized adjudicating bodies for all administrative disputes.
3. A hybrid approach, allocating specific types of administrative disputes to either civil courts or newly established adjudicating bodies.

The trajectory of administrative law development continued with the 1960 Decree No. II/MPRS/1960 issued by the General Assembly of the Provisional People's Consultative Assembly (MPRS), which mandated the establishment of an administrative court. In response, the National Law Development Institute (LPHN) drafted a law on administrative courts in the same year. A significant legislative milestone was reached in 1964 with the enactment of Law No. 19/1964. This law explicitly recognized the administrative court as one of the judicial branches in Indonesia (Article 7, paragraph 1). Building on this foundation, the minister of justice issued Decree No. J.S.8/12/17 in 1965, establishing a working committee tasked with drafting the administrative court law.

The journey toward establishing administrative courts in Indonesia was marked by a series of legislative attempts and political transitions. In 1966, the LPHN approved a draft bill on administrative courts. However, political instability during the transition from the Old Order to the New Order prevented its presentation to the Provisional People's Representative Council (DPR-GR).

The New Order era saw renewed efforts to establish administrative courts. A significant milestone was the enactment of Law No. 14/1970 on the Basic Provisions of Judicial Power, which explicitly recognized administrative courts as part of the judicial system. This was further reinforced by MPR Decrees No. IV/MPR/1978 and No. 11/1983 on the General Guidelines of State Policy (GBHN), which emphasized the urgency of establishing administrative courts. In 1982, the minister of justice submitted a draft law on administrative courts to the DPR. However, time constraints due to the impending end of government and parliamentary terms prevented its completion. An agreement was reached on September 4, 1982, to postpone the discussion, acknowledging the complexity of the draft and its novel status in the Indonesian legal system.

The process was further delayed following the 1982 elections and the formation of the Fourth Development Cabinet. The government revised its initial draft, and on April 16, 1986, resubmitted a new version through Presidential Letter No. R. 04/PU/IV/1986. This revised draft underwent extensive discussion in the DPR, incorporating public input over approximately eight months. The culmination of these efforts came on December 29, 1986, with the enactment of Law No. 5 of 1986 on Administrative Courts. This law, along with its explanatory notes, was published in the *State Gazette of the Republic of Indonesia* of 1986, Number 77, and the supplement to the *State Gazette of the Republic of Indonesia*, Number 3344.

Reformation Era and Contemporary Juridical Advancements

After the New Order era, significant changes occurred in Indonesia's state administrative law. The 1998 Reformation led toward democratization, transparency, and governmental accountability, demanding substantial changes in the structure and practice of state administrative law. One of the critical milestones in improving governance was the implementation of Law No. 28/1999 on State Administration, stipulating a state administrative law system that is clean and free from corruption, collusion, and nepotism. Structural changes were represented through Law No. 22/1999 on Regional Governance, marking a shift toward a decentralized government system and expanded regional autonomy. This regional governance law was subsequently updated through Law No. 32/2004, and finally, Law No. 23/2014. Decentralization and regional autonomy granted greater authority to local governments to manage their affairs independently. This expanded authority influenced the development of administration at the local level. In practice, the central government played a key role in monitoring this local implementation. However, the approach used by the central government in decentralization emphasized collaborative use. The foundation for formulating regulations and public policies was based on the principles of transparency, participation, and accountability, which are essential to good governance.

These structural and practical changes in state administration also changed the rules governing administrative courts. Generally, there were three shifts in the authority of administrative courts. Firstly, there was a change in the meaning of administrative decrees (KTUN) related to the expansion of government actions that could be sued or requested for determination, increasing the number of objects under administrative courts. Secondly, the scope of objects under administrative courts for government actions that could be sued was narrowed by removing certain government action objects, meaning that the original concept of KTUN no longer applied. Thirdly, restrictions were imposed on the examination and adjudication of state administrative disputes, which were limited to certain levels and did not extend to the cassation level of the supreme court.

The amendments to the 1945 Constitution were a key factor in adjusting the content of the law on administrative courts. The amendments to Law No. 5/1986 on the Administrative Courts established the policy that all technical judicial and nonjudicial matters of the administrative courts fall under the jurisdiction of the supreme court. In addition, the jurisdiction and function of administrative courts in Indonesia are further delineated and affected by several subsequent legislative enactments. These include Law No. 31/1997 on Military Courts, Law No. 14/2002 on Tax Courts, and Law No. 30/2014 on Government Administration. Notably, Consideration Letter (e) of Law No. 31/1997 stipulates that, pursuant to Law No. 2/1988 on Armed Forces Personnel, military courts are vested with the authority to examine, adjudicate, and resolve administrative disputes pertaining to members of the armed forces.

Thus, this law interprets the provisions of the law on administrative courts and Law No. 2/1988. In addition, Law No. 14/2002 serves as the basis for the establishment of tax courts under the supreme court of justice to ensure justice and legal certainty in tax disputes. Finally, Law No. 30/2014 on Government Administration explains in one of its considerations (Letter (b) of Law No. 30/2014) that the resolution of issues related to the management and regulation of government administration is expected to provide legal protection for both the public and government officials. As a result, the legal implications of the changes in the competence of administrative courts have led to the synchronization and harmonization of the provisions governing administrative courts.

Structural Analysis of the Administrative Court System

Dispute Resolution Mechanisms: Administrative Courts and Legal Remedies

Based on Law No. 5/1986 on Administrative Courts, legal protection resulting from administrative decisions is pursued through two avenues: administrative courts and administrative remedies. There is a distinction between administrative courts and administrative remedies. The term, "administrative court," denotes a judicial process within the government conducted through independent institutions. This independence is manifested in the professionalism of administrative judges and their legal status; they are appointed for life, provisions regarding their review are stipulated by law, and dismissal (in cases of misconduct) can only be effected through a court decision. This institution only assesses governmental actions based on the law. Administrative remedies are concerned with the judicial process within the administrative environment. The administrative remedies institution is a government organ equipped with governmental accountability. In this context, governmental actions are assessed based on both the law and certain policy aspects.

Administrative remedies comprise two categories:

1. Administrative appeals: The resolution of administrative disputes conducted by a superior authority or an alternative institution to the one that issued the contested decision.
2. Objection procedures: The resolution of administrative disputes conducted by the same institution that issued the disputed decision.

The enactment of Law No. 30/2014 on Government Administration precipitated a significant procedural shift, leading to the supreme court's implementation of Supreme Court Regulation No. 6/2018, which delineates procedures for addressing government administrative disputes.[20] This regulation intro-

20 Riawan Tjandra, *Hukum Acara Peradilan Tata Usaha Negara: Filosofi, Teori, Dan Praktik* (Yogkakarta: Kanisius, 2023).

duces a crucial prerequisite: individuals seeking justice must now exhaust administrative remedies before filing a lawsuit in the state administrative court.

Specifically, Article 3 of Supreme Court Regulation No. 6/2018 stipulates that the court is empowered to accept, investigate, adjudicate, and resolve government administrative disputes only after administrative remedies have been pursued. Furthermore, the court processes claims related to government administration disputes in accordance with the established procedural law, except where specific provisions in applicable laws and regulations dictate otherwise.

Jurisdictional Competence of the State Administrative Court

The jurisdiction of the administrative court in Indonesia is bifurcated into relative and absolute competence. Relative competence pertains to the court's territorial jurisdiction, while absolute competence relates to its subject matter jurisdiction.

1. Relative Competence

The relative competence of administrative courts is delineated in Article 6 of Law No. 5/1986:

- Administrative courts are established in municipalities or district capitals, with jurisdiction over the respective municipal or district areas.
- High administrative courts are situated in provincial capitals, exercising jurisdiction over the entire province.

The apex of the administrative court system, as stipulated in Article 5(2) of Law No. 5/1986, is the supreme court, mirroring other judicial systems in Indonesia, including the general courts, the religious courts, and the military courts.

Article 54(1-6) further elucidates the relative competence concerning disputing parties, prescribing the appropriate court for filing disputes based on the domicile of defendants and plaintiffs. This includes provisions for cases involving multiple defendants or international parties. Article 55 imposes a 90-day limitation period for filing lawsuits from the date of receipt or announcement of the administrative body's or official's decision.

2. Absolute Competence

The absolute competence of the State Administrative Court (PTUN) is delineated in Article 1(3) of Law No. 5/1986, characterized by:

- Disputes between individuals or legal entities and administrative bodies or officials

- Contestation of administrative decisions issued by administrative bodies or officials
- Decisions containing administrative legal actions
- Decisions that are concrete, pertaining to either individuals or legal entities

Evolutionary Trajectory of State Administrative Court Competence

The law on administrative courts has undergone two amendments in the past three decades:

1. Law No. 9/2004
2. Law No. 51/2009

However, the most significant change in the competence of the administrative courts occurred with the enactment of Law No. 30/2014 on Government Administration. This legislation substantially expanded the courts' jurisdiction in several key areas:

1. Expanded Jurisdiction over KTUN:
   - Article 87 extends the courts' jurisdiction to include challenges against Keputusan Tata Usaha Negara or State Administrative Decisions (KTUN) that have general applicability to citizens.
   - This removes the requirement for individual specificity in the elements of KTUN, empowering the administrative courts to examine and adjudicate on KTUNs of a general nature.
2. Broadened Objects of Administrative Disputes:
   - The scope now includes factual actions by the government.
   - Examination and adjudication of unlawful actions by state administrative bodies or officials are further regulated in Supreme Court Regulation No. 2/2019.
3. Inclusion of General Principles of Good Governance (AUPB):
   - AUPB are now considered objects of administrative disputes.
4. Expanded Authority:
   - The courts can now examine and decide on applications regarding alleged abuse of power by applicants.
   - This changes the nature of disputes from unidirectional (citizens as plaintiffs and state administrative officials as defendants) to bidirectional (state administrative officials can also be applicants).
5. Restoration of Competence in Tax Disputes:
   - The administrative court has regained competence in tax disputes as a specialized court.

A Case Study: Juridical Analysis of the Tamansari Land Dispute

A land conflict in Tamansari, Bandung, exemplifies a case in which the state administrative court played a pivotal and determinative role in dispute resolution.[21] This case illustrates the function of administrative courts as the primary forum for adjudicating complex land-use conflicts between citizens and government entities. As part of its urban renewal initiative aimed at eradicating slums, the Bandung City Government designated RW 11 Tamansari for redevelopment. Resident opposition emerged following the issuance of Decision Letter DPKP3 No. 538.2/1325A/DPKP3/2017, which delineated building compensation, relocation procedures, and plans for the construction of row houses.

In 2019, affected residents initiated legal proceedings in the administrative court. Subsequently, on December 12th of that year, an eviction operation involving police, military, and city law enforcement personnel was met with resistance from the residents, who perceived the eviction as unilateral and lacking proper communication. This contentious action precipitated another lawsuit in the Bandung City Administrative Court. During the judicial proceedings, neither party presented conclusive land ownership documentation. The residents submitted evidence of long-term tax payments, while the city government relied on a 1930 land purchase agreement and asserted a pending land certificate from the National Land Agency.

The court's final ruling on Case Number 0001/Ling.Pem/VII/2018/DPMPTSP, Pertaining to the Tamansari Row Houses Environmental Permit, dismissed all claims brought by the residents[3]. The judicial panel determined that no regulatory violations were present in the city's construction plans, thereby rendering the decision legally binding. Notwithstanding the court's decision, the eviction process was deemed to contravene the transparency principle of AUPB and was found to be in conflict with various human rights laws and constitutional provisions. Despite these findings, the residents were ordered to bear the court fees, and the eviction was classified as an administrative sanction of governmental coercion.

Conclusion

In carrying out administrative tasks in Indonesia, there is a possibility for the government to take actions perceived as detrimental or violating the rights of citizens, leading to conflicts of interest, disputes, or disagreements between government agencies or officials and the public that may harm or hinder the national development process. To anticipate the emergence of such disputes, it is necessary to have a judicial body with special absolute competence, namely a state administrative court or an administrative judiciary, which is capable of upholding justice, truth, order, and legal certainty, and thereby protecting the public, especially in the relationship between government agencies or officials and the public.

21 Shanisa Berliana Indah Sari, "Sengketa Wilayah Tamansari, Bandung dalam Perspektif Asas Umum Pemerintahan Yang Baik," *Lontar Merah* 5, no. 1 (2022): 432–41.

Theoretically, the existence of the administrative judiciary is recognized as one of the requirements of a dynamic rule of law (welfare state). Thus, there is an urgent need for the administrative judiciary or administrative courts to anticipate the possibility of disputes between the government and its citizens or with private legal entities arising from government activities. In other words, it can also be argued that there is an urgent need for the administrative court (the Pengadilan Tata Usaha Negara or PTUN) to implement constitutional provisions that guarantee the equality of citizens, both in their relations with each other and with their government.

References

Anggara, Sahya. *Hukum Administrasi Negara*. Bandung: CV. Pustaka Setia, 2018.

Angkouw, Kevin. "Fungsi Mahkamah Agung Sebagai Pengawas Internal Tugas Hakim Dalam Proses Peradilan." *Lex Administratum* 2, no. 2 (2014). https://ejournal.unsrat.ac.id/v3/index.php/administratum/article/view/4746

Ashari, Muhammad Iqbal. "Theory and Practice of State Administrative Law." *Riwayat: Educational Journal of History and Humanities* 6, no. 3 (2023): 823–30. https://jurnal.usk.ac.id/riwayat/article/view/33562

Basah, Sjachran. *Eksistensi Dan Tolak Ukur Badan Peradilan Administrasi Di Indonesia*. Bandung: Alumni, 1989.

Berge, J. B. J. M. ten, N. M. Spelt, and Philipus M. Hadjon. *Pengantar Hukum Perizinan*. Surabaya: Yuridika, 1993.

Faridy, Faridy. "Menuju Kekuasaan Kehakiman Yang Bebas Dan Mandiri." *HAKAM: Jurnal Kajian Hukum Islam Dan Hukum Ekonomi Islam* 2, no. 2 (2018). https://ejournal.unuja.ac.id/index.php/hakam/article/view/452

Hambali, H M. "Politik Hukum Undang-Undang Kekuasaan Kehakiman." *Supremasi Hukum: Jurnal Kajian Ilmu Hukum* 1, no. 2 (2012). https://doi.org/10.14421/sh.v1i2.1908

Ihwan, Miftakhul. "Jawade Hafidz Arsyad's Perspective on Corruption in the Perspective of State Administrative Law." *Law Research Review Quarterly* 5, no. 1 (2019): 91–106. https://doi.org/10.15294/snh.v5i01.29708

Jailani, Sofyan. "Independensi Kekuasaan Kehakiman Berdasar Undang-Undang Dasar 1945." *Fiat Justisia: Jurnal Ilmu Hukum* 6, no. 3 (2012). https://doi.org/10.25041/fiatjustisia.v6no3.360

Jiwantara, Firzhal Arzhi. "Upaya Administratif Dan Penerapannya Dalam Penyelesaian Sengketa Administrasi." *Jatiswara* 34, no. 2 (2019): 131–42. https://doi.org/10.29303/jtsw.v34i2.203

Machmud, Syahrul. "Tindakan Preventif Dan Represif Non-Yustisial Penegakan Hukum Administrasi Oleh Eksekutif." *Jurnal Hukum Media Justitia Nusantara (MJN)* 7, no. 2 (2017): 62–77. https://ojs.uninus.ac.id/index.php/MJN/article/view/660

Marzuki, H. M. Laica. "Penggunaan Upaya Administratif Dalam Sengketa Tata Usaha Negara." *Jurnal Hukum Dan Pembangunan* 22, no. 2 (1992). https://doi.org/10.21143/jhp.vol22.no2.373

Prodjodikoro, Wirjono. *Asas-Asas Ilmu Negara Dan Politik*. Bandung: PT. Eresco, 1971.

Rahardjo, Satjipto. *Ilmu Hukum [Legal Studies]*. Bandung: Citra Aditya Bakti, 2014.

Rakhmat, Muhamad. *Hukum Administrasi Negara Indonesia*. Majalengka: Universitas Majalengka, 2014.

Ridwan, H. R. *Hukum Administrasi Negara*. Jakarta: Rajawali Press, 2018.

Sari, Shanisa Berliana Indah. “Sengketa Wilayah Tamansari, Bandung dalam Perspektif Asas Umum Pemerintahan yang Baik.” *Lontar Merah* 5, no. 1 (2022): 432–41. https://jom.untidar.ac.id/index.php/lontarmerah/article/view/2571

Simanjuntak, Enrico. *Hukum Acara Peradilan Tata Usaha Negara: Transformasi & Refleksi*. Jakarta: Sinar Grafika, 2021.

Soekanto, Soerjono. *An Introduction to Sociology*. Jakarta: Rajawali Press, 2012.

Tjandra, Riawan. *Hukum Acara Peradilan Tata Usaha Negara: Filosofi, Teori, Dan Praktik*. Yogkakarta: Kanisius, 2023.

Vallerio, Patrick. “Executive Preview Dalam Sistem Pengawasan Preventif Terhadap Peraturan Daerah.” *Jurnal Kewarganegaraan* 7, no. 2 (2023): 2389–95. https://journal.upy.ac.id/index.php/pkn/article/view/5760

5 State Administrative Law in Corruption Eradication

Introduction

Administrative law is closely connected with the study of corruption crimes, as state administrative law plays a crucial and strategic role in realizing clean and good governance. State administrative law, both in preventive and repressive terms, is expected to function as the primary legal instrument in establishing a government free from corruption, collusion, and nepotism. Furthermore, corruption crimes often occur due to the misuse of authority by public officials or officeholders as outlined in applicable laws. Given this premise, understanding state administrative law in the context of corruption crimes is essential.

Contemporary legal studies indicate a limited understanding of state administrative law's contribution to corruption studies, with most research focusing on criminal law. This chapter is divided into two main sections. The first section elucidates the concept of authority, followed by a discussion of the role of authority according to state administrative law, the sources of authority, and the criteria for misuse of authority in acts of corruption as defined by state administrative law. The subsequent section presents state administrative law's contribution to the prevention of corruption crimes.

Intersectionality of State Administrative Law and Corruption

The interrelation between authority and corruption within the framework of state administrative law presents a number of complex legal aspects.[1] State administrative law serves as an intermediary between administrative and criminal law, facilitating the enforcement of societal norms through criminal sanctions. This interconnection is characterized by the, "poison at the tail" phenomenon,[2] wherein administrative acts are potentially subject to criminal repercussions. Hadjon elucidates this relationship by positing a tripartite

1 Abdul Latief, *Hukum Administrasi Dalam Praktik Tindak Pidana Korupsi* (Jakarta: Kencana, 2016).

2 W. F. Prins and R. Kosim Adisapoetra, *Pengantar Ilmu Hukum Administrasi Negara, Cet* (V. Jakarta: PT. Pradnya Paramita, 1993).

DOI: 10.4324/9781003518563-5

system of norms: those which are for the government, by the government, and against the government.[3] Therefore, state administrative law encompasses governmental authority norms, the exercise of such norms, and both preventive and repressive legal protections for individuals and society.

To address corruption, state administrative law assumes a pivotal role due to its focus on governmental authority and government regulation. From a preventive standpoint, state administrative law serves as a primary legal instrument in three dimensions: establishing governance norms, particularly concerning governmental authority; regulating governmental actions, both regulatory and concrete; and ensuring legal protection for citizens. State administrative law is paramount to repress corruption, as corruption invariably involves state financial losses resulting from maladministration in the exercise of authority that has predominantly manifested from abuses of power.

It is crucial to note that corruption extends beyond mere financial losses to the state resulting from maladministration in the exercise of governmental authority. Corruption also encompasses instances where civil servants or state officials promise or provide inducements to act or refrain from acting in their official capacity, in contravention of their obligations, or when they engage in activities contrary to their duties irrespective of whether these actions fall within their official capacity. Thus, not all instances of corruption are solely attributable to state financial losses caused by maladministration.

Maladministration, as a form of deviation by public officials, can be conceptualized as substandard service delivery.[4] From a juridical perspective, the provisions regarding maladministration are delineated in Article 1(3) of Law No. 3/2008. This legislation defines maladministration as behaviors or actions that contravene the law, exceed authority, or utilize authority for purposes beyond the intended scope of the law. This definition also encompasses negligence or disregard for legal obligations in the implementation of public services by state and government officials, resulting in material and/or immaterial losses to society and individuals.

In the context of corruption, maladministration represents a deviation from the legitimate use of authority by government officials, which is subject to criminal sanctions. The misuse of authority, therefore, constitutes a key element of corruption—an unlawful act that contravenes applicable laws, legal principles, and societal norms. Corruption has far-reaching implications, including the disruption of governance and development, the violation of

3 Philipus M. Hadjon and Tatiek Sri Djatmiati, *Hukum Administrasi Dan Tindak Pidana Korupsi* (Yogkakarta: Gadjah Mada University Press, 2011).

4 Cevyn Oktavianus Taroreh, "Kedudukan Dan Peranan Ombudsman Republik Indonesia Dalam Sistem Ketatanegaraan Republik Indonesia," *Lex Crimen* 11, no. 3 (2022), https://ejournal.unsrat.ac.id/v3/index.php/lexcrimen/article/view/40580; Eivandro Wattimury and Madaskolay Viktoris Dahoklory, "Hakikat Kedudukan Lembaga Ombudsman Dalam Struktur Ketatanegaraan Republik Indonesia," *Jurnal Pendidikan Tambusai* 6, no. 3 (2022): 17169–76.

human rights intended to benefit the state and society, and state losses that adversely impact the national economy. It is noteworthy that in European and American jurisdictions, the discourse surrounding the abuse of authority and corruption centers not on policy interpretation, but on the nexus between authority and bribery. In contrast, corruption cases in Indonesia primarily revolve around the misuse of authority and other unlawful acts, which often leads to the criminalization of policies.

In Dutch administrative law scholarship, the concept of authority remains a crucial focal point for the foundation of state administrative law, given its centrality to public law notifications.[5] Authority is the fundamental concept in both constitutional and administrative law, comprising three essential components within public law: influence, legal basis, and legal conformity.

The influence component pertains to the utilization of authority to regulate the behavior of legal subjects, aiming to prevent state officials from exceeding their legislatively prescribed authority. The legal basis component mandates that all authority must have a legal foundation, ensuring that every governmental or state official action is grounded in law. The legal conformity component necessitates specific standards for various types of authority, establishing general benchmarks for all authority types which ensure the legality of actions.

State administrative law literature delineates two primary methods of obtaining governmental authority: attribution and delegation, with mandating considered a distinct method. Attribution refers to the original authority derived from constitutional law provisions, allowing for direct decision-making authority based on substantive law. Attribution also involves the establishment and assignment of specific authority to a particular organ, empowered by legislation establishing governmental authority.

The attribution of governmental authority distinguishes between original and delegate legislators. In the Indonesian context, original legislators include the People's Consultative Assembly as the constitutive body, and the House of Representatives in conjunction with the government as central law-making bodies. At the regional level, this role is fulfilled by the Regional Representatives Council in collaboration with the regional government. Delegate legislators refer to the president, who, based on statutory provisions, issues government regulations that create and delegate governmental authorities to specific state administrative bodies or positions.

The reformation of state law enforcement, a crucial pillar of democracy, is influenced by the following four key factors.[6] Firstly, there is the law itself, encompassing both substantive regulations and procedural laws for enforcement. Secondly, there is the professionalism of law enforcement personnel.

5 Philipus Hadjon, *Hukum Administrasi Dan Good Governance*. Jakarta: Universitas Trisakti, 2010.

6 Sri Nur Hari Susanto, "Good Governance Dalam Konteks Hukum Administrasi," *Administrative Law and Governance Journal* 2, no. 2 (2019): 205–17.

Thirdly, there is the adequacy of infrastructure and facilities. Fourthly, there is the public's perception of the legal system.

Administrative law governs the legal relationship between government entities and citizens, characterized by administrative acts distinct from those in civil law. Unlike in the civil law, administrative law relationships are indirectly derived from statutory regulations. This aligns with the conceptualization of administrative law as being primarily concerned with governmental functions. While the law may command or prohibit certain actions, it is challenging to frame this as a direct legal relationship between the government (as the authority) and citizens. Rather, a relationship exists external to the body responsible to the authority (the government), and the execution of this relationship is not inherently a governmental function.[7] State administrative law plays a significant role in both preventing and eradicating corruption in Indonesia. The functions and roles of state administrative law in this context are multifaceted.[8]

1. Legal Oversight of Government Administration

Oversight, from a legal perspective, serves to evaluate the compliance of duty execution with applicable legal norms and the achievement of objectives within these normative constraints. In the context of state finances, this oversight entails the examination and assessment of financial acquisition, utilization, and resolution processes in accordance with legal norms.[9]

The supervision of state finances encompasses both internal and external mechanisms. Internal oversight is conducted by bodies within the governmental structure, while external oversight is performed by organizations independent of the governmental structure. Furthermore, oversight is categorized into *a priori* and *a posteriori* forms. *A priori* oversight precedes governmental decision-making, whereas *a posteriori* oversight follows governmental decision-making. Additionally, oversight is differentiated based on legal and utilitarian aspects. Legal oversight focuses solely on the legality of governmental actions, while utilitarian oversight assesses the efficacy of these actions. Judicial oversight in state administrative law exhibits the following distinct characteristics:

1. It is external, being conducted by entities outside the governmental structure.
2. It is *a posteriori*, occurring subsequent to the action under scrutiny.
3. It is primarily legal in nature, assessing actions from a legal perspective.

7 Aju Putrijanti, "Jurisprudence of State Administrative Courts in The Development of State Administrative Law," *Jurnal Penelitian Hukum De Jure* 21, no. 2 (2021): 161; Muhamad Rakhmat, *Hukum Administrasi Negara Indonesia* (Majalengka: Universitas Majalengka, 2014).

8 Harsanto Nursadi, *Hukum Administrasi Negara Sektoral* (Depok: Badan Penerbit FHUI, 2019).

9 Aju Putrijanti and Kadek Cahya Susila Wibawa, "The Implementation of E-Court in Administrative Court to Develop Access to Justice in Indonesia," *Journal of Environmental Treatment Techniques* 9, no. 1 (2021): 105–9.

Legal oversight, conducted by the judiciary, evaluates the congruence of governmental actions with applicable legal norms. Concurrently, political oversight, exercised by the legislature, assesses the alignment between governmental authority utilization and the public will. Moreover, citizens play an active role in overseeing governmental administration.[10]

To prevent and eradicate corruption in Indonesia, enhancing regulatory oversight of governmental administration is crucial. The government must be subject to both direct and indirect control mechanisms. Direct oversight manifests through public participation in monitoring governmental administration, particularly in forumulating policies. Indirect oversight is exercised through the legislature's supervisory function over the executive branch. This comprehensive approach to direct and indirect oversight serves as a potent tool in corruption prevention and eradication.

2. *Realization of Transparency and Accountability in Government Administration*

The evolution of governmental responsibility is intrinsically linked to the historical development of state regulation. Siagian delineates three distinct state regulatory paradigms, each characterized by unique governmental roles and functions:[11]

1. The Political State, wherein the monarch wields absolute governmental power.
2. The Legal State, wherein the government's role is confined to law enforcement.
3. The Welfare State, wherein governmental purview expands to encompass public welfare, necessitating discretionary powers.[12]

The pursuit of good governance in Indonesia is inextricably intertwined with the nation's democratic ethos. Democracy, as a cornerstone of good governance, is predicated on continuous public engagement and decision-making networks that involve diverse political units acting through transparent processes. This framework facilitates public control and initiative through established channels within the political system.

10 Enny Agustina, "Legal Malfunctions and Efforts in Reconstructing the Legal System Service: A State Administrative Law Perspective," *Jurnal Dinamika Hukum* 18, no. 3 (2018): 357–64.

11 Sondra P Siagian, *Development Administration, Earth Literacy* (Jakarta: Aksa Earth, 2003).

12 Saut P Panjaitan, "Makna Dan Peranan Freies ErmessenDalam Hukum Administrasi Negara Dalam SF Marbun Dkk," in *Dimensi-Dimensi Pemikiran Hukum Administrasi Negara*, ed. S. F. Marbun (Yogyakarta: UII Press, 2001), n.d.; Raden Roro Theresia Tri Widorini et al., "Shift of Power Abuse That Inflict State Losses from the Perspective of Criminal Law into Administrative Law," *Perspectives of Law and Public Administration* 9 (2020): 38.

The exercise of power and authority necessitates adherence to principles of accountability, transparency, and openness. This aligns with the Ford Foundation's proposition that effective governance derives its legitimacy from broad participation, fairness, and accountability. Extrapolating from the conceptualization of governance as a method of implementation or utilization, good governance implies both distant and effective administration and encompasses actions and behaviors of stakeholders in governance. Fundamentally, governance is underpinned by these ethical and moral considerations.[13]

The realization of good governance is contingent upon the establishment of a clean government, and this can only be achieved through the implementation of good governance practices. These practices are fundamentally predicated on the principles of transparency and accountability.[14]

The concept of accountability, as elucidated by Ndraha, is intrinsically linked to the notion of authority as it refers to legitimate power structures.[15] Weber's typology of authority delineates three ideal types: the traditional, the charismatic, and the legal-rational.[16] The legal-rational model of authority, grounded in rational law, forms the basis of governmental authority. Barnard's subsequent conceptualization of authority emphasizes the imperative of accountable authority utilization.[17]

Accountability was initially conceived as a mechanism to ensure appropriate allocation and utilization of public funds, and has since evolved to encompass the assessment of government program efficiency. This expanded scope includes the identification of inefficiencies in staffing, procedures, and resource allocation. Essentially, the doctrine of accountability serves as a system of checks and balances within the state administrative law framework.

Transparency, as defined by Mardiasmo, refers to governmental openness in disseminating information pertaining to the management of public resources. This governmental obligation extends to the provision of financial information to relevant stakeholders to realize informed decision-making.[18] Therefore, the realization of accountability and transparency principles in governmental

13 Weda Kupita, "State Administrative Court as a Means to Realize Justice," in *SHS Web of Conferences*, vol. 54 (EDP Sciences, 2018), 3007, https://doi.org/10.1051/shsconf/20185403007.

14 Aju Putrijanti, "The Competence of the Administrative Court and Administrative Justice," *FIAT JUSTISIA: Jurnal Ilmu Hukum* 14, no. 2 (2020): 97.

15 Taliziduhu Ndraha, *Konsep Administrasi Dan Administrasi Di Indonesia* (Jakarta: Bina Aksara, 1989).

16 Martin E. Spencer, "Weber on Legitimate Norms and Authority," *The British Journal of Sociology* 21, no. 2 (1970): 123–34; Claus Wendt, *Max Weber and Institutional Theory* (London: Springer, 2016).

17 Aju Putrijanti and Kadek Cahya Susila Wibawa, "The Implementation of E-Court in Administrative Court to Develop Access to Justice in Indonesia," *Journal of Environmental Treatment Techniques* 9, no. 1 (2021): 105–9.

18 Aju Putrijanti, "Jurisprudence of State Administrative Courts in The Development of State Administrative Law," *Jurnal Penelitian Hukum De Jure* 21, no. 2 (2021): 161.

administration emerges as a crucial strategy for preventing and eradicating corruption in Indonesia.

3. Reformation

Bureaucratic reform has gained significant traction in recent years, permeating all aspects of governance in Indonesia. This heightened focus is particularly salient given the substantial contributions of the pre-reform governmental bureaucracy in response to the protracted multidimensional crisis that has beset Indonesian society. The pre-reform bureaucratic structure fostered a culture rife with corruption, collusion, and nepotism. The post-reform government has not uniformly guaranteed its successful implementation.

A perceived lack of commitment to bureaucratic reform in the post-reform government appears commensurate with inadequate dedication to combating corruption, a persistent malady within the Indonesian government. Public perception of the post-reform government's commitment to bureaucratic reform remains predominantly negative. Paradoxically, this has led to a sense of nostalgia among some segments of the population for the superficial stability of the New Order-era government.[19]

Sofyanoor delineates the role of state administrative law in bureaucratic reform as follows:[20]

1. Synchronization and harmonization of all laws regulating bureaucracy, as stipulated in Law No. 3/1999 Concerning Human Resource Principles, which ensures consistency when implementing regulations.
2. Adherence to the hierarchical order of legislation as stipulated in Law No. 12/2011, encompassing the 1945 Constitution, the People's Consultative Assembly Decisions, Laws and Government Regulations in Lieu of Laws, Government Regulations, Presidential Decrees, Provincial Regulations, and District and City Regulations.

This framework aligns with the Principles of Good Governance, which advocate for the application of laws to protect the public interest without excessive regulation. The establishment of clear implementation procedures through state administrative law is expected to facilitate this bureaucratic reform.

Key aspects of reform include the neutralization of civil servants from political affiliations and the development of a professional civil service, as mandated by Article 3 of Law No. 43/1999. The proposed state administrative court

19 Ralph C. Chandler, *The Public Administration Dictionary* (New York: John Wiley & Sons, 1982).

20 Andin Sofyanoor, "Peran Hukum Administrasi Negara Dalam Pemberantasan Korupsi Di Indonesia," *Sibatik Journal: Jurnal Ilmiah Bidang Sosial, Ekonomi, Budaya, Teknologi, Dan Pendidikan* 1, no. 2 (2022): 21–30.

law must explicitly delineate civil servant neutrality and professionalism. This necessitates the resignation of civil servants appointed to political positions for the duration of their tenure in such roles, thereby preserving the professionalism of the civil service.[21]

Article 17(2) of Law No. 43/1999 stipulates that civil servant appointments should be based on principles of professionalism, competence, work performance, and job hierarchy, without discrimination based on gender, ethnicity, religion, race, or group affiliation. State administrative law must also reflect these provisions so as to ensure their concrete implementation in the selection of bureaucratic officials. The realization of these principles must align with the good governance objectives of actualizing human rights and preventing excessive bureaucratic regulations that may impede market mechanisms.

Preventive Measures against Bureaucratic Corruption through State Administrative Acts

The pervasiveness of corruption extends beyond Indonesia's borders, afflicting numerous countries in the Southeast Asian region. The ideal of a rule of law state aspires to engender state activities, including governmental bureaucracy and citizen interactions, to be predicated on principles of justice, peace, and utility. This conceptual framework transcends the traditional notion of the state as a mere guardian of security and order, positioning it instead as an active participant in myriad aspects of citizens' lives.[22]

The logical corollary of this expanded state role rests in the establishment of diverse institutions to execute these multifaceted functions. In this context, state administrative law serves a crucial regulatory function, as it oversees administrative performance and scrutiny of state bureaucratic institutions in their exercise of authority and fulfillment of public responsibilities. The efficacy of state administrative law in Indonesia remains suboptimal, with inadequate bureaucratic firmness in addressing and overseeing implementation.

Firmansyah and Syam posit that numerous central and regional institutions continue to exhibit instances of abuse of authority, particularly at the leadership level.[23] These abuses permeate policy-making, implementation, and state administration. This weakness in state administrative law inadvert-

21 Anom Wahyu Asmorojati, "The Urgency to Establish State Administrative Court to Actualize the Concept of State Law in Indonesia," in *International Conference on Law Reform (INCLAR 2019)* (North Holland: Atlantis Press, 2020), 54–58, https://doi.org/10.2991/aebmr.k.200226.011.

22 Vicky Zaynul Firmansyah and Firdaus Syam, "Penguatan Hukum Administrasi Negara Pencegah Praktik Korupsi Dalam Diri Pemerintahan Indonesia," *Integritas: Jurnal Antikorupsi* 7, no. 2 (2021): 325–44.

23 Vicky Zaynul Firmansyah and Firdaus Syam, "Penguatan Hukum Administrasi Negara Pencegah Praktik Korupsi Dalam Diri Pemerintahan Indonesia," *Integritas: Jurnal Antikorupsi* 7, no. 2 (2021): 325–44.

ently creates opportunities for corrupt practices among officials. Transparency International's Corruption Perceptions Index (CPI) for 2022 also corroborates this observation, ranking Indonesia 110th out of 180 surveyed countries and indicating a significant regression in anti-corruption efforts since 1995.[24]

The implementation of good governance principles serves as a bridge between the government bureaucratic system and the tenets of state administrative law. A closed system approach provides enhanced control over officials and state institutions. This system involves conducting state affairs in a manner insulated from external influences such as political systems, power dynamics, vested interests, and favoritism. State administrative law, in this context, assumes a supervisory and disciplinary role, regulating bureaucratic officials in their duties and exercise of authority.

Furthermore, state administrative law establishes a framework for government-citizen relations that circumscribes excessive influence on state officials. This closed system has the potential to enhance the operational regulation of state administration, encompassing aspects from human resource allocation to budget management. The closed system aligns with principles of good governance administration as delineated in the General Principles of Good Governance. Corruption within Indonesia's governmental bureaucracy frequently manifests within the state administration system, involving state officials, institutions, and government functionaries. This prevalence is attributable to systemic weaknesses in policy regulation and administrative law enforcement. Strengthening state administrative law, as an integral component of public law, is pivotal in regulating and controlling the authority of state officials to ensure compliance with applicable laws and regulations. In the following section, the author introduces strategies to combat corrupt practices within state administrative law.

Cultivation of Leadership Ethos for Good Governance

State administrative law serves as the regulatory framework governing the actions of governmental entities, including both state institutions and officials, while simultaneously delineating the relationships between the government and its citizens and inter-governmental interactions. It comprehensively regulates the position, duties, functions, responsibilities, rights, and obligations of both institutions and government officials. Furthermore, the implementation of effective leadership training, grounded in the General Principles of Good Governance, is paramount for public officials. As bearers of power and a public mandate, these individuals must cultivate and exhibit leadership qualities

24 International Transparency, "Indeks Persepsi Korupsi Indonesia 2022," 2023, https://ti.or.id/indeks-persepsi-korupsi-indonesia-2022-mengalami-penurunan-terburuk-sepanjang-sejarah-reformasi/.

commensurate with their responsibilities in shaping and directing the bureaucratic apparatus.

Institutional Enhancement of Government Agencies

The primary function of state administrative law is to realign and reinforce the roles, duties, and authority of state institutions in accordance with extant legal frameworks. This approach transcends mere programmatic alterations, emphasizing instead systemic changes in governmental organization to preemptively combat corruption. The focus, therefore, shifts toward enhancing the government's operational efficacy in executing its quotidian responsibilities. This recalibration necessitates a multifaceted strategy involving the following actions:

1. Ameliorating the negative public perception of government through targeted initiatives.
2. Disseminating comprehensive information to the citizenry regarding their entitlements to governmental services.
3. Publishing accessible handbooks for civil servants serving as informational resources for the public and for contractors interfacing with relevant governmental agencies.
4. Introducing dynamic elements such as periodic staff rotation and implementing recognition systems for honest and competent employees.
5. Enhancing the administrative framework through the development of a superior, effective, and efficient public service system.

It is imperative to recognize that the state is neither a source of unlimited wealth nor a commercial enterprise. State institutions and officials, as custodians of public trust, must discharge their duties and responsibilities in alignment with the General Principles of Good Governance. These principles encompass professionalism, accountability, transparency, excellent service, democracy and participation, efficiency and effectiveness, and the rule of law. The conscientious application of these principles in the execution of official duties is anticipated to minimize opportunities for corrupt practices. The ultimate goal is to foster a culture of dedicated public service that is oriented toward achieving collective prosperity, justice, and welfare.

The reinforcement of state institutions through the fortification of the state administrative law system is envisioned as a bulwark against administrative violations, with a particular emphasis on corruption prevention.

The reformation of state institutional bureaucracy encompasses three critical aspects:[25]

25 Bambang Waluyo, "Optimalisasi Pemberantasan Korupsi Di Indonesia," *Jurnal Yuridis* 1, no. 2 (2014): 162–69.

1. The Institutional Aspect: The reinforcement of the institutional system necessitates a comprehensive reorganization of organizational structures, adhering to the principle of, "right sizing." This recalibration aims to establish an optimally functioning organization that is appropriately scaled to its responsibilities. The ultimate objective is to create a modern organizational framework capable of supporting the effective, efficient, transparent, and accountable execution of tasks and functions.[26]
2. The Procedural Aspect: Procedural reforms are imperative to ensure that all tasks and functions—whether technical, legal, or administrative—are guided by clear, measurable protocols. This entails the development and implementation of unambiguous, orderly, and nonoverlapping systems, processes, and standard operating procedures (SOPs) that adhere to the General Principles of Good Governance.
3. The Human Resources Aspect: This dimension focuses on the enhancement of human capital within state institutions through targeted training and education programs. The human resources reform strategy encompasses three key areas: a) The Mindset Transformation involves instilling a deep understanding among state officials of their primary role in optimizing public service delivery, and requires a shift from bureaucratic inertia to a citizen-centric approach in governance; b) The Work Culture Modificationentails fostering a culture of responsibility, particularly in the execution of daily tasks, andemphasizes judicious management of time, budgetary resources, equipment, and other operational aspects; c) The Behavioral Adjustmentfocuses on cultivating exemplary behaviors and ethical standards among public servants, who while demonstrating virtuous conduct and high ethical standards, are thereby setting a positive example for both colleagues and the public.

Legal Framework Reinforcement

The imperative for combating corruption through law enforcement necessitates a paradigm prioritizing fairness and clarity for all stakeholders. This legislative framework must transcend mere creation and must be implemented in such a way so as to reinforce the integrity and efficacy of anti-corruption statutes. This entails the articulation of unambiguous protocols for prosecuting corrupt acts and delineating sanctions with precision and firmness.

The current state of criminal laws on corruption in Indonesia appears to be susceptible to manipulation by political elites. The ambiguity and leniency of existing sanctions have failed to generate a significant deterrent effect, seemingly providing inadvertent protection to corrupt actors.

26 Regina Syafriani Boru Sitorus, Ayu EfritaDewi, and Heni Widiyani, "Optimalisasi Pemberantasan Korupsi Di Indonesia," *Jurnal Pahlawan* 6, no. 2 (2023): 1–8.

The reformation of criminal law regulations on corruption must be insulated from interventions by people in positions of power or with access authority. This imperative should be given serious consideration by institutions vested with legislative authority. One potential avenue for enhancement is the expansion of the Corruption Eradication Commission's (KPK) jurisdiction at both the central and regional levels. Sanctions for corruption suspects must be clear, binding, and multifaceted, encompassing moral sanctions, community service, and confiscation of personal wealth as a guarantee to the state.

The development of specialized criminal laws addressing sanctions for corrupt individuals is crucial. Such a legislative framework will foster an environment where state officials execute their functions and duties with earnestness and responsibility. While law enforcement is undeniably important, strategies that focus exclusively on punitive measures are likely to fall short of creating an ethical environment that inherently rejects corrupt behavior. Therefore, the participation of civil society in combating public sector corruption is of paramount importance.[27]

Ethical and Integrity Augmentation in State Administration

The lack of integrity and ethical standards prevalent among state officials emerge as a primary catalyst for deviations and abuses of authority or power.[28] Given that the state apparatus and state officials are integral to the establishment of a good, clean, and corruption-free administrative bureaucracy, there is an imperative for both government officials and society at large to cultivate and enhance integrity and anti-corruption ethics. This initiative is intrinsically linked to the broader agenda of human resources reform within the public sector.

The process of instilling integrity and anti-corruption ethics in individuals is inherently complex and requires a sustained, long-term approach. A key strategy in this endeavor is the integration of an integrity-focused curriculum, predicated on Pancasila ideology, into both school and university educational frameworks.[29] The noble values enshrined in Pancasila must be actualized in every facet of state administration in order to foster integrity and build ethical foundations for the state apparatus. This actualization should manifest

27 Jawade Hafidz, *Korupsi Dalam Perspektif Hukum Administrasi Negara* (Jakarta: Sinar Grafika, 2013).

28 Regina Syafriani Boru Sitorus, Ayu EfritaDewi, and Heni Widiyani, "Optimalisasi Pemberantasan Korupsi Di Indonesia," *Jurnal Pahlawan* 6, no. 2 (2023): 1–8.

29 Pancasila, as the state foundation, philosophical underpinning, ethical system, guideline, national identity, and embodiment of the nation's developmental aspirations, offers a robust framework for shaping and enhancing the quality of human resources. The implementation of Pancasila's values has the potential to foster strong and resilient individuals capable of upholding ethical standards in public service.

concretely in quotidian activities, ultimately cultivating a cadre of state officials who are both professional and highly disciplined.

Fostering Public Awareness and Participatory Governance

The cornerstone of effective anti-corruption efforts relies on the collective courage and resolute determination of both the state apparatus and society at large to confront corrupt practices. A significant impediment to this effort is the persistent reluctance among many prosecutors to pursue charges, particularly when corruption implicates individuals of considerable influence and power. This underscores the critical need for cultivating a shared commitment to challenging and rectifying injustices, with the ultimate aim of elevating legal consciousness within society. In the sociocultural context, two distinct behavioral paradigms emerge:

1. The Culture of Shame: This paradigm is characterized by a behavioral pattern wherein an individual's sense of identity and social role is threatened by public exposure of wrongdoing. In this context, guilt is primarily induced when misconduct is discovered by others, be they peers, superiors, or financial oversight bodies. The deterrent effect is thus contingent upon the fear of social repercussions rather than upon internalized ethical standards.
2. The Culture of Wrongdoing: Conversely, this paradigm is rooted in an individual's internal moral compass. It manifests as a sense of wrongdoing when engaging in moral deviations, irrespective of external awareness or social consequences. This internalized ethical framework serves as a more robust defense against corrupt tendencies, as it operates independently of external surveillance or social pressure.

The cultivation and widespread application of a culture of wrongdoing represents the most formidable bulwark against corrupt practices. This cultural approach shifts the locus of ethical behavior from external social pressures to internal moral convictions, thereby creating a more sustainable and pervasive resistance to corruption.

Institutional Development and Fortification of Anti-Corruption Entities

To pursue the effective enforcement and prosecution of corruption-related offenses, the Indonesian state has established autonomous bodies vested with specific mandates in the anti-corruption domain. While diverse institutional models exist, it is imperative that any adopted framework be sufficiently resourced with competent personnel. Failure to properly resource this initiative risks exacerbating the already extensive roster of ineffectual and incompetent anti-corruption entities. Given the pervasive nature of corruption, it is crucial to reinforce institutions such as the Corruption Eradication Commission (KPK) through the conferral of independence.

The role of the press in combating corruption is also of paramount importance. Media activities should be facilitated without undue governmental interference. An ideal press should function as a conduit for public sentiment, a mechanism for identifying administrative malfeasance, and as a medium for bilateral communication between the citizenry and the government. The press's role should transcend mere oversight of developmental programs, as comprehensive surveillance cannot be entrusted solely to structural or functional supervisory units.

As codified in Presidential Regulation No. 54/2018 on the National Strategy for Corruption Prevention, the KPK is designated as a *sui generis* institution, endowed with coordinative and supervisory authority in corruption prevention and eradication as prescribed by the law. The National Corruption Prevention Strategy delineates three primary focal areas: licensing and commerce, state finances, and law enforcement and bureaucratic reform. The efficacy of corruption prevention efforts is enhanced when they are concentrated on strategic sectors that significantly impact developmental performance and public trust in governmental institutions. Furthermore, these efficiency of corruption prevention measures can be augmented through the reduction of administrative encumbrances and redundancies, facilitated by enhanced collaboration among ministries, agencies, local governments, other relevant stakeholders, and the KPK.[30]

Law No. 19/2019, which constitutes the Second Amendment to the Corruption Eradication Commission Law, situates the KPK within the executive branch, specifically categorizing it as a governmental institution. This amendment serves to elucidate the KPK's institutional position, emphasizing its role in executing governmental authority and consequently influencing corruption enforcement mechanisms. The revision to the KPK law provides clarity regarding the KPK's status as a component of the governmental apparatus, functioning in concert with law enforcement entities such as the police and prosecutors. This alignment facilitates a more systematic and structured approach to corruption prevention and eradication, thereby mitigating disparities in enforcement practices among various law enforcement agencies.

Notwithstanding the contentious nature of the 2019 KPK law's enactment, which was perceived by some as potentially undermining the KPK's efficacy, this amendment effectuates institutional reform and transformation within the KPK. It signifies a strategic shift from a predominantly repressive approach to corruption eradication toward a more preventive paradigm. This transition can be interpreted as an effort to reinforce the rule of law, particularly in the realm of state administrative law and from within the KPK's operational framework.

30 Chandra Bayu, "Transformasi Kelembagaan KPK: UU KPK Sebagai Kebijakan Pencegahan Korupsi Di Indonesia," *Jurnal Dinamika Sosial Budaya* 23, no. 1 (2021): 84–97.

However, the successful implementation of the new KPK law also necessitates collaborative efforts, not just from the KPK and other governmental bodies, but also from across all of Indonesian society.

The KPK's mandate extends beyond mere law enforcement. It must ensure a well-functioning, anti-corruption educational institution. It is imperative that anti-corruption education, socialization, and character formation be expeditiously integrated into both bureaucratic structures and throughout Indonesian society. The implementation of an anti-corruption curriculum at the tertiary education level represents a concrete initiative which warrants continued application. In its capacity as a anti-corruption enforcement entity, the KPK assumes a dual role of monitoring and providing educational outreach to government officials and to the general public.

The persistent occurrence of corruption cases annually remains a significant challenge within the Indonesian bureaucratic apparatus. A recent case involved the head of the Banjarnegara Regency, who was apprehended in a sting operation on suspicion of corruption related to procurement processes for the local government. The suspect's allegedly rationalized the corrupt practices due to insufficient remuneration, which exemplifies the inadequate internalization and implementation of good governance principles and anti-corruption education. This case exposes the apparent weaknesses in the application of state administrative law within regional governments demonstrates the prevalence of corruption cases involving local officials. There is a clear and collective societal responsibility to maintain vigilant oversight of administrative processes.

Decentralization of Anti-Corruption Institutional Framework

The corruption cases that emerged in 2021 illuminated the pervasive nature of administrative malfeasance within regional governmental structures. According to data provided by the KPK, multiple regional officials were apprehended on allegations of corruption in 2021, as evidenced in the jurisdictions of Bintan, Banjarnegara, and Probolinggo Regencies. This pattern of misconduct indicates a persistent vulnerability in regional administrative governance and suggests inadequate oversight mechanisms for agencies and regional officials in the execution of their mandated duties.

Arrsa explains a tripartite framework elucidating the factors that contribute to corruption within regional governments.[31] Firstly, there exists an abuse of power, perpetrated by officials vested with specific authority derived from legal legitimacy and who engage in collusive practices involving bribery, standard manipulation, or financial inflation. This form of the abuse of authority is typically characterized as nonpolitical and is predominantly executed by lower-echelon officials. Secondly, there is a discretionary abuse of power, wherein

31 Ria Casmi Arrsa, "Urgensi Membentuk KPK Di Daerah," *Integritas: Jurnal Antikorupsi* 2, no. 1 (2016): 215–34.

regional executives misappropriate their authority to promulgate specific policies, facilitating collusion with associates, interest groups, or familial connections. Thirdly, an ideological abuse of power occurs when officials pursue particular objectives or interests aligned with their affiliated groups or political parties, often accompanied by support for strategic positioning within bureaucratic or executive agencies which results in *quid pro quo* arrangements colloquially termed as, "cunning political favors."

In contemplating the establishment of KPK-analogous institutions at the regional level, it is instructive to consider the Danish model. Denmark, a nation characterized by low corruption indices, has implemented anti-corruption institutions within every governmental agency and regional entity. The Danish bureaucratic system places significant emphasis on local governments as the vanguard of its democratic framework. This structural arrangement confers direct authority and relational proximity between local governments and their constituents. Therefore, Denmark has instituted anti-corruption bodies within each institutional entity and local governmental structure.

In its endeavors to mitigate corrupt practices, Denmark prioritizes the establishment of a robust anti-corruption educational foundation within its governmental framework. This approach encompasses the dissemination of comprehension, education, legal frameworks, and exemplifications of diverse corrupt acts. Notably, each governmental agency in Denmark formulates its own anti-corruption policy, thereby centralizing regulations designed to address the abuse of authority and corruption.

The transparency inherent in Denmark's bureaucratic system yields impressive outcomes. Citizens engaged in administrative processes are accorded the right to monitor and access governmental information. Furthermore, there is a synergy between an effective democratic system and the public oversight of administrative functions, which engenders public trust in the government. Denmark's governance system is characterized by its systematic and robust nature, with integrity serving as the cornerstone of its anti-corruption bureaucratic framework. The fortification of anti-corruption enforcement agencies in Denmark, in conjunction with law enforcement entities, has garnered high levels of public trust. A fair legal system, devoid of rights violations and marked by impartiality, ensures equitable treatment in judicial proceedings.

Danish governance facilitates the establishment of an exemplary public service administration system, wherein public service providers can execute their duties with integrity and are supported by concise and transparent accounting procedures, regulations, and systems. Drawing from this paradigm, the establishment of anti-corruption institutions at the regional level represents a strategic effort to suppress corrupt practices that are frequently observed in regional governments. These anti-corruption institutions, beyond their enforcement and investigative functions, also serve as purveyors of anti-corruption education and act as supervisory controls over administrative operations. Given the susceptibility of regional officials to corrupt practices due to a weakened state administrative law system, the establishment of anti-corruption institutions at the regional level constitutes a manifestation of state administrative law implementation. These institutions not only enforce anti-corruption measures but also function as control and oversight systems for governance in every agency. The anticipated outcome of this institutional establishment is the creation of a system of checks and balances in administration, coupled with the development of an exemplary, effective, and efficient public service system.

Critical Legal Analysis of State Administrative Law in Corruption Crimes after Law No. 30/2014

The preceding discourse delineated the theoretical and idealized framework of state administrative law, encompassing anti-corruption institutions from the central to regional governments. This section progresses to an examination of the implications of Law No. 30/2014 on Government Administration vis-à-vis the role of administrative courts in adjudicating corruption cases and thereby providing a comprehensive actualization of state administrative law within the Indonesian context. Law No. 30/2014 serves as both the substantive foundation for administrative courts in their adjudicatory function and the normative basis for governmental actions and decision-making processes. Notwithstanding its significance, this legislation is not without controversy, particularly regarding theoretical inconsistencies and practical challenges in administrative jurisprudence. A salient issue arises from the law's treatment of actions and decisions. While state administrative law traditionally distinguishes between these two concepts, Law No. 30/2014 places them on equal footing within the hierarchy of governmental activities. This conflation potentially engenders conceptual ambiguities in legal interpretation and application.

Moreover, the practical implementation of Law No. 30/2014 in administrative judiciary proceedings involving corruption cases reveals a jurisdictional conflict with Law No. 31/1999 on the Eradication of Corruption Crimes. These two statutes offer divergent approaches to the abuse of authority, prescribing disparate sanctions and resolution mechanisms. Article 17 of Law No. 30/2014 proscribes the abuse of authority by government bodies and/or officials, categorizing such conduct as an administrative infraction. In contrast, Article 3 of Law No. 31/1999 criminalizes the abuse of authority resulting in state financial loss, classifying it as clear corruption and imposing severe penalties, including life imprisonment or a minimum incarceration period of one year.

The supreme court's promulgation of Regulation (Perma) No. 7/2015 establishes the precedence of criminal proceedings over administrative cases. However, this regulation presents theoretical inconsistencies with the principle of *lex specialis derogat legi generali.* The logical extension of this principle would dictate that corruption cases should be adjudicated without regard to administrative court determinations. Nevertheless, the current legal landscape is characterized by a notable absence of normative provisions governing criminal cases, including those pertaining to corruption. Therefore, corruption cases have bifurcated into parallel streams of adjudication: administrative judicial proceedings and corruption crime court proceedings. This bifurcation engenders the potential for divergent outcomes. Administrative courts may conclude an absence of the abuse of authority, while corruption crime courts may concurrently classify the same conduct as constituting criminal acts of corruption.

The jurisdictional and interpretive conflict at hand necessitates an unequivocal resolution to delineate the respective purviews of administrative law and criminal law in addressing corrupt acts perpetrated by public officials or governmental bodies. The current administrative lacuna presents an opportunity for exploitation, potentially facilitating corrupt practices under the guise of administrative infractions. If left unaddressed, this legal intersection may contribute to the proliferation of corruption among officials and governmental entities, potentially compromising the integrity of Indonesia's administrative judiciary system.

The case of Ikhwanudin exemplifies the problematic duality inherent in the concurrent application of administrative and criminal law. Ikhwanudin, in his capacity as head of the National Unity and Political Agency of South Sumatra Province, was convicted of embezzling grant funds intended for community organizations. The Palembang District Court, in Decision Number 10/PID.TPK/2017/PT.PLG, imposed a sentence of four years and six months' imprisonment, accompanied by a financial penalty. Subsequently, the governor, in Decree Number 2070/KPTS/BKD.I/2018, implemented an administrative sanction, terminating Ikhwanudin's civil service status.

The defendant leveraged his dismissal as grounds for appeal to the administrative court. The court's Decision Number 74/B/2019/PT.TUN-MDN favored the appellant, annulling the dismissal decree. Although the governor pursued further legal recourse through an appeal to the supreme court, the apex court's Ruling Number 436K/TUN/2019 invalidated the dismissal decision, effectively reinstating the defendant's civil service status.

The integrity of the administrative judiciary faced a significant challenge in March 2024, with the exposure of a corruption scandal involving a supreme court justice and several judicial officials. This case, centered on the illicit trading of cases to manipulate court decisions, represents a grave breach of judicial ethics and the rule of law. The KPK investigations spanning 2018 to 2022 unveiled a complex network of gratuity payments, amounting to approximately 15 billion Indonesian Rupiah, which was facilitated through intricate financial maneuvers involving multiple money changers and proxy identities. Indonesian Corruption Watch (ICW) has highlighted the supreme court's suboptimal performance in maintaining appropriate sentences for corruption convicts.[32] Notable examples include:

32 ICW, "Hakim Agung Terjerat Korupsi: Momentum Bersih-Bersih Mafia Peradilan," 2022, https://antikorupsi.org/id/hakim-agung-terjerat-korupsi-momentum-bersih-bersih-mafia-peradilan.

1. The case of the lawyer, Lucas, whose initial five-year sentence was reduced to three years upon supreme court appeal.
2. Acquittals at the cassation level in high-profile cases such as the Bank Indonesia Liquidity Assistance (BLBI) case.
3. An acquittal in the bribery case involving the Riau Power Plant project in the first instance at trial.

ICW's analysis delineates a tripartite structure of judicial corruption:

1. Case Registration: Illicit payments to secure priority case numbers.
2. Pre-Trial Phase: Selection of sympathetic judges to influence case outcomes.
3. Trial Proceedings: Direct bribery of judges to secure favorable rulings.

Given the current state of the administrative judiciary, a comprehensive and multifaceted approach is imperative to eradicate corruption within the judicial system and restore public trust. This approach should encompass rigorous internal evaluations of the administrative judiciary, interinstitutional collaboration among all judicial bodies to comprehensively map corruption networks and practices, and development and implementation of robust oversight policies based on the findings of these collaborative efforts.

Conclusion

The role of state administrative law in optimizing government bureaucracy in Indonesia can be elucidated through the following multifaceted framework:[33]

1. Legal Certainty: State administrative law serves as a cornerstone for legal certainty. As an operational extension and technical specialization of constitutional law, it emanates from state sovereignty as the functional implementation of statutory provisions. This body of law assumes a pivotal role in administrative oversight, delineating the structural and functional aspects of state administration. It encompasses the enforcement of disciplinary regulations governing state officials in the execution of their duties and the exercise of their authority.
2. Bureaucratic Legal Frameworks: State administrative law fortifies bureaucratic legal frameworks by scrutinizing the nexus between specific legal matters pertaining to state administration and to state institutions. It also regulates both the internal dynamics among government institutions and

33 Abid Zamzami, "Pelaksanaan Fungsi Hukum Administrasi Negara Dalam Mewujudkan Pemerintahan Yang Baik," *Jurnal Fakultas Hukum Universitas Islam Malang*, 2020. https://doi.org/10.33474/yur.v3i2.6736

their external interactions with the public, thereby fostering a cohesive and accountable administrative ecosystem.

3. Diverse Domains: State administrative law holds significant import for the diverse domains of developmental administration, civil service management, state financial governance, and national defense. In these spheres, state administration law serves as a regulatory mechanism for governmental intervention in societal affairs, guiding planned changes and ensuring orderly progress.
4. Environmental Administration: The purview of state administrative law extends to environmental administration. This aspect focuses on environmental law enforcement by authorized government agencies, encompassing permit issuance, supervisory mechanisms, application of administrative sanctions, and the initiation of state administrative lawsuits within the bureaucratic milieu.[34] As exemplified in Law No. 32/2009 on Environmental Management and Protection, environmental administrative law aims to achieve compliance with statutory regulations through both preventive and repressive measures, including administrative, criminal, and civil sanctions.
5. Good Governance: State administrative law plays an instrumental role in fostering good governance and cultivating exemplary state officials. There exists a normative framework for the establishment of good governance practices and the formation of a government characterized by integrity, fairness, and authority. This legal framework aims to ensure a government free from legal defects, collusion, corruption, and nepotism. Additionally, it strives to cultivate a bureaucracy insulated from undue political influences, partisan interests, and commercial pressures. Within the realm of public service, state administrative law furnishes guidelines, oversight mechanisms, ethical standards, and frameworks for maximizing the roles and responsibilities of government officials.

Criminal corruption is conceptualized as an egregious act that inflicts substantial harm on state finances and permeates various facets of national life. The fundamental premise of anti-corruption efforts elucidates that corruption constitutes a criminal offense occurring within state institutions or the governmental apparatus, wherein an individual misappropriates their vested authority and executes tasks and responsibilities in contravention of legal provisions.

Law No. 19/2019, which serves as the Second Amendment to Law No. 30/2002 on the Komisi Pemberantasan Korupsi or Corruption Eradication Commission (the KPK), provides a comprehensive definition of corruption eradication. It delineates this process as a series of activities encompassing

34 Latifah Amir, "Analisis Yuridis Hak Gugat Pemerintah Terhadap Pelaku Pencemaran/Perusakan Lingkungan Hidup Berdasarkan UU NO. 32 Tahun 2009," *Jurnal Penelitian Universitas Jambi: Seri Humaniora* 15, no. 2 (2013): 43473.

prevention and eradication of corrupt practices through coordinated efforts, supervision, monitoring, investigation, prosecution, and trial proceedings, with the integral participation of the community in accordance with extant legislative provisions. Combatting corruption has been elevated to a primary governance objective, one aimed at enhancing public welfare, reinforcing the integrity of the Republic of Indonesia (NKRI), and advancing national goals.[35]

Article 6 of the KPK law vests the commission with the authority and duty to implement preventive measures against corrupt acts. This preventive mandate is further elaborated in Article 7, which delineates the commission's specific powers in the following actions:[36]

1. Registration and examination of wealth reports submitted by state officials.
2. Receipt and determination of gratuity statuses.
3. Implementation of anti-corruption education programs across all educational tiers.
4. Planning and execution of anti-corruption socialization initiatives.
5. Conduct of public anti-corruption campaigns.
6. Engagement in bilateral or multilateral cooperation for combating corruption.

Corruption, as elucidated in the provided text, can be conceptualized as a multifaceted phenomenon with profound implications for societal, political, and economic structures. Corruption is also fundamentally defined as a deviation from the official duties associated with a state position, motivated by personal, familial, or group interests. This characterization of corruption as antisocial, immoral, and unlawful emphasizes its transgressive nature across multiple domains of societal norms and legal frameworks.

Therefore, reform of anti-corruption laws is necessary. Strengthening the legal system with clear, firm, and fair laws is essential. Imposing sanctions on corruptors needs to be reinforced with moral and social accountability systems, including community service, moral sanctions, and confiscation of corruptors' assets as guarantees to the state. The prevalence of corruption crimes as extraordinary crimes against the state requires extraordinary measures to prevent and eradicate wrongdoing.[37]

Corrupt behavior can be categorized into three main areas: behavior carried out in a public position, behavior involving market conditions, and behavior directly affecting public interests. Examples of corrupt behavior have included

35 Bambang Waluyo, "Optimalisasi Pemberantasan Korupsi Di Indonesia," *Jurnal Yuridis* 1, no. 2 (2014): 162–69.

36 Hariman Satria Satria, "Kebijakan Kriminal Pencegahan Korupsi Pelayanan Publik," *Integritas: Jurnal Antikorupsi* 6, no. 2 (2020): 169–86.

37 Hariman Satria Satria, "Kebijakan Kriminal Pencegahan Korupsi Pelayanan Publik," *Integritas: Jurnal Antikorupsi* 6, no. 2 (2020): 169–86.

the misappropriation of state funds for personal use, embezzlement in office, cheating, bribery, extortion, gratuities, and conflicts of interest in procurement and policies.

Corruption invariably exerts a negative impact on democratization and development processes, delegitimizing and reducing public trust in the political process through financially motivated politics. Corruption also distorts decision-making in public policy, undermining public accountability and the rule of law. Epistemologically, the different types of corruption frequently encountered in government environments, whether they occur at the central or at the regional level, are often related to the public service.[38] This negative impact on the public service intersects with bureaucratic environments and public-facing services, creating signficant administrative obstacles. Furthermore, corruption leads to various low-quality development projects and public facilities that fail to meet their intended needs, thus hindering long-term sustainable development.[39]

References

Agustina, Enny. "Legal Malfunctions and Efforts in Reconstructing the Legal System Service: A State Administrative Law Perspective." *Jurnal Dinamika Hukum* 18, no. 3 (2018): 357–64. https://dinamikahukum.fh.unsoed.ac.id/index.php/JDH/article/view/2117

Amir, Latifah. "Analisis Yuridis Hak Gugat Pemerintah Terhadap Pelaku Pencemaran/ Perusakan Lingkungan Hidup Berdasarkan UU NO. 32 Tahun 2009." *Jurnal Penelitian Universitas Jambi: Seri Humaniora* 15, no. 2 (2013): 43473. https://media.neliti.com/media/publications/43473-ID-analisis-yuridis-hak-gugat-pemerintah-terhadap-pelaku-pencemaran-perusakan-lingk.pdf

Arrsa, Ria Casmi. "Urgensi Membentuk KPK Di Daerah." *Integritas: Jurnal Antikorupsi* 2, no. 1 (2016): 215–34. https://doi.org/10.32697/integritas.v2i1.132

Asmorojati, Anom Wahyu. "The Urgency to Establish State Administrative Court to Actualize the Concept of State Law in Indonesia." In *International Conference on Law Reform (INCLAR 2019)*, 54–58. North Holland: Atlantis Press, 2020. https://doi.org/10.2991/aebmr.k.200226.011

Bayu, Chandra. "Transformasi Kelembagaan KPK: UU KPK Sebagai Kebijakan Pencegahan Korupsi Di Indonesia." *Jurnal Dinamika Sosial Budaya* 23, no. 1 (2021): 84–97. https://journals.usm.ac.id/index.php/jdsb/article/view/2935

Chandler, Ralph C. *The Public Administration Dictionary*. New York: John Wiley & Sons, 1982. https://doi.org/10.1111/j.1754-7121.1982.tb02096.x

Firmansyah, Vicky Zaynul, and Firdaus Syam. "Penguatan Hukum Administrasi Negara Pencegah Praktik Korupsi Dalam Diri Pemerintahan Indonesia." *Integritas:*

38 Hariman Satria Satria, "Kebijakan Kriminal Pencegahan Korupsi Pelayanan Publik," *Integritas: Jurnal Antikorupsi* 6, no. 2 (2020): 169–86.

39 I Wayan Joniarta, "Banalitas Korupsi Di Indonesia," *Jurnal Ilmiah Dinamika Sosial* 2, no. 1 (2018): 149–56.

Jurnal Antikorupsi 7, no. 2 (2021): 325–44. https://doi.org/10.32697/integritas.v7i2.817

Hadjon, Philipus M. *Hukum Administrasi Dan Good Governance*. Jakarta: Universitas Trisakti, 2010.

Hadjon, Philipus M., and Tatiek Sri Djatmiati. *Hukum Administrasi Dan Tindak Pidana Korupsi*. Yogkakarta: Gadjah Mada University Press, 2011.

Hafidz, Jawade. *Korupsi Dalam Perspektif Hukum Administrasi Negara*. Jakarta: Sinar Grafika, 2013.

ICW. "Hakim Agung Terjerat Korupsi: Momentum Bersih-Bersih Mafia Peradilan," *ICW*, September 23, 2022. https://antikorupsi.org/id/hakim-agung-terjerat-korupsi-momentum-bersih-bersih-mafia-peradilan.

Joniarta, I Wayan. "Banalitas Korupsi Di Indonesia." *Jurnal Ilmiah Dinamika Sosial* 2, no. 1 (2018): 149–56. https://journal.undiknas.ac.id/index.php/fisip/article/view/358

Klitgaard, Robert. Membasmi Korupsi, Terj. Yogyakarta: Hermojo, Yayasan Obor Indonesia, 2005.

Kupita, Weda. "State Administrative Court as a Means to Realize Justice." In *SHS Web of Conferences*, 54:3007. EDP Sciences, 2018. https://doi.org/10.1051/shsconf/20185403007

Latief, Abdul. *Hukum Administrasi Dalam Praktik Tindak Pidana Korupsi*. Jakarta: Kencana, 2016.

Muttaqin, M Zaenul. *Corruption in the Public Sector: An International Perspective: By Krishna K. Tummala*. Bingley, UK: Emerald Publishing Limited, 2021. Taylor & Francis, 2023. https://doi.org/10.1080/10999922.2022.2038464

Ndraha, Taliziduhu. *Konsep Administrasi Dan Administrasi Di Indonesia*. Jakarta: Bina Aksara, 1989.

Nursadi, Harsanto. *Hukum Administrasi Negara Sektoral*. Depok: Badan Penerbit FHUI, 2019.

Ohoiwutun, Yosephina, M. Zaenul Muttaqin, Ilham Ilham, and Vince Tebay. "Electronic-Based Service Innovation: Evidence From the Jayapura City Population and Civil Registration Office, Indonesia." In *Global Perspectives on Social Media Usage Within Governments*, 214–25. IGI Global, 2023. https://doi.org/10.4018/978-1-6684-7450-1.ch014

Panjaitan, Saut P. "Makna Dan Peranan Freies ErmessenDalam Hukum Administrasi Negara." In *Dimensi-Dimensi Pemikiran Hukum Administrasi Negara*, edited by S. F. Marbun. Yogyakarta: UII Press, 2001.

Prins, W. F., and R. Kosim Adisapoetra. *Pengantar Ilmu Hukum Administrasi Negara, Cet.* V. Jakarta: PT. Pradnya Paramita, 1993.

Putrijanti, Aju. "Jurisprudence of State Administrative Courts in The Development of State Administrative Law." *Jurnal Penelitian Hukum De Jure* 21, no. 2 (2021): 161. https://doi.org/10.30641/dejure.2021.V21.161-174

Putrijanti, Aju. "The Competence of the Administrative Court and Administrative Justice." *FIAT JUSTISIA: Jurnal Ilmu Hukum* 14, no. 2 (2020): 97. https://doi.org/10.25041/fiatjustisia.v14no2.1890

Putrijanti, Aju, and Kadek Cahya Susila Wibawa. "The Implementation of E-Court in Administrative Court to Develop Access to Justice in Indonesia." *Journal of Environmental Treatment Techniques* 9, no. 1 (2021): 105–9. https://doi.org/10.47277/JETT/9(1)109

Quah, Jon S. T. "Corruption Scandals in Six Asian Countries: A Comparative Analysis." *Public Administration and Policy* 23, no. 1 (2020): 7–21. https://doi.org/10.1108/PAP-01-2020-0002

Rakhmat, Muhamad. *Hukum Administrasi Negara Indonesia*. Majalengka: Universitas Majalengka, 2014.

Satria, Hariman Satria. "Kebijakan Kriminal Pencegahan Korupsi Pelayanan Publik." *Integritas: Jurnal Antikorupsi* 6, no. 2 (2020): 169–86. https://jurnal.kpk.go.id/index.php/integritas/article/view/660

Siagian, Sondra P. *Development Administration. Earth Literacy*. Jakarta: Aksa Earth, 2003.

Sitorus, Regina Syafriani Boru, Ayu EfritaDewi, and Heni Widiyani. "Optimalisasi Pemberantasan Korupsi Di Indonesia." *Jurnal Pahlawan* 6, no. 2 (2023): 1–8. https://doi.org/10.31004/jp.v6i2.22810

Sofyanoor, Andin. "Peran Hukum Administrasi Negara Dalam Pemberantasan Korupsi Di Indonesia." *Sibatik Journal: Jurnal Ilmiah Bidang Sosial, Ekonomi, Budaya, Teknologi, Dan Pendidikan* 1, no. 2 (2022): 21–30. https://doi.org/10.54443/sibatik.v1i2.9

Spencer, Martin E. "Weber on Legitimate Norms and Authority." *The British Journal of Sociology* 21, no. 2 (1970): 123–34. https://doi.org/10.2307/588403

Susanto, Sri Nur Hari. "Good Governance Dalam Konteks Hukum Administrasi." *Administrative Law and Governance Journal* 2, no. 2 (2019): 205–17. https://doi.org/10.14710/alj.v2i2.205-217

Taroreh, Cevyn Oktavianus. "Kedudukan Dan Peranan Ombudsman Republik Indonesia Dalam Sistem Ketatanegaraan Republik Indonesia." *Lex Crimen* 11, no. 3 (2022). https://ejournal.unsrat.ac.id/v3/index.php/lexcrimen/article/view/40580

Transparency, International. "Indeks Persepsi Korupsi Indonesia 2022." *Transparency International Indonesia*, January 31, 2023. https://ti.or.id/indeks-persepsi-korupsi-indonesia-2022-mengalami-penurunan-terburuk-sepanjang-sejarah-reformasi/.

Tummala, Krishna K. "India's Continuing Fight Against Corruption: The Modi Regime's First Five-Year Saga." In *Corruption in the Public Sector: An International Perspective*, vol. 34, 23–42. Bingley: Emerald Publishing Limited, 2021. https://doi.org/10.1108/S2053-769720210000034004

Waluyo, Bambang. "Optimalisasi Pemberantasan Korupsi Di Indonesia." *Jurnal Yuridis* 1, no. 2 (2014): 162–69. https://media.neliti.com/media/publications/282159-optimalisasi-pemberantasan-korupsi-di-in-6faf3218.pdf

Wattimury, Eivandro, and Madaskolay Viktoris Dahoklory. "Hakikat Kedudukan Lembaga Ombudsman Dalam Struktur Ketatanegaraan Republik Indonesia." *Jurnal Pendidikan Tambusai* 6, no. 3 (2022): 17169–76. https://jptam.org/index.php/jptam/article/view/6186

Wendt, Claus. *Max Weber and Institutional Theory*. Berlin: Springer, 2016.

Widorini, Raden Roro Theresia Tri, I. Nyoman Nurjaya, Bambang Sugiri, and Ismail Navianto. "Shift of Power Abuse That Inflict State Losses from the Perspective of Criminal Law into Administrative Law." *Perspectives of Law and Public Administration* 9 (2020): 38. https://openurl.ebsco.com/EPDB%3Agcd%3A12%3A26539084/detailv2?sid=ebsco%3Aplink%3Acrawler&id=ebsco%3Agcd%3A146799971

Zamzami, Abid. "Pelaksanaan Fungsi Hukum Administrasi Negara Dalam Mewujudkan Pemerintahan Yang Baik." *Jurnal Fakultas Hukum Universitas Islam Malang* (2020). https://doi.org/10.33474/yur.v3i2.6736

6 Omnibus Law and Its Influence on State Administrative Law

Introduction

In February 2020, the Indonesian executive branch presented a draft of the Job Creation Bill (RUU Cipta Kerja) to the House of Representatives (DPR).[1] The proposed legislation, comprising 174 articles with accompanying explanations and supplementary academic texts totaling 1,981 pages, adopted the omnibus law approach as an innovative legislative strategy. This methodology aims to consolidate multiple regulations into a single, comprehensive legislative package. The Job Creation Bill was subsequently enacted into law in November 2020 and remains in force at the time of this book's publication, codified as Law No. 11/2020 on Job Creation, *State Gazette* No. 245/2020, with Supplement to the *State Gazette* No. 6573.

As delineated in Article 4 of the Job Creation Law, the legislation addresses a wide array of legal domains concurrently, including but not limited to: labor regulations, government administration, investment protocols, protection and empowerment of Micro, Small, and Medium Enterprises (MSMEs), business facilitation measures, research and innovation support, land acquisition procedures, economic zone regulations, acceleration of national strategic projects, and relevant sanctions.

The expansive scope of this omnibus legislation raises concerns regarding potential conceptual inconsistencies and overlaps with existing statutes, notably Law No. 13/2003 on Employment and Law No. 30/2014 on Government Administration. From an administrative law perspective, the clustered structure of the Job Creation Law presents several significant issues. Critics argue that the adoption of the omnibus law method in this context may be unconstitutional, its delineation of authority between central and regional governments lacks clarity, and the standards for licensing remain ambiguous.

1 Muhammad Adiguna Bimasakti, "Several Conceptual Errors in the Job Creation Law in the Light of the Science of Administrative Law," *Jurnal Hukum Peratun* 4, no. 1 (2021): 45–66, https://doi.org/https://doi.org/10.25216/peratun.412021.45-66.

DOI: 10.4324/9781003518563-6

The Omnibus Law Methodology within Indonesian Jurisprudential Framework

The implementation of the omnibus law methodology within the Job Creation Law has engendered significant discourse among legal scholars in Indonesia. A cohort of experts contends that this legislative approach is incongruous with the established norms of Indonesian statutory construction. However, proponents of the method argue that the law offers a more streamlined approach to the legislative process.

Opposition to the Job Creation Law emanates from a consortium of academics representing 67 Indonesian tertiary institutions.[2] These scholars posit that the law's enactment was disproportionately influenced by economic and political imperatives, thereby circumventing the mandated public participation as stipulated in Article 96 of Law No. 12/2011, and as amended by Law No. 15/2019 Concerning the Formation of Legislation.

Three prominent academics have articulated the following specific critiques:[3]

1. Professor Susi Dwi Harijanti, of the Faculty of Law at Padjadjaran University, asserts that the Job Creation Law is marred by substantive deficiencies. She contends that its provisions contravene established legislative procedures, demonstrate a disregard for environmental considerations, and that the law's expedited enactment, in the face of public opposition, constitutes a derogation of human rights.
2. Zainal Arifin Mochtar, a constitutional law scholar at Gadjah Mada University, corroborates Professor Harijanti's concerns, emphasizing the lack of transparency in the drafting process, which extended to the exclusion of certain state institutions from accessing the draft legislation.
3. Professor Maria Sumardjono, of the Faculty of Law at Gadjah Mada University, has expressed her opposition to the extent of initiating judicial review proceedings before the constitutional court.

Furthermore, constitutional law expert Bivitri Susanti argues that the formulation of the Omnibus Law Job Creation Law contravenes fundamental constitutional principles.[4] She characterizes the law's formation as a paradigmatic example of legislative malfeasance, violating both procedural norms and the principle of transparency integral to post-reform democratic morality. This

2 Petrus Riski and Fathiyah Wardah, "Akademisi Tolak UU Cipta Kerja," *Voa-Indonesia*, October 08, 2020.

3 Petrus Riski and Fathiyah Wardah, "Akademisi Tolak UU Cipta Kerja," *Voa-Indonesia*, October 08, 2020.

4 Tsarina Maharani and Kristian Erdianto, "Pakar Hukum: Pembentukan UU CIpta Kerja Merupakan Proses Legislasi Terburuk," *Kompas.com*, October 17, 2020, https://nasional.kompas.com/read/2020/10/17/11113141/pakar-hukum-pembentukan-uu-cipta-kerja-merupakan-proses-legislasi-terburuk.

academic dissent finds resonance within the legislative sphere. Nasir Djamil, a member of Commission III of the House of Representatives, posits that public opposition to the Job Creation Law stems from the law's perceived prioritization of business interests over those of the citizenry, particularly in relation to labor rights.[5]

However, some experts have agreed with the Omnibus Law. Yustinus Prastowo, Special Staff to the Minister of Finance for Strategic Communications, enumerates the following benefits:[6]

1. Facilitation of simultaneous revisions to multiple laws
2. Effective integration of diverse regulations into a single, comprehensive rule
3. Concurrent reference to multiple, technical laws

Legal scholars Arief and Sutrisni, from Wiraraja University, posit that the Job Creation Law, through its utilization of the omnibus law technique, presents a potential solution to the persistent issue of regulatory overlap.[7] They argue that the Omnibus Law technique enhances both the drafting process and the implementation of the rules, leading to increased efficiency in governance.

Constitutional law expert Sodikin expands upon this perspective, asserting that the Job Creation Law not only consolidates disparate regulations, it also serves to mitigate regulatory proliferation and redundancy. Sodikin contends that this streamlining has the potential to expedite governmental performance across various sectors, including the economic, health, and administrative domains.[8]

The discourse surrounding the omnibus law technique in the context of the Job Creation Law crystallizes around the novelty of the omnibus technique within the Indonesian legal framework. Potential inconsistencies have arisen within the established legal hierarchy, resulting in the potential misuse of administrative actions in the law's implementation. Sodikin further emphasizes that the legitimacy of the omnibus law technique, as applied in the Job Creation Law, necessitates adjustments to the existing hierarchy of regulations. The introduction of concepts and theories diverging from established

5 DPR-RI, "Peringati 'May Day', Nasir Djamil Sebut UU Ciptaker Lebih Berpihak Ke Pengusaha," DPR.go.id, May 9, 2023, https://emedia.dpr.go.id/2023/05/09/peringati-may-day-nasir-djamil-sebut-uu-ciptaker-lebih-berpihak-ke-pengusaha/.

6 Yustinus Prastowo, "Mujarabkah Omnibus Law Sebagai Obat Lesu Ekonomi?," in *Makalah Disampaikan Dalam Seminar Yang Diselenggarakan Oleh Ikatan Akuntan Indonesia Bekerjasama Dengan CITA*, edited by Fajry Akbar and Fatih Amar Maulana. (Jakarta: Center for Indonesia Taxation Analysis, 2019).

7 Moh Zainol Arief and Sutrisni Sutrisni, "Analisis Politik Hukum Tentang Omnibus Law Di Indonesia," *Jurnal Jendela Hukum* 8, no. 1 (2021): 19–28.

8 Sodikin, "Paradigm of Law in The Omnibus Law Concept Relating To Legal Norm Applicable in Indonesia," *Jurnal RechtsVinding: Media Pembinaan Hukum Nasional* 9, no. 1 (2020): 143–60.

national legal models and norms suggests that the omnibus law approach may precipitate significant alterations to the national legislative system.

The legislative process in Indonesia has historically been governed by Law No. 12/2011, as amended by Law No. 5/2019, Concerning the Formation of Legislation. This framework establishes a hierarchical structure for the nation's legal norms, as delineated in Article 7(1) of Law No. 12/2011. The resulting hierarchy, in descending order of precedence, is as follows:

1. The 1945 Constitution
2. Decisions of the People's Consultative Assembly
3. Laws and Government Regulations in Lieu of Laws (Perpu)
4. Government Regulations
5. Presidential Regulations
6. Provincial Regulations
7. District and City Regulations

Article 7(2) of Law No. 12/2011 explicitly stipulates that the legal force of legislation in Indonesia is contingent upon this hierarchical structure. This structure is further reinforced by Article 22A of the 1945 Constitution, which mandates that the formulation of formal laws by the legislature must adhere to procedures established by the law. Therefore, any legislative process that deviates from the procedures outlined in Law No. 12/2011 may be deemed formally defective.

The theoretical underpinning of this hierarchical approach to legislation finds its roots in the works of the prominent legal theorist, Hans Kelsen. Kelsen's theory of the hierarchy of norms posits that in the creation of laws, lower norms must derive their validity from, and conform to, higher norms.[9] Hans Nawiasky further refined this concept by proposing a more detailed stratification of legal norms. According to Nawiasky's theory, legal norms in legislation are arranged in the following ascending order: a) Implementing regulations and autonomous regulations; b) Laws in the formal sense; c) The constitution of the state; d) The fundamental norms of the state.[10] Therefore, both the substantive content and the formal process of law-making must align with higher legal norms, specifically the decisions of the People's Consultative Assembly and the 1945 Constitution.

The formation of the omnibus legislation, such as the Job Creation Law in Indonesia, necessitates a comprehensive approach to public involvement, underscoring the principle of transparency that is fundamental to democratic

9 Lars Vinx, *Hans Kelsen's Pure Theory of Law: Legality and Legitimacy* (Oxford: Oxford University Press, 2007), https://doi.org/10.1093/acprof:oso/9780199227952.001.0001; Hans Kelsen, *The Essence and Value of Democracy* (Rowman & Littlefield, 2013).

10 Hans Nawiasky, *Allgemeine Rechtslehre Als System Lichen Grundbegriffe* (Zurich: Benziger, 1948).

governance.[11] This imperative for broad public participation is intrinsically linked to the legal fiction principle, which presumes universal understanding and adherence to enacted regulations. Jimly Asshiddiqie, a prominent legal scholar, has identified several potential negative consequences associated with the omnibus law methodology, particularly concerning public participation (diminution in the quality of public engagement, erosion of public trust in parliamentary institutions, and fragmentation and disorganization of public discourse).[12]

In response to these concerns, the revision of Law No. 12/2011 through the enactment of Law No. 13/2022 represents a significant legislative effort to reinforce meaningful public involvement and participation. This strengthening of public engagement is predicated on an orderly and responsible process, encompassing three fundamental prerequisites:

1. The right to be heard: Ensuring that public voices and perspectives are actively solicited and received in the legislative process.
2. The right to be considered: Mandating that public input is genuinely evaluated and taken into account in policy formulation.
3. The right to be explained: Requiring that decisions and outcomes are elucidated to the public, providing clarity on how their input influenced the legislative outcome.

It is crucial to recognize that the omnibus law methodology is inextricably linked to the evolving political-legal landscape in Indonesia. This process represents a transition from the current legal framework (*ius constitutum*) toward aspirational future objectives.

Theoretical Legal Approaches to Omnibus Law

Asshiddiqie's analysis of omnibus law practices across various jurisdictions reveals two predominant patterns of application.[13] Firstly, there is the utilization of a single legislative act to amend multiple existing laws concurrently, modifying specific provisions without wholesale repeal. Secondly, there is an integration of several laws into a unified, comprehensive statute, simultaneously repealing (or invalidating) related prior legislation while selectively modifying content as necessary.

11 Suwandi Arham and Ahmad Saleh, "Omnibus Law Dalam Perspektif Hukum Indonesia," *Petitum* 7, no. 2 Oktober (2019): 72–81.

12 Jimly Asshiddiqie, *Omnibus Law Dan Penerapannya Di Indonesia* (Jakarta: Konstitusi Press, 2020).

13 Jimly Asshiddiqie, *Omnibus Law Dan Penerapannya Di Indonesia* (Jakarta: Konstitusi Press, 2020).

A comprehensive analysis of the Omnibus Law methodology necessitates consideration beyond the vertical aspect of legislative legitimacy. Two theoretical frameworks offer valuable perspectives. Firstly, there is Montesquieu's theory, which posits that all beings have their own laws; that natural laws cannot be changed or rejected; that religious laws comes from God; and that moral laws rely on philosophers who can make and change the laws. Political law (constitutional structure, the relationship between rulers and the ruled, the combination of power, superiority, and authority), is distinct from civil law (the relationship between individual desires).[14] The omnibus law method in Montesquieu's approach relates to constitutional policy and is based on a political configuration of the executive and legislative regimes to facilitate foreign investment. This foreign investment allows lawmakers to operate more freely in Indonesia, without considering the fundamental rights of society. These societal rights have a close relationship with every process of legal regulation. Individual rights, for example, are related to employment, which in the Omnibus Law cannot guarantee the constitutional relationship between workers and employers. Secondly, Hans Kelsen's theory states that the legal system is a hierarchy with tiered rules.[15] Lower laws must align with higher legal norms, and the highest legal rules must be based on the most essential norms. According to this theory, the Omnibus Law must undergo a systematic review to align with the Indonesian Constitution, Pancasila, and the 1945 Constitution. The concept of harmonizing legal norms through the Omnibus Law by the government must, therefore, seek a hierarchical basis in the constitution so that the Omnibus Law maintains the dignity of the constitution. However, in the 1945 Constitution, no material mentions the basis for formulating the Omnibus Law.[16]

The Indonesian legal system exemplifies a hybrid framework, predominantly rooted in the continental European tradition, while accommodating Indonesia's diverse ethnic, racial, religious, and cultural tapestry. Indonesia's pluralism persists despite the historical principle of concordance, which sought

14 Anne M. Cohler, Basia Carolyn Miller, and Harold Samuel Stone, *Montesquieu: The Spirit of the Laws* (Cambridge: Cambridge University Press, 1989); Sharon R. Krause, "Laws, Passion, and the Attractions of Right Action in Montesquieu," *Philosophy & Social Criticism* 32, no. 2 (2006): 211–30; Mark H. Waddicor, *Montesquieu and the Philosophy of Natural Law*, vol. 37 (Berlin: Springer Science & Business Media, 2012).

15 Lars Vinx, "Hans Kelsen and the Material Constitution of Democracy," *Jurisprudence* 12, no. 4 (2021): 466–90; Lars Vinx, *Hans Kelsen's Pure Theory of Law: Legality and Legitimacy* (Oxford: Oxford University Press, 2007), https://doi.org/10.1093/acprof:oso/9780199227952.001.0001; Hans Kelsen, "On the Pure Theory of Law," *Israel Law Review* 1, no. 1 (1966): 1–7; Hans Kelsen, "What Is the Pure Theory of Law?," in *Law and Morality* (London: Routledge, 2017), 101–8, https://doi.org/10.4324/9781315092003-6.

16 Henry Donald Lumbantoruan, "Pembentukan Regulasi Badan Usaha Dengan Model Omnibus Law," *To-Ra* 3, no. 1 (2017): 463–72.

to extend European (specifically Dutch) legal norms to various societal segments within the Dutch East Indies, the precursor to modern Indonesia.[17]

As a constitutional state, Indonesia adheres to fundamental legal principles, including the supremacy of the law,[18] equality before the law,[19] and constitutional protection of individual rights.[20] In light of these principles, the implementation of omnibus legislation necessitates careful consideration, particularly with respect to administrative structures. The potential for systematic marginalization of regional autonomy also warrants a thorough examination. The consolidation of disparate policies into overarching statutory provisions, as envisaged by the omnibus law concept, may inadvertently constrain the latitude of regional governments. This potential constraint arises from the hierarchical nature of the legal system, which requires all subordinate legislation to conform to the general provisions of the Omnibus Law. Any centralization may impinge upon localized cultural traditions, including customary laws, which resist uniform national application.

It is imperative to note that conflicts between legal norms, while significant, should not be the sole impetus for omnibus legislation. The government must undertake a comprehensive assessment, encompassing teleological, philosophical, and juridical perspectives, to preserve societal values of justice. Should the omnibus legislation be deemed to be the optimal solution, it is incumbent upon the government to meticulously codify each substantive element of any conflicting laws, ensuring a coherent and harmonized legal framework.

Jurisprudential Debates Surrounding Omnibus Law

According to Zakaria, the issues surrounding the formation of the Omnibus Law have led certain parties to file for a judicial review in the constitutional court.[21] A judicial review petition was then partially granted by the constitutional court. In Decision Number 91/PUU-XVIII/2020, the constitutional court ruled that the implementation of the Job Creation Law should be suspended due to formal defects in the legislative process of the law. In response, lawmakers enacted Law No. 13/2022 Concerning the Second Amendment to Law No. 12/2011 Concerning the Formation of Legislation (Second

17 Fajar Nurhardianto, "Sistem Hukum Dan Posisi Hukum Indonesia," *Jurnal Tapis: Jurnal Teropong Aspirasi Politik Islam* 11, no. 1 (2015): 33–44.

18 Hayat Hayat, "Keadilan Sebagai Prinsip Negara Hukum: Tinjauan Teoritis Dalam Konsep Demokrasi," *PADJADJARAN Jurnal Ilmu Hukum (Journal of Law)* 2, no. 2 (2015), https://doi.org/10.22304/pjih.v2n2.a10.

19 Haposan Siallagan, "Penerapan Prinsip Negara Hukum Di Indonesia," *Sosiohumaniora* 18, no. 2 (2016): 122–28.

20 Atang Hermawan Usman, "Kesadaran Hukum Masyarakat Dan Pemerintah Sebagai Faktor Tegaknya Negara Hukum Di Indonesia," *Jurnal Wawasan Yuridika* 30, no. 1 (2015): 26–53.

21 Erlangga Zakaria, "Penerapan Omnibus Law Dalam Sistem Legislasi Nasional Menurut Undang-Undang Nomor 13 Tahun 2022," *Innovative: Journal Of Social Science Research* 3, no. 3 (2023): 10719–33.

Amendment Law). This law serves as the basis for lawmakers to use the omnibus method in drafting legislative proposals.

Debates and discussions regarding the Omnibus Law in Indonesia began after President Joko Widodo urged the House of Representatives to cooperate in drafting a single bill that could amend several laws simultaneously, comprising even dozens of laws, which became known as omnibus law. The Job Creation Omnibus Law was subsequently realized through the enactment of the Job Creation Bill. President Joko Widodo signed the Job Creation Bill on November 2, 2020, at which time it became Law No. 11/2020 Concerning Job Creation.

However, Law No. 11/2020 was later annulled and conditionally declared unconstitutional by the constitutional court. In response, the president issued Government Regulation in Lieu of Law No. 2/2022 Concerning Job Creation. This government regulation was subsequently ratified through the enactment of Law No. 6/2023 Concerning the Determination of Government Regulations in Lieu of Law Number 2 of 2022 (the Job Creation Law of 2023).

Government Regulation No. 2/2022 Concerning Job Creation employed the omnibus method similarly to the previous Job Creation Law. This is evidenced by the numerous related laws covered in the regulation's articles. The structure of the government regulation comprises 15 chapters and 186 articles with explanationsamending, abolishing, or establishing new regulations across 75 laws, while also revoking and declaring invalid three laws, including Law No. 11/2020 Concerning Job Creation.

The omnibus method, as stipulated in Article 64(1b) of Law Number 13 of 2022, states that the omnibus method is a method of drafting legislation with three criteria:

1. Contains new content
2. Modifies content that is related and/or necessary in various laws of the same type and hierarchy
3. Revokes laws of the same type and hierarchy

New content in the omnibus method consists of: a) content that was previously not regulated in legislation using the omnibus method; and/or b) the addition of content in legislation amended through the omnibus method. There is an example of new content, as referred to in Letter (a) of the Job Creation Government Regulation, in which the provisions in Article 6 and Article 178 of Government Regulation No. 2/2022 relate to investment and business activities. These two articles represent new formulations that have emerged simultaneously by enacting the Job Creation Government Regulation. They are not articles taken from other laws.

The new content, as referred to in Letter (b), represents an addition of content to the legislation as amended through the Job Creation Omnibus

Law. An example is in the addition of Articles 46 A-E in the revision of Law Number 40 of 2004 Concerning the National Social Security System. The authors argue that the addition of this new content has indirect consequences for the number and structure of articles in the National Social Security System Law. Therefore, in the overall implementation of the National Social Security System Law, attention must be paid to the additional formulations contained in Articles 46 A-E.

In addition to containing new content, the omnibus method also modifies related and/or necessary content in various laws provided they have the same type and hierarchy. The Government Regulation Concerning Job Creation in terms of content and in terms of hierarchy is the same as several related laws whose content is amended by the Job Creation Government Regulation. Content that is related to and/or necessary for the Job Creation Government Regulation to be modified includes Article 81 of the Employment Chapter, which in turn amends Article 13 of Law No. 13/2003 Concerning Employment.

The enactment of the Job Creation Government Regulation, through the application of the omnibus method, also revokes several laws. The revocation of laws through the Job Creation Government Regulation is carried out for three laws, which are Staatsblad Year 1926 Number 226 and Staatsblad Year 1940 Number 450 Concerning Disturbance Law (*Hinder Ordonnantie*); Law Number 3 of 1982 Concerning Mandatory Company Registration; and Law Number 11 of 2020 Concerning Job Creation. Each of these laws is repealed successively in Article 110, Article 116, and Article 185. Revoking these three laws also simultaneously removes their binding force through the narrative: "revoked and declared invalid."

Critical Analysis of the Job Creation Law

Conceptual Framework of Governmental Authority

Authority in Indonesian administrative law often overlaps with the term, '"power." The terms "authority" and "power" have different meanings. Both terms have been definitively classified historically through Law No. 30/2014 Concerning Government Administration. According to this law, authority constitutes the power of a state body or state administrator to act under public law. Authority is the inherent right vested in a governmental body or in a state administrator to make decisions and take actions in the execution of governmental administration. This concept finds parallel expression in the 1945 Constitution of Indonesia, which interprets authority within the framework of the *Trias Politica* doctrine and state administrative law, the latter being a fundamental area of study within the broader field of public law. *Trias Politica*, according to Article 4(1) of the 1945 Constitution, states that the power or authority of the government lies with the president as head of the executive branch. The legislative and judicial branches' roles are as stated in Article 20(1) and Article 24(1). Article 20(1) of the 1945 Constitution states that the power or authority to formulate laws lies in the hands of the DPR (House of Representatives). Article 24(1) further states that the power or authority of the judiciary lies with the supreme court and judicial bodies under the supreme court, within the general judiciary, religious judiciary, military judiciary, state administrative judiciary, and constitutional court.

Regional governments in the Job Creation Law emphasize their role as an extension of the central government, which in this case primarily indicates the president as head of the executive branch. This distinction can be seen in Article 174 of the Job Creation Law, which states:

> With the enactment of this Law, the authority of ministers, heads of institutions, or regional governments that have been stipulated in the Law to implement or establish regulations must be interpreted as the implementation of the president's authority.

Based on this provision, the central government still overshadows the implementation of regional autonomy. This contradicts the provisions of the 1945 Constitution, which adhere to the principle of decentralization as a means to implement regional autonomy. As a principle of regional autonomy, decentralization assumes the dispersion of authority and the separation of powers between the central and regional governments.[22] Regional governments, as stated in Articles 18 and 18A of the 1945 Constitution, have the authority to manage regional affairs and are not under the central government's authority. Furthermore, Article 18(2) emphasizes that provincial, district, and city governments regulate and manage their own governance affairs based on the principles of autonomy and the delegation of tasks.

The authority of the central government (represented by the president) in the context of regional governance is limited to aspects of supervision, as per the principle of, "no autonomy without supervision," through executive review functions that involve the examination of autonomous regulations of regional regulations, regulations of regional heads, and other regulations related to regional government administration.[23] This supervision aspect itself is a characteristic that shows the difference between a federal state and a unitary state. In a unitary state, regional autonomy entails central government oversight of regional governments. Thus, the substance of the Job Creation Law systematically embodies the principle of centralization, which contradicts the spirit of regional autonomy after the New Order era.

22 Bagir Manan, *Menyongsong Fajar Otonomi Daerah* (Yogkakarta: Pusat Studi Hukum (PSH) Fakultas Hukum UII, 2001).
23 HR Ridwan, *Hukum Administrasi Negara* (Jakarta: Rajawali Press, 2018).

Discretionary Powers: A Legal Perspective

As explained in the previous section, the state administrative law system in Indonesia has changed over time, alongside developmental progress in all areas. The use of discretion has also colored this development. The government's desire to accelerate the domestic economy through investment gave birth to the enactment of Law No. 11/2020 Concerning Job Creation. To facilitate investment, this law directly shifts the system of government administration. Article 175 of the Job Creation Law specifically utilizes discretion, which is believed to have catalyzed the executive government's flexibility in exercising discretion. Before this law came into effect, the practice of government discretion in licensing and investment was considered to have narrowed the scope of government officials' maneuverability.

Before the enactment of this law, Indonesia had several investment constraint issues.[24] Firstly, there was inconsistency in policy regulations regarding investment, which was often due to conflicting interests. Secondly, bureaucratic obstacles, especially at the local level, resulted in increased investment costs and the proliferation of corruption.[25] Thirdly, there were concerns about unabsorbed productive human resources in the labor market due to low skilled labor and poor work ethic. Fourthly, inadequate investment protection led investors to hesitate to contribute to domestic economic development. Fifthly, there was a demonstrable lack of coordination between institutions due to unclear roles and functions at all levels of government, with overlapping policies between central and regional governments especially indicating this constraint.

The Job Creation Law, as a legal basis for the use of the omnibus law method in Indonesia's legal system, serves as an alternative to overcome these obstacles. The omnibus law technique, which underpins the seminal law, brings about changes in legislation, including the repeal and enactment of various provisions from multiple regulations. In short, the state can change several laws with just one regulation in order to facilitate specific policies. Consequently, the omnibus law technique guides the government to change other investment-related laws.

According to the government administration law, discretion enables the decisions and/or actions determined or taken by government officials to address specific issues encountered in the administration of government. This helps facilitate government administration and provide legal certainty when any legislation providing options lackscomprehensiveness, remains unclear, or

24 Subadi Subadi and Tiara Oliviarizky Toersina, "Perkembangan Konsep Atau Pemikiran Teoritik Tentang Diskresi Berbasis Investasi Di Daerah," *Mimbar Hukum-Fakultas Hukum Universitas Gadjah Mada* 30, no. 1 (2018): 17–31.

25 Benny Irawan Natasasmita, "Diskresi Sebagai Tindak Pidana Korupsi: Kajian Kriminologi Dan Hukum Terhadap Fenomena Pejabat Otoritas," *MIMBAR: Jurnal Sosial Dan Pembangunan* 27, no. 2 (2011): 143–49.

has resulted from government stagnation.[26] Therefore, the utilization of discretion by government officials aims to fill certain legal gaps resulting from absent or lacking rules regarding an issue in government administration, thereby providing benefits for the public interest.

Government officials who decide to exercise discretion under the government administration law are subject to limitations designed to prevent the abuse of power by government officials. These limitations are manifested in the conditions for using discretion andmust be adhered to by government officials when exercising discretion. These conditions consist of the following:

- Conditions must adhere to the purpose of discretion as regulated in Article 22(2) of the government administration law.
- Discretion must not contradict the provisions found in the legislation.
- Discretion must comply with the General Principles of Good Governance.
- Discretion must be based on objective reasoning.
- Discretion must not create conflicts of interest.
- When utilizingdiscretion, officials must act with good intention.

These conditions for utilizing discretion in decision-making are established with clear limitations. If the use of discretion is not restricted, maladministration may occur due to the abuse of authority, leading to criminal acts and corruption.

With the evolution of the Indonesian government's desire to boost economic growth through investments to stay competitive with other countries, the enactment of Law No. 11/2020 Concerning Job Creation was passed as a means to facilitate investment. The impact of the enactment of this law has led to several shifts in the administration of government affairs, one of which concerns discretion as regulated in Article 175. This shift in the concept of discretion is due to the government's belief that the existing concept of discretion has narrowed the scope for government officials to issue discretionary decisions related to licensing in their efforts to expedite investment. Thus, in the Job Creation Law, the concept of discretion has changed from being initially limited to being now expanded. However, this change in the scope of discretion has sparked controversy in society, because the alteration in the concept of discretion contained in the Job Creation Law is considered overly broad and has potentially negative repercussions for the stability of government administration.

Essentially, investment can boost economic growth, accelerate development, and empower communities by creating more job opportunities through

26 Mery Farida, "Problematika Konsep Diskresi Dalam Penyelenggaraan Administrasi Pemerintahan Pasca Undang-Undang Cipta Kerja," *Jurnal Ilmiah Hukum Dan Hak Asasi Manusia* 1, no. 1 (2021): 11–20.

investments. However, in Indonesia, there are a number of obstacles to investing caused by the following factors:[27]

- Inconsistencies in policy regulations regarding investment
- Bureaucratic obstacles, particularly at the local level, resulting in increased investment costs, extortion, and corruptionadversely affecting investment in Indonesia
- Issues related to human resources, particularly in the labor sector, including low productivity of Indonesian workers, lack of skills, and poor work ethic
- Low levels of investment protection guarantees
- Lack of coordination among institutions stemming from an ambiguity regarding the roles and functions of government agencies and leading to disharmonious coordination between agencies and the overlapping of policies between the central and regional governments

Therefore, the Job Creation Law was enacted to address these investment obstacles. The Job Creation Law was established using the omnibus law method, which was previously only known in countries following the common law system. The omnibus law method is a legislative technique to address issues caused by overlapping regulations or excessive regulation.[28] Audrey O'Brien and Marc Bosc define "omnibus law" as a legislative technique involving the repeal, amendment, and/or enactment of several provisions from various laws, enabling changes to multiple laws through a single piece of legislation facilitating a specific policy adopted by the state.[29] Consequently, with the enactment of the Job Creation Law, changes will occur in other Indonesian laws related to expediting investment.

One piece of legislation amended by the enactment of the Job Creation Law is the law on government administration, regulated in Article 175 of the Job Creation Law. This was done because the law on government administration was considered to contain provisions that hindered investment development in Indonesia. Changes to the law on government administration, particularly those related to discretion, aim to facilitate government officials in issuing discretionary decisions related to the speed of investment, especially in licensing matters.

Discretion, also known as, *freies ermessen*, is the freedom of action granted to government officials according to their authority and exercised for society's

27 Subadi Subadi and Tiara Oliviarizky Toersina, "Perkembangan Konsep Atau Pemikiran Teoritik Tentang Diskresi Berbasis Investasi Di Daerah," *Mimbar Hukum-Fakultas Hukum Universitas Gadjah Mada* 30, no. 1 (2018): 17–31.

28 Antoni Putra, "Penerapan Omnibus Law Dalam Upaya Reformasi Regulasi," *Jurnal Legislasi Indonesia* 17, no. 1 (2020): 1–10.

29 Bayu Dwi Anggono, "Omnibus Law Sebagai Teknik Pembentukan Undang-Undang: Peluang Adopsi Dan Tantangannya Dalam Sistem Perundang-Undangan Indonesia," *Jurnal RechtsVinding* 9, no. 1 (2020): 17–37.

benefit. As stated by Sjachran Basah, *freies ermessen* is the freedom to act on one's own initiative and in accordance with the law, as established by the rule of law based on Pancasila.[30] The law on government administration delineates the scope and circumstances under which government officials are authorized to exercise discretion. Article 23 of this law stipulates that discretionary power may be invoked in situations characterized by regulatory incompleteness, ambiguity, absence, or in a legal vacuum, necessitating decisive action. Furthermore, discretion is permissible when government stagnation impedes the realization of broader public interests.

This legislative framework confers upon government officials the *droit function*, empowering them to interpret legislation within the bounds of their discretionary authority. However, this power is not absolute and is subject to legal constraints and judicial oversight. Any discretionary action that results in societal harm may be subject to challenge through administrative or general courts, as elucidated by S.F. Marbun and Moh Mahfud M.D. in their seminal work, *Pokok-Pokok Administrasi Hukum Administrasi Negara*.[31]

The law on government administration originally imposed specific limitations on the exercise of discretion, which included the following:

1. Adherence to the objectives of discretion as stipulated in Article 22(2) of the law.
2. Compliance with existing legislative provisions.
3. Conformity with the General Principles of Good Governance (AUPB).
4. Objective justification for discretionary decisions.
5. Avoidance of conflicts of interest.
6. Exercise of discretion in good faith.

These constraints were designed to prevent abuse of discretionary power and to ensure its judicious application within the framework of administrative law.

However, the enactment of the Job Creation Law introduced a significant paradigm shift in the conceptualization and application of administrative discretion. Notably, it eliminated a crucial limitation: the requirement that discretionary decisions must not contravene existing legislation. This legislative change substantially broadens the scope of discretionary power available to government officials, effectively removing the constraint of strict legislative compliance.

The rationale underpinning this expansion of discretionary authority, as articulated in the academic discourse surrounding the Job Creation Law, stems from a perceived inefficacy of the previous, more restricted model of

30 Sjachran Basah, *Eksistensi Dan Tolak Ukur Badan Peradilan Administrasi Di Indonesia* (Bandung: Alumni, 1989).

31 S. F. Marbun and Moh Mahfud MD, *Pokok-Pokok Administrasi Hukum Administrasi Negara* (Yogyakarta: Liberty, 2006).

discretion. The limitations imposed by the law on government administration were deemed to constrain the ability of government officials to facilitate investment licensing processes effectively, thus necessitating a more expansive approach to discretion.

The expansion of discretionary powers in the Job Creation Law represents a significant shift in Indonesian administrative law, one aimed at enhancing governmental flexibility in decision-making and particularly in the realm of investment facilitation. This legislative change is intended to broaden the scope of maneuverability for government officials, potentially enabling novel legal approaches to accelerate investment at both the central and regional levels and thereby stimulating national economic growth.

The expansion of discretionary authority presents a complex dichotomy in administrative governance. As noted in the discourse, an overly restrictive approach to discretion may impede effective governance, by constraining officials' ability to make timely and context-appropriate decisions. Conversely, excessively broad discretionary powers may lead to actions exceeding legitimate authority (*excess du pouvoir*), potentially resulting in malfeasance and corruption.[32] The Job Creation Law's approach to discretion thus emerges as a double-edged sword. While the law may enhance Indonesia's investment climate by allowing for more agile and responsive governance, it simultaneously increases the risk of abuse by government officials.

Public criticism of the expanded discretion concept in the Job Creation Law stems from concerns about the law's potentially detrimental impact on governmental administration. The fundamental principle of legality in Indonesian administrative law, which dictates that all official actions must be grounded in the law, appears to be challenged by this legislative change.[33] The removal of the provision requiring discretionary actions to align with existing legislation has raised significant societal concerns. Sjachran Basah's assertion that the exercise of discretion must remain rooted in the law, even as it provides flexibility in governance, highlights the traditional approach to limited discretion in Indonesia.[34] Basah's perspective suggests that discretionary actions should not arbitrarily contravene higher-level legislation, on the principle that it seems at odds with the Job Creation Law's expanded concept of discretion.

This shift toward broader discretionary powers in the Job Creation Law represents a departure from Indonesia's traditional adherence to the concept of limited discretion. The consequent changes also raise fundamental questions

32 Benny Irawan Natasasmita, "Diskresi Sebagai Tindak Pidana Korupsi: Kajian Kriminologi Dan Hukum Terhadap Fenomena Pejabat Otoritas," *MIMBAR: Jurnal Sosial Dan Pembangunan* 27, no. 2 (2011): 143–49.

33 Lutfil Ansori, "Diskresi Dan Pertanggungjawaban Pemerintah Dalam Penyelenggaraan Pemerintahan," *Jurnal Yuridis* 2, no. 1 (2015): 135–50.

34 Sjachran Basah, *Eksistensi Dan Tolak Ukur Badan Peradilan Administrasi Di Indonesia* (Bandung: Alumni, 1989).

about the balance between administrative flexibility, legal certainty, and the potential for increased vulnerability to abuse.

Potential Constitutional Implications of Discretionary Powers

The expansion of discretionary powers in the Job Creation Law presents a significant challenge to Indonesia's constitutional framework, particularly in relation to the principle of rule of law enshrined in Article 1(3) of the 1945 Constitution. This constitutional provision mandates that governance must be rooted in the law, rather than in the arbitrary authority vested in government officials. The broadened scope of discretion afforded to regional government officials under the Job Creation Law raises legitimate concerns about the potential for the unconstitutional use of discretion.

Unconstitutional discretion, as Indra Wicaksono elucidates, refers to the creation of legal products that contravene the 1945 Constitution.[35] The removal of the explicit requirement that discretionary actions must not contradict existing legislation significantly increases the risk of such unconstitutional outcomes. The expansion of discretionary powers may allow political interests to unduly influence decision-making processes, potentially leading to actions that conflict with constitutional principles. The elimination of the legislative compliance requirement in the exercise of discretion has been widely criticized as overly broad. This change also potentially undermines the hierarchical structure of the Indonesian legal system, in which the 1945 Constitution stands as the supreme law. The concern is that discretionary actions, when no longer explicitly bound by legislative constraints, may conflict with constitutional provisions, thereby compromising the integrity of the legal system and the principle of the rule of law.

Jimly Ashidiqqie emphasizes the role of the 1945 Constitution in economic policymaking, which is particularly pertinent in this context.[36] The constitution serves not only as a reference point for governance but also as an instrument for balancing market dynamics and engineering economic development toward the common goals of justice, shared prosperity, and freedom. The constitution further functions as a mediator between state, societal, and market interests. Therefore, while the Job Creation Law aims to improve the economy and streamline investment processes, it must do so without compromising constitutional integrity. Economic policies, no matter how urgent or potentially beneficial, cannot supersede or violate constitutional provisions.

35 Indra Wicaksono, "Optimalisasi Peran Mahkamah Konstitusi Dalam Pembangunan Hukum Nasional Dengan Model Preventive Review," *Majalah Hukum Nasional* 49, no. 1 (2019): 91–116.

36 Elviandri Elviandri, Khuzdaifah Dimyati, and Absori Absori, "Quo Vadis Negara Kesejahteraan: Meneguhkan Ideologi Welfare State Negara Hukum Kesejahteraan Indonesia," *Mimbar Hukum* 31, no. 2 (2019): 252–66.

Contradictions with Principles of Good Governance

The Principles of Good Governance (AUPB) serves as a constraining factor in the formation of administrative discretion, necessitating that such discretionary actions do not contravene the AUPB. Moreover, the AUPB functions as a mechanism to guide and ensure that the authority exercised by government officials remains subject to control and is safeguarded against potential abuses of power.[37] Therefore, discretionary decisions issued by government officials should not impinge upon societal interests. The AUPB delineates specific criteria for discretion, including: fair play; diligence; purity of purpose; balance; and legal certainty.

Within the context of governmental administration, the AUPB finds statutory expression in Article 10 of the administration of government law, which enumerates the following principles: legal certainty; utility; impartiality; diligence; non-abuse of authority; transparency; public interest; and good service. These principles, as applied to the exercise of discretion, may be construed as a test for determining the alignment of discretionary actions with the broader public interest. Should a discretionary decision be found to contravene the AUPB, it may be subject to nullification.

However, a novel legal quandary has emerged consequent to the modification of the discretion concept within the Job Creation Law, which potentially permits deviations from the principle of legal certainty. This principle is fundamental to the rule of law, prioritizing the foundation of statutory provisions, propriety, precision, and justice in governmental administrative policies. The elimination of the requirement that discretion must not contradict legislation, as stipulated in the Job Creation Law, may result in discretionary actions lacking a clear legal basis and thereby engendering legal uncertainty in governmental administration. Furthermore, according to Gustav Radbruch's legal philosophy, legal certainty pertains to certainty about the law itself.

Thus, to align with Radbruch's conceptualization of legal certainty, the discretionary framework within the Job Creation Law should, at a minimum, satisfy four criteria:[38]

1. Positive law: The law must be grounded in legislation.

37 Elisa J. B. Sumeleh, "Implementasi Kewenangan Diskresi Dalam Perspektif Asas-Asas Umum Pemerintahan Yang Baik (AUPB) Berdasarkan Undang-Undang No. 30 Tahun 2014 Tentang Administrasi Pemerintahan," *Lex Administratum* 5, no. 9 (2017), https://ejournal.unsrat.ac.id/index.php/administratum/article/view/18158.

38 Gustav Radbruch, "Law's Image of the Human," *Oxford Journal of Legal Studies* 40, no. 4 (2020): 667–81; Gustav Radbruch, "Five Minutes of Legal Philosophy (1945)," *Oxford Journal of Legal Studies* 26, no. 1 (2006): 13–15; Fahmi Ramadhan Firdaus and Anna Erliyana, "Perlindungan Kebijakan Diskresi Dalam Penanganan Covid-19 Menurut Undang-Undang No. 2 Tahun 2020," *Jurnal Palar (Pakuan Law Review)* 6, no. 02 (2020).

2. Factual basis: The law should be predicated on facts (*Tatsachen*), rather than on subjective judicial formulations (e.g. good faith and propriety).
3. Clarity and implementability: The facts must be articulated with sufficient clarity to preclude misinterpretation or multiple interpretations, and they must be readily implementable.
4. Stability: Positive law should not be subject to frequent modifications.

Upon analysis, the discretionary concept embodied in the Job Creation Law appears to fall short of these criteria, particularly in its legislative basis, thereby potentially engendering a distortion of legal certainty in governmental administration. The revised discretionary concept may also contravene the principle of non-abuse of authority enshrined in the AUPB, and its expansive nature could potentially facilitate misuse of power by administrative officials.

The formation of discretion in governmental administration continues to be plagued by instances of abuse of power, often culminating in corruption. According to data released by the KPK up to 2021, 143 regional leaders were implicated in corruption cases, with discretionary power untempered by integrity cited as a contributing factor.[39] Despite the administration of government law's clear delineation of discretionary limits, misuse persists, carrying legal consequences and accountability across criminal, civil, and administrative domains.[40]

The misuse of discretion can be attributed, in part, to insufficient oversight from both central government and public entities. The expansion of discretionary powers in the Job Creation Law, without commensurate increases in oversight mechanisms, may exacerbate this issue by potentially allowing government officials to issue discretionary decisions that contravene existing legislation. Consequently, absent enhanced scrutiny over discretionary actions, the revised concept may prove counterproductive and perpetuate corruption within governmental administration.

Thus, the concept of discretion as articulated in the Job Creation Law presents significant challenges that require expeditious resolution to ensure that discretionary powers support the law's intended objective of stimulating investment, rather than facilitating further abuses of authority. Discretionary actions and policy regulations may be deemed invalid or aberrant under several circumstances:[41]

39 Henry Hilmawan Wibowo, Dimas Fahmi Rizalqi, and Sri Husda Yani, "Pengaruh Revisi Undang-Undang Kpk Dalam Kegiatan Pemberantasan Korupsi Di Indonesia," *Jurnal Sosial Dan Sains* 1, no. 8 (2021): 943–50.

40 Made Suteja, "Pengawasan Terhadap Penyalahgunaan Wewenang Polri Mengadakan Tindakan Lain Menurut Hukum Yang Bertanggung Jawab (Diskresi)," *Jurnal Magister Hukum Udayana* 2, no. 2 (2013): 44073.

41 Nehru Asyikin and Adam Setiawan, "Tanggung Jawab Jabatan Dan Tanggung Jawab Pribadi Dalam Penggunaan Diskresi," *Jurnal Hukum & Pembangunan* 50, no. 3 (2020): 633–46.

1. Contravention of existing legislation and legal principles (*rechtsbeginsel*)
2. Where there are elements constituting abuse of authority or arbitrariness
3. Violation of principles of rationality and/or human rights
4. Contradiction of principles of good governance or good government (*Goed Bestuur*)
5. Presence of elements indicative of maladministration

The urgency of addressing these issues in the discretionary framework cannot be overstated. A recalibration of these concepts is imperative to create better alignment with the foundational principles of administrative law and good governance.

Implications for the Role of Administrative Courts

The impact of the enactment of the Job Creation Law in Indonesia not only changes the procedures for the administration of state affairs and extends discretion, it also alters the role and competence of the Administrative Court (PTUN) in adjudicating administrative cases. Public attention to these regulations focuses on the shortened time limit for the approval of applications by government bodies or officials, reduced from ten working days to five days. There is also attention being paid to regulations regarding electronic-based decision requests as stipulated in Article 53 of Law No. 30/2014 Concerning Government Administration, and to the diminishing role and authority of PTUN as the court that decides disputes regarding positive fictitious decisions. These changes raise questions about licensing disputes that should fall within PTUN's absolute competence to examine, adjudicate, and make decisions. PTUN, as a judicial body, has relative and absolute competencies. Relative competence refers to jurisdictional areas, while absolute competence refers to the types of cases that can be adjudicated.[42]

The number of PTUNs scattered across Indonesia is limited to 26, with only four administrative high courts located in Makassar, Surabaya, Jakarta, and Medan. Since the enactment of the Administration of Government Law in 2020, the five PTUNs in Indonesia have handled 152 cases.[43] These applications are not solely related to licensing but also involve positive fictitious decisions (silence or disregard of administrative officials who fail to issue written administrative decisions requested by individuals or legal entities).

42 Enrico Simanjuntak, *Hukum Acara Peradilan Tata Usaha Negara: Transformasi & Refleksi* (Jakarta: Sinar Grafika, 2021).

43 Ishviati Joenaini Koenti and Vinny Victoria Tanawani, "Komparasi Putusan Pengadilan Tata Usaha Negara Terhadap Gugatan Keputusan Fiktif Negatif, Permohonan Terhadap Keputusan Fiktif Positif Dan Perubahannya Pasca Undang-Undang Cipta Kerja," in *Perkembangan Bidang Sosial Humaniora Pertanian Dan Teknologi Mendukung Sustainable Development Goals*, ed. Untoro Budi Surono and Bayu Megaprastio (Yogkakarta: Kepel Press, 2023), 348–65.

Licensing-related applications amounted to 124 cases, with eight applications related to positive fictitious decisions in PTUN. Research by Koenti and Tanawani shows that out of all applications, PTUN granted 64%, while the rest were withdrawn or rejected.[44]

Law No. 30/2014 Concerning Government Administration, as amended by Law No. 11/2020 on Job Creation, significantly altered the scope of administrative governance. Article 175 of the Job Creation Law, as amended by the provisions in Article 53 of the government administration law regarding the PTUN authority to accept positive fictitious decision requests. Consequently, the Job Creation Law effectively eliminates PTUN's jurisdiction over positive fictitious requests, thereby removing its legal basis for adjudication in such matters. Article 175 of the Job Creation Law stipulates that further provisions concerning Article 53 of the government administration law shall be regulated by presidential regulation, which is considered legally binding.

The objective of administrative dispute resolution under the government administration law encompasses Administrative Decisions (KTUN). These include written determinations covering factual actions, and decisions of executive, legislative, judicial, and other state organs that are based on statutory provisions and the Principles of Good Governance. Such decisions are final in the broadest sense, potentially resulting in legal consequences which are also applicable to citizens (Article 87 of Law No. 30/2014).

In practice, decisions of government bodies or officials giving rise to disputes in PTUN may also include decisions on licensing (e.g. building permits, mining and forestry permits), determinations of legal status, rights and obligations, and employment-related decisions.[45] Following the enactment of the Job Creation Law, PTUN has lost its authority to adjudicate positive fictitious requests, thereby relinquishing its absolute competence in this area. The Job Creation Law explicitly states that the examination and adjudication of cases within PTUN's jurisdiction shall be further regulated through a presidential regulation. This implies that the technical aspects of positive fictitious requests will be delineated in the forthcoming presidential regulation. However, at the time of this writing, the presidential regulation concerning the technical aspects of positive fictitious requests has not been promulgated.

44 Ishviati Joenaini Koenti and Vinny Victoria Tanawani, "Komparasi Putusan Pengadilan Tata Usaha Negara Terhadap Gugatan Keputusan Fiktif Negatif, Permohonan Terhadap Keputusan Fiktif Positif Dan Perubahannya Pasca Undang-Undang Cipta Kerja," in *Perkembangan Bidang Sosial Humaniora Pertanian Dan Teknologi Mendukung Sustainable Development Goals*, ed. Untoro Budi Surono and Bayu Megaprastio (Yogkakarta: Kepel Press, 2023), 348–65.

45 Abdul Qodir Jaelani Jaelani, "Kewenangan Peradilan Tata Usaha Negara Dalam Mengadili Sengketa Keputusan Fiktif Negatif Dan Fiktif Positif," *Supremasi Hukum: Jurnal Kajian Ilmu Hukum* 6, no. 2 (2017); Yodi Martono Wahyunadi, "Kompetensi Absolut Pengadilan Tata Usaha Negara Dalam Konteks Undang-Undang Nomor 30 Tahun 2014 Tentang Administrasi Pemerintahan," *Jurnal Hukum Dan Peradilan* 5, no. 1 (2016): 135–54.

In a significant development, the constitutional court, through Decision No. 91/PUU-XVIII/2020, partially granted a formal review request against the Job Creation Law, declaring that this legislation suffered from formal defects. To address the resulting legal vacuum, the supreme court issued Circular Letter No. 2/2021, which provisionally allowed positive fictitious requests to continue to be submitted to the PTUN pending the issuance of the derivative presidential regulation mandated by the Omnibus Law.

Subsequently, the supreme court issued Circular Letter No. 5/2021 as a guideline for the judiciary's implementation of duties. This latter circular letter stipulates that the positive fictitious institution falls outside the jurisdiction of PTUN, ostensibly reinforcing the objectives of the Job Creation Law and providing guidance to other governmental agencies. However, it is crucial to note that circular letters lack the requisite legal force to compel PTUN judges to accept applications, thus necessitating robust arguments and systematic reasoning for their implementation. Besides, the reliance on a presidential regulation for the settlement of administrative cases may be deemed neither effective nor efficient, as it potentially diminishes the inherent authority of PTUN as the designated administrative judicial body.

The controversies surrounding the Omnibus Law on Job Creation law were not confined to its post-enactment period but extended to its drafting phase, particularly concerning alleged human rights violations related to information transparency and communication. In response, the Jakarta Legal Aid Institute (LBH), in conjunction with the Indonesian Workers' Union Confederation (KPBI), the Agrarian Reform Consortium (KPA), and the Mining Advocacy Network (Jatam), initiated legal proceedings against the president's letter (Surpres) on the Omnibus Law on Job Creation.[46] This lawsuit was filed with the administrative court under Case Number 97/G/2020/PTUN-JKT. During the trial proceedings on September 15, 2020, the plaintiffs presented expert testimony, including that of a commissioner from the National Commission on Human Rights (Komnas HAM). The expert witness elucidated that the drafting process of the Job Creation Bill, which formed the basis for the issuance of the Surpres, was characterized by a lack of transparency and discriminatory practices.

The Komnas HAM noted that the government imposed restrictions on public access to the Job Creation Bill. According to the expert witness, discriminatory practices in the law's drafting process were evident in the restriction or preferential treatment afforded to certain interest groups, a practice that fundamentally contravenes human rights principles. This preferential treatment was exemplified by the involvement of business interests in the formation of the

46 LBH-Jakarta, "Gugatan Surpres Omnibus Law: Komnas HAM Berikan Keterangan Nyatakan Penyusunan RUU Cipta Kerja Diskriminatif," 2020, https://bantuanhukum.or.id/gugatan-surpres-omnibus-law-komnas-ham-berikan-keterangan-nyatakan-penyusunan-ruu-cipta-kerja-diskriminatif/.

Omnibus Law Task Force, as established through the Minister of Economic Affairs Decree No. 378/2019. On the other hand, community stakeholders such as indigenous peoples, workers, and farmers were neither granted access to nor provided opportunities for contributing input on the draft legislation. These infringements on citizens' rights were deemed to constitute discriminatory practices.

On October 19, 2020, the Jakarta Administrative Court rendered a final ruling declaring the lawsuit inadmissible. Mukti et al. observe that while the lawsuit satisfied the requirements regarding the parties involved—with the plaintiffs being non-governmental organizations and the defendant being the president in his capacity as the highest administrative official—the objective of the lawsuit failed to meet the criteria for a KTUN.[47] The court determined that the president's letter (*Surpres*) concerning the Job Creation Bill did not constitute a form of policy regulation. The administrative court judges emphasized that KTUN, while issued by administrative officials, does not fall within the purview of administrative law but rather within the domain of constitutional law. In this context, the *Surpres* on the Job Creation Bill pertained to a horizontal relationship between the executive branch, represented by the president, and the legislative branch, represented by the House of Representatives.

However, Mukti et al. explained that the administrative court, in this case, did not use the dismissal process or screening process for incoming lawsuits as stipulated in Article 62 paragraph (1) of Law No. 51/2009 on Administrative Courts. In reality, the administrative court allowed this case to proceed, leading to legal uncertainty and a lengthy examination and proof process.

As previously explained, the Job Creation Law is unrelated to human rights violations. However, the shift in the administrative court's authority to decide on positive fictitious requests, which waned after the enactment of the Job Creation Law, opened the door to weakening human rights protection, particularly land rights and the rights of indigenous people.[48] Article 175 of the Job Creation Law, which amends the provisions of Article 53 paragraph (4) of Law No. 30/2014 on Government Administration, underscores this by stating that positive fictitious decisions will be regulated by a presidential regulation,

47 Surya Mukti Pratama, Adrian E. Rompis, and R. Adi Nurzaman, "Kewenangan PTUN Dalam Memeriksa Surat Presiden Tentang RUU Cipta Kerja Dan Implikasi Putusannya," *Risalah Hukum* (2021): 11–25, https://doi.org/10.30872/risalah.v17i1.516.

48 Nur Eka Fatimatuz Zahro and Ahmad Hasan Basri, "Konsep Permohonan Keputusan Fiktif Positif Pasca Berlakunya Pasal 175 Angka 7 Undang-Undang Nomor 6 Tahun 2023 Tentang Penetapan Peraturan Pengganti Undang-Undang Nomor 2 Tahun 2022 Tentang Cipta Kerja," *Journal of Law and Islamic Law* 1, no. 1 (2023): 1–23; Muhammad Alvin Nashir Alvin Nashir, "Pudarnya Kewenangan Peradilan Tata Usaha Negara Dalam Sengketa Perizinan Atas Undang-Undang Cipta Kerja (Omnibus Law)," *TARUNALAW: Journal of Law and Syariah* 2, no. 01 (2024): 84–95; Jusak Sindar, Jakobus Ronald Mawuntu, and Donna Okthalia Setiabudhi, "Penyelesaian Sengketa Keputusan Fiktif Positif Pasca Undang-Undang Cipta Kerja," *Jurnal Pendidikan Dan Konseling (JPDK)* 5, no. 2 (2023): 6045–51.

which has yet to be issued. The implication is that applicants do not have the means to process positive fictitious requests due to legal uncertainty and gaps.

According to the National Commission on Human Rights documents, the Job Creation Law eliminates several environmental permitting mechanisms, leading to conflicts between communities and companies.[49] For example, agrarian disputes involving indigenous groups' communal land rights and mining and palm oil companies in Papua. At specific points, indigenous people, as citizens, also have to face the state. After enactment of the Job Creation Law, opportunities for corporations and political oligarchs to influence investment permits in Papua have widened. In November 2020, the expansion using deforestation methods of PT Korindo, the largest palm oil company in Papua, negatively impacted indigenous communities.[50] Since 2001, this company has controlled 57,000 hectares of Papua's forest area.

Another case involves a palm oil plantation project on communal land owned by the Awyu tribe in Fofi District, Boven Digoel, Papua.[51] Initially, the Awyu tribe from the Woro clan filed an information dispute lawsuit with the Papua Public Information Commission (KIP) in August 2022. After the lawsuit was rejected in March 2023, the Awyu tribe filed a lawsuit with the Jayapura Administrative Court regarding the environmental feasibility permit issued by the Investment and One-Stop Integrated Services Office (DPMPTSP) to PT Indo Asiana Lestari. In Lawsuit No. 6/G/LH/2023/PTUN.JPR, the plaintiffs requested that the court to annul the DPMPTSP permit and respect the rights of indigenous communities over the disputed area covering 39,000 hectares. Aji, a legal representative from Greenpeace, stated that the environmental impact analysis documents for the palm oil plantation were manipulated, including coercion for residents to approve the palm oil project and exclusion of residents' opposition from the analysis documents. In this case, the Jayapura Administrative Court judges rejected the residents' lawsuit, represented by Hendrikus Woro, the leader of the Woro clan from the Awyu tribe. The judges considered that the environmental feasibility assessment team from the provincial forestry and environmental agency had conducted proper assessments and evaluations of the environmental impacts. Additionally, the issuance of the permit by DPMPTSP was deemed to comply with required procedures and the Principles of Good Governance (AUPB).

49 The Indonesian National Human Rights Commission, *4th Universal Periodic Review: 41st Session of The Working Group on the UPR Human Rights Council* (Jakarta: Komnas HAM, 2022).

50 Grace Frestisa Irena Hutabarat, "Kajian Green Politic Theory dalam Upaya Menangani Deforestasi Papua terkait Aktivitas Ekspansi," *Jurnal Polinter: Kajian Politik Dan Hubungan Internasional* 7, no. 2 (2022): 59–76.

51 BBC, "Hakim PTUN Jayapura Tolak Gugatan Suku Awyu Di Papua Yang Menentang Perkebunan Sawit," November 02, 2023, https://www.bbc.com/indonesia/articles/cm5k548801zo.

Conclusion

The Central Government Authority (represented by the president), in the context of limited local governance, manifests in the aspect of supervision by adhering to the principle of, "no autonomy without supervision" through executive review. This involves testing autonomous regulations, including regional regulations, regional head regulations, and regulations related to regional administration.[52] This supervisory aspect distinguishes a unitary state from a federal state. In a unitary state, regional autonomy is characterized by central government oversight of regional governments. Consequently, the substance of the Job Creation Law systematically embodies the principle of centralization, which contradicts the spirit of regional autonomy after the New Order era.

Furthermore, the expansion of the discretion concept in the Job Creation Law broadens the scope of government officials' maneuverability in issuing discretionary decisions. This may introduce new legal breakthroughs in accelerating investment at both the central and local levels, potentially increasing national economic growth. However, it is crucial to understand that in exercising discretionary authority, a narrowed scope may impede the smooth administration of government affairs, as officials face difficulties in decision-making. Conversely, overly broad discretion may lead to actions that exceed authority (*excess du pouvoir*), resulting in unlawful acts and corruption.[53]

Therefore, the expansion of the discretion concept in the Job Creation Law is akin to a double-edged sword. While it can potentially improve Indonesia's investment climate, it simultaneously increases the risk of abuse by government officials. The discretion concept in the Job Creation Law, which eliminates the requirement that discretion not conflict with statutory regulations, may cause numerous societal problems. This is because Indonesia fundamentally adheres to a concept of limited discretion, rather than a broad discretion that could facilitate abuse of authority.

The Job Creation Law has affected all levels of the law in Indonesia, including the implementation and enforcement of state administrative law. The elimination of PTUN authority in the Job Creation Law (Articles 175 and 176), which amends Article 53 of Law No. 30/2014 Concerning Government Administration, results in a deadlock for non-executable decisions and undermines the principles of a simple and low-cost judiciary. This provision also applies to permits such as environmental permits, as stated in Law No. 32/2009 Concerning Regulation of Environmental Permits, with the PTUN's authority to adjudicate environmental permits having been removed by Article 175 of the Job Creation Law.

52 HR Ridwan, *Hukum Administrasi Negara* (Jakarta: Rajawali Press, 2018).

53 Benny Irawan Natasasmita, "Diskresi Sebagai Tindak Pidana Korupsi: Kajian Kriminologi Dan Hukum Terhadap Fenomena Pejabat Otoritas," *MIMBAR: Jurnal Sosial Dan Pembangunan* 27, no. 2 (2011): 143–49.

The state administration settlement mechanism, according to the Job Creation Law, addresses more positive fictitious claims by reducing the settlement time to five working days. If this specified time passes, the application is deemed to have been received in full by the designated government agency or official. While this time reduction can be seen as a positive measure that encourages administrative agencies or officials to work more efficiently in public services, it is important to recognize that such time constraints may negatively impact the quality of application requirement examinations, potentially leading to hasty decision-making by the government.

Positive fictitious decisions in the Job Creation Law indicate that applications are no longer being submitted to the PTUN. This change effectively eliminates the PTUN's absolute authority in deciding on applications. It is the author's view that the elimination of the PTUN's role removes a crucial judicial body's control mechanism over government actions which ignore certain requests addressed to them. Furthermore, the removal of the PTUN's authority to process and decide positive fictitious cases demonstrates the government's unresponsive attitude and may foster a culture of maladministration. At a more extreme level, the erosion of the PTUN's role appears to negatively impact processes governing positive fictiious claims and decisions. While the existence of the PTUN is still recognized, it is left without a clear legal basis, potentially to the detriment of society.

References

Anggono, Bayu Dwi. "Omnibus Law Sebagai Teknik Pembentukan Undang-Undang: Peluang Adopsi Dan Tantangannya Dalam Sistem Perundang-Undangan Indonesia." *Jurnal RechtsVinding* 9, no. 1 (2020): 17–37. https://doi.org/10.33331/rechtsvinding.v9i1.389

Ansori, Lutfil. "Diskresi Dan Pertanggungjawaban Pemerintah Dalam Penyelenggaraan Pemerintahan." *Jurnal Yuridis* 2, no. 1 (2015): 135–50. https://ejournal.upnvj.ac.id/Yuridis/article/view/165

Arham, Suwandi, and Ahmad Saleh. "Omnibus Law Dalam Perspektif Hukum Indonesia." *Petitum* 7, no. 2 (October 2019): 72–81. https://jurnal.uit.ac.id/JPetitum/article/view/652

Arief, Moh Zainol, and Sutrisni Sutrisni. "Analisis Politik Hukum Tentang Omnibus Law Di Indonesia." *Jurnal Jendela Hukum* 8, no. 1 (2021): 19–28. https://doi.org/10.24929/fh.v8i1.1331

Asshiddiqie, Jimly. *Omnibus Law Dan Penerapannya Di Indonesia*. Jakarta: Konstitusi Press, 2020.

Asyikin, Nehru, and Adam Setiawan. "Tanggung Jawab Jabatan Dan Tanggung Jawab Pribadi Dalam Penggunaan Diskresi." *Jurnal Hukum & Pembangunan* 50, no. 3 (2020): 633–46. https://doi.org/10.21143/jhp.vol50.no3.2759

Basah, Sjachran. *Eksistensi Dan Tolak Ukur Badan Peradilan Administrasi Di Indonesia*. Bandung: Alumni, 1989.

BBC. "Hakim PTUN Jayapura Tolak Gugatan Suku Awyu Di Papua Yang Menentang Perkebunan Sawit." November 02, 2023. https://www.bbc.com/indonesia/articles/cm5k548801zo

Bimasakti, Muhammad Adiguna. "Several Conceptual Errors in The Job Creation Law in The Light of the Science of Administrative Law." *Jurnal Hukum Peratun* 4, no. 1 (2021): 45–66. https://doi.org/https://doi.org/10.25216/peratun.412021.45-66.

Cohler, Anne M., Basia Carolyn Miller, and Harold Samuel Stone. *Montesquieu: The Spirit of the Laws.* Cambridge: Cambridge University Press, 1989.

DPR-RI. "Peringati 'May Day', Nasir Djamil Sebut UU Ciptaker Lebih Berpihak Ke Pengusaha." *DPR.go.id*, May 09, 2023. https://emedia.dpr.go.id/2023/05/09/peringati-may-day-nasir-djamil-sebut-uu-ciptaker-lebih-berpihak-ke-pengusaha/

Elviandri, Elviandri, Khuzdaifah Dimyati, and Absori Absori. "Quo Vadis Negara Kesejahteraan: Meneguhkan Ideologi Welfare State Negara Hukum Kesejahteraan Indonesia." 2019. https://doi.org/10.22146/jmh.32986

Farida, Mery. "Problematika Konsep Diskresi Dalam Penyelenggaraan Administrasi Pemerintahan Pasca Undang-Undang Cipta Kerja." *Jurnal Ilmiah Hukum Dan Hak Asasi Manusia* 1, no. 1 (2021): 11–20. https://doi.org/10.35912/jihham.v1i1.412

Firdaus, Fahmi Ramadhan, and Anna Erliyana. "Perlindungan Kebijakan Diskresi Dalam Penanganan Covid-19 Menurut Undang-Undang No. 2 Tahun 2020." *Jurnal Palar (Pakuan Law Review)* 6, no. 02 (2020). https://journal.unpak.ac.id/index.php/palar/article/view/2128

Hans Nawiasky. *Allgemeine Rechtslehre Als System Lichen Grundbegriffe.* Zurich: Benziger, 1948.

Hayat, Hayat. "Keadilan Sebagai Prinsip Negara Hukum: Tinjauan Teoritis Dalam Konsep Demokrasi." *PADJADJARAN Jurnal Ilmu Hukum (Journal of Law)* 2, no. 2 (2015). https://doi.org/10.22304/pjih.v2n2.a10

Hutabarat, Grace Frestisa Irena. "Kajian Green Politic Theory dalam Upaya Menangani Deforestasi Papua terkait Aktivitas Ekspansi." *Jurnal Polinter: Kajian Politik dan Hubungan Internasional* 7, no. 2 (2022): 59–76. https://doi.org/10.52447/polinter.v7i2.5488

The Indonesian National Human Rights Commision. *4th Universal Periodic Review: 41st Session of The Working Group on the UPR Human Rights Council.* Jakarta: Komnas HAM, 2022.

Jaelani, Abdul Qodir Jaelani. "Kewenangan Peradilan Tata Usaha Negara Dalam Mengadili Sengketa Keputusan Fiktif Negatif Dan Fiktif Positif." *Supremasi Hukum: Jurnal Kajian Ilmu Hukum* 6, no. 2 (2017). https://doi.org/10.14421/sh.v6i2.2019

Kelsen, Hans. *The Essence and Value of Democracy.* Lanham: Rowman & Littlefield, 2013.

Kelsen, Hans. "On the Pure Theory of Law." *Israel Law Review* 1, no. 1 (1966): 1–7. https://doi.org/10.1017/S0021223700013595

Kelsen, Hans. "What Is the Pure Theory of Law?" In *Law and Morality*, 101–8. London: Routledge, 2017. https://doi.org/10.4324/9781315092003-6

Koenti, Ishviati Joenaini, and Vinny Victoria Tanawani. "Komparasi Putusan Pengadilan Tata Usaha Negara Terhadap Gugatan Keputusan Fiktif Negatif, Permohonan Terhadap Keputusan Fiktif Positif Dan Perubahannya Pasca Undang-Undang Cipta Kerja." In *Perkembangan Bidang Sosial Humaniora Pertanian Dan Teknologi Mendukung Sustainable Development Goals*, edited by Untoro Budi Surono and Bayu Megaprastio, 348–65. Yogkakarta: Kepel Press, 2023.

Krause, Sharon R. "Laws, Passion, and the Attractions of Right Action in Montesquieu." *Philosophy & Social Criticism* 32, no. 2 (2006): 211–30. https://doi.org/10.1177/0191453706061093

LBH-Jakarta. "Gugatan Surpres Omnibus Law: Komnas HAM Berikan Keterangan Nyatakan Penyusunan RUU Cipta Kerja Diskriminatif." September 15, 2020. https://bantuanhukum.or.id/gugatan-surpres-omnibus-law-komnas-ham-berikan-keterangan-nyatakan-penyusunan-ruu-cipta-kerja-diskriminatif/

Lumbantoruan, Henry Donald. "Pembentukan Regulasi Badan Usaha Dengan Model Omnibus Law." *To-Ra* 3, no. 1 (2017): 463–72. http://ejournal.uki.ac.id/index.php/tora/article/view/1118/947

Maharani, Tsarina, and Kristian Erdianto. "Pakar Hukum: Pembentukan UU CIpta Kerja Merupakan Proses Legislasi Terburuk." *Kompas.com*, October 17, 2020. https://nasional.kompas.com/read/2020/10/17/11113141/pakar-hukum-pembentukan-uu-cipta-kerja-merupakan-proses-legislasi-terburuk

Manan, Bagir. *Menyongsong Fajar Otonomi Daerah.* Yogkakarta: Pusat Studi Hukum (PSH) Fakultas Hukum UII, 2001.

Marbun, S. F., and Moh Mahfud MD. *Pokok-Pokok Administrasi Hukum Administrasi Negara.* Yogyakarta: Liberty, 2006.

Nashir, Muhammad Alvin Nashir Alvin. "Pudarnya Kewenangan Peradilan Tata Usaha Negara Dalam Sengketa Perizinan Atas Undang-Undang Cipta Kerja (Omnibus Law)." *TARUNALAW: Journal of Law and Syariah* 2, no. 01 (2024): 84–95. https://doi.org/10.54298/tarunalaw.v2i01.178

Natasasmita, Benny Irawan. "Diskresi Sebagai Tindak Pidana Korupsi: Kajian Kriminologi Dan Hukum Terhadap Fenomena Pejabat Otoritas." *MIMBAR: Jurnal Sosial Dan Pembangunan* 27, no. 2 (2011): 143–49. https://ejournal.unisba.ac.id/index.php/mimbar/article/view/322

Nurhardianto, Fajar. "Sistem Hukum Dan Posisi Hukum Indonesia." *Jurnal Tapis: Jurnal Teropong Aspirasi Politik Islam* 11, no. 1 (2015): 33–44. https://ejournal.radenintan.ac.id/index.php/TAPIs/article/view/840

Prastowo, Yustinus. "Mujarabkah Omnibus Law Sebagai Obat Lesu Ekonomi?" In *Makalah Disampaikan Dalam Seminar Yang Diselenggarakan Oleh Ikatan Akuntan Indonesia Bekerjasama Dengan CITA*, edited by Fajry Akbar and Fatih Amar Maulana. Jakarta: Center for Indonesia Taxation Analysis, 2019.

Pratama, Surya Mukti, Adrian E. Rompis, and R. Adi Nurzaman. "Kewenangan PTUN Dalam Memeriksa Surat Presiden Tentang RUU Cipta Kerja Dan Implikasi Putusannya." *Risalah Hukum* (2021): 11–25. https://doi.org/10.30872/risalah.v17i1.516

Putra, Antoni. "Penerapan Omnibus Law Dalam Upaya Reformasi Regulasi." *Jurnal Legislasi Indonesia* 17, no. 1 (2020): 1–10. https://doi.org/10.54629/jli.v17i1.602

Radbruch, Gustav. "Five Minutes of Legal Philosophy (1945)." *Oxford Journal of Legal Studies* 26, no. 1 (2006): 13–15. https://doi.org/10.1093/ojls/gqi042

Radbruch, Gustav. "Law's Image of the Human." *Oxford Journal of Legal Studies* 40, no. 4 (2020): 667–81. https://doi.org/10.1093/ojls/gqaa026

Ridwan, H. R. *Hukum Administrasi Negara.* Jakarta: Rajawali Press, 2018.

Riski, Petrus, and Fathiyah Wardah. "Akademisi Tolak UU Cipta Kerja." *Voa-Indonesia*, October 08, 2020.

Siallagan, Haposan. "Penerapan Prinsip Negara Hukum Di Indonesia." *Sosiohumaniora* 18, no. 2 (2016): 122–28. https://doi.org/10.24198/sosiohumaniora.v18i2.9947

Simanjuntak, Enrico. *Hukum Acara Peradilan Tata Usaha Negara: Transformasi & Refleksi*. Jakarta: Sinar Grafika, 2021.

Sindar, Jusak, Jakobus Ronald Mawuntu, and Donna Okthalia Setiabudhi. "Penyelesaian Sengketa Keputusan Fiktif Positif Pasca Undang-Undang Cipta Kerja." *Jurnal Pendidikan Dan Konseling (JPDK)* 5, no. 2 (2023): 6045–51. https://journal.universitaspahlawan.ac.id/index.php/jpdk/article/view/17168

Sodikin. "Paradigm of Law in The Omnibus Law Concept Relating To Legal Norm Applicable in Indonesia." *Jurnal RechtsVinding: Media Pembinaan Hukum Nasional* 9, no. 1 (2020): 143–60. https://doi.org/10.33331/rechtsvinding.v9i1.393

Subadi, Subadi, and Tiara Oliviarizky Toersina. "Perkembangan Konsep Atau Pemikiran Teoritik Tentang Diskresi Berbasis Investasi Di Daerah." *Mimbar Hukum-Fakultas Hukum Universitas Gadjah Mada* 30, no. 1 (2018): 17–31. https://doi.org/10.22146/jmh.29222

Sumeleh, Elisa J. B. "Implementasi Kewenangan Diskresi Dalam Perspektif Asas-Asas Umum Pemerintahan Yang Baik (AUPB) Berdasarkan Undang-Undang No. 30 Tahun 2014 Tentang Administrasi Pemerintahan." *Lex Administratum* 5, no. 9 (2017). https://ejournal.unsrat.ac.id/index.php/administratum/article/view/18158

Suteja, Made. "Pengawasan Terhadap Penyalahgunaan Wewenang Polri Mengadakan Tindakan Lain Menurut Hukum Yang Bertanggung Jawab (Diskresi)." *Jurnal Magister Hukum Udayana* 2, no. 2 (2013): 44073. https://ojs.unud.ac.id/index.php/jmhu/article/view/7283

Usman, Atang Hermawan. "Kesadaran Hukum Masyarakat Dan Pemerintah Sebagai Faktor Tegaknya Negara Hukum Di Indonesia." *Jurnal Wawasan Yuridika* 30, no. 1 (2015): 26–53. https://core.ac.uk/download/pdf/287307509.pdf

Vinx, Lars. *Hans Kelsen's Pure Theory of Law: Legality and Legitimacy*. Oxford: Oxford University Press, 2007. https://doi.org/10.1093/acprof:oso/9780199227952.001.0001

Vinx, Lars. "Hans Kelsen and the Material Constitution of Democracy." *Jurisprudence* 12, no. 4 (2021): 466–90. https://doi.org/10.1080/20403313.2021.1921493

Waddicor, Mark H. *Montesquieu and the Philosophy of Natural Law*. Vol. 37. Berlin: Springer Science & Business Media, 2012.

Wahyunadi, Yodi Martono. "Kompetensi Absolut Pengadilan Tata Usaha Negara Dalam Konteks Undang-Undang Nomor 30 Tahun 2014 Tentang Administrasi Pemerintahan." *Jurnal Hukum Dan Peradilan* 5, no. 1 (2016): 135–54. https://doi.org/10.25216/jhp.5.1.2016.135-154

Wibowo, Henry Hilmawan, Dimas Fahmi Rizalqi, and Sri Husda Yani. "Pengaruh Revisi Undang-Undang Kpk Dalam Kegiatan Pemberantasan Korupsi Di Indonesia." *Jurnal Sosial Dan Sains* 1, no. 8 (2021): 943–50. https://doi.org/10.36418/sosains.v1i8.187

Wicaksono, Indra. "Optimalisasi Peran Mahkamah Konstitusi Dalam Pembangunan Hukum Nasional Dengan Model Preventive Review." *Majalah Hukum Nasional* 49, no. 1 (2019): 91–116. https://doi.org/10.33331/mhn.v49i1.94

Zahro, Nur Eka Fatimatuz, and Ahmad Hasan Basri. "Konsep Permohonan Keputusan Fiktif Positif Pasca Berlakunya Pasal 175 Angka 7 Undang-Undang Nomor 6 Tahun

2023 Tentang Penetapan Peraturan Pengganti Undang-Undang Nomor 2 Tahun 2022 Tentang Cipta Kerja." *Journal of Law and Islamic Law* 1, no. 1 (2023): 1–23. https://doi.org/10.31869/plj.v0i0.3819

Zakaria, Erlangga. "Penerapan Omnibus Law Dalam Sistem Legislasi Nasional Menurut Undang-Undang Nomor 13 Tahun 2022." *Innovative: Journal of Social Science Research* 3, no. 3 (2023): 10719–33. https://j-innovative.org/index.php/Innovative/article/view/2490

Index

MIX
Papier | Fördert gute Waldnutzung
FSC® C083411

Kolibri 360 GmbH
Ferdinand-Jühlke-Straße 7
99095 Erfurt, Deutschland
produktsicherheit@kolibri360.de